The World Atlas of
TREES
AND
FORESTS

The World Atlas of
TREES
AND
FORESTS

EXPLORING EARTH'S FOREST
ECOSYSTEMS

Herman Shugart, Peter White,
Sassan Saatchi, and Jérôme Chave

PRINCETON UNIVERSITY PRESS
PRINCETON AND OXFORD

Published by Princeton University Press
41 William Street, Princeton, New Jersey 08540
99 Banbury Road, Oxford OX2 6JX
press.princeton.edu

Library of Congress Control Number 2022934357

ISBN 978-0-691-22674-3
Ebook ISBN 978-0-691-23593-6

Typeset in Ulises and Autor

Printed and bound in China
10 9 8 7 6 5 4 3 2 1

British Library Cataloging-in-Publication
Data is available

This book was conceived, designed, and
produced by **UniPress Books Limited**
Publisher: Nigel Browning
Commissioning editor: Kate Shanahan
Project manager: Caroline Earle
Designer and illustrator: Paul Oakley, Fogdog
Picture researcher: Sharon D'Ortenzio

Jacket art: Matt Avery; tree outline: iStock
Jacket design: Monograph / Matt Avery
Back cover photos: Shutterstock/Oleg Senkov
(top), /Ken Griffiths (bottom)

Contents

Introduction   8

1 SEEING THE FOREST FOR THE TREES   14

2 SCALE AND THE FOREST ECOSYSTEM   54

3 THE FOREST AS A DYNAMIC MOSAIC   78

4 MAPPING THE FORESTS OF THE WORLD   110

5 THE DIVERSITY OF THE WORLD'S FORESTS   140

6 TROPICAL RAIN FORESTS   174

7 THE BOREAL FOREST OR TAIGA   208

8 SAVANNAS AND DRY FORESTS 238

9 TEMPERATE FORESTS 268

10 FOREST CHANGE OVER MILLENNIA 304

11 CLIMATE CHANGE AND FORESTS 332

12 THE FUTURE: SEEING FORESTS WITH NEW EYES 362

Appendices 386

Glossary 388

Resources 391

Notes on Contributors 394

Index 396

Picture Credits 400

Introduction

This book is about forests—their extent, diversity, function, beauty, variation, and vital planetary significance. In so many dimensions, forests are remarkable. The juxtapositions of chaos and calm, serenity and change, and shelter and danger manifested in the forest experience touch the deepest roots of our consciousness. *Homo sapiens* originated from a forest species and subsequently adapted to the savanna woodlands of Africa. An appreciation of trees and forests is in our very bones.

▶ **Primeval forests**

Old forests are not always composed of towering, large trees. Part of their magic is just how far the processes that created patterns read back into the deep past, such as this ancient Dartmoor woodland. On July 24, 1240 under direction of Henry III, the Sheriff of Devon and 12 knights walked around the forest to determine its bounds (the 1240 "Perambulation"). Dartmoor's early human use dates back to the late Neolithic/early Bronze Age and is written upon the landscape in land patterns, standing stones, stone circles, and cairns.

The issues we treat here are biological, ecological, and geographical, but an understanding of forests as a tactile, visible assemblage is equally important. While forest ecologists might view this understanding as an "ecosystem approach," poets and balladeers appreciate the forest in this sense perhaps better than anyone. In his epic *Evangeline—A Tale of Acadie* (1847), American poet Henry Wadsworth Longfellow paints a picture of a timeless sylvan kingdom:

> THIS is the forest primeval. The murmuring pines and the hemlocks,
> Bearded with moss, and in garments green, indistinct in the twilight,
> Stand like Druids of eld, with voices sad and prophetic.

Forests have an ancientness that conjures up images of nature lost and beauty changed by progress, and of the passage of human history. Taming the forest wilderness was once synonymous with human progress; restoring the wilderness may prove our hope for the future. To this hope, we seek to understand trees and the forests they form as working mechanisms that are both significant and necessary to a functioning living planet.

If forests can produce a meditative calm, perhaps it is because the trees that define them are such venerable objects. If we lived longer and moved slower ourselves, perhaps our view would be different. In Longfellow's *Evangeline*, the "forest primeval" emerges from its deep past, the ancient ecosystem remaining as natural processes gradually erase signs of human habitation following the removal of the local population. However, his image of this and other ancient forests as unchanging does not reflect the deaths of thousands of trees as they wrestle for access to sunlight to become the few canopy-dominant individuals.

▶ Reaching for the sky

Trees seek the autumn sun warmly shining through the canopy of beech (Fagus) trees with gold foliage. Hidden, on the ground below, an incredibly complex system of fungi, arthropods, worms, and coworkers, both allies and enemies, convert the dead organic material falling from the canopy to create and modify the soil.

The words of English author Thomas Hardy's "In a Wood" (1898) conjure up a more dynamic image, with trees engaged in a conflict much like the humans around them:

> Heart-halt and spirit lame,
> City-opprest,
> Unto this wood I came
> As to a nest;
> Dreaming that sylvan peace
> Offered the harrowed ease—
> Nature a soft release
> From men's unrest.
> But, having entered in,
> Great growths and small
> Show them to be men akin—
> Combatants all!
> Sycamore shoulders oak,
> Bines the slim sapling yoke,
> Ivy-spun altars choke
> Elms stout and tall.

The struggles among trees to gain space by increasing their height eventually results in the unyielding dominance of a winner. With the ultimate death of this champion, myriad battles again break out among the remaining, smaller trees in a bid to gain dominance. The poetry of Hardy is echoed in the prose of Alex S. Watt, the Scottish ecologist who developed just such a theoretical basis for the understanding of forest dynamics.

Scale is at the root of these poetic differences in forest descriptions. In scientific discussions, the nature, pattern, and drivers of forest dynamics are conditional on scale. In the poetic example, whether a forest is constant or changing depends on scale—the dimensions in time and in space that are considered frame our view of it. In building hypotheses about forests, ecologists often use an explicit recognition of scale to restrict the domains in space and time—the patterns forests form and the internal and external processes that cause them to change these patterns. We have followed this approach in developing this book.

▼ **Patterns**

A pine forest on Madeira island, Portugal. The patterns in the landscape produce puzzles on which processes formed the forest. Why do the evergreens have a straight-line boundary? What caused the similar sizes of patches of deciduous trees? If one likes riddles, then reading a forest is a joy.

Canopy light

A tall, open forest with bright morning sunlight beaming through the open subcanopy. This forest geometry can occur when there is sufficient light coming through the upper canopy to support seedlings, shrubs, and herbaceous plants, but not enough to support medium-sized saplings.

Humans appreciate forests through all our senses: the rustle of leaves in a breeze or the crack of a falling branch, the fresh smell of new growth or the acrid odor after a fire, the feel of smooth or rough bark, and the taste of fruits and seeds at harvesttime. That said, we rely on our vision in particular—so much so, in fact, that "Do you see what I mean?" conflates sight with comprehension. For this reason, we are particularly pleased that this book presents visually rich images to inform what we are trying to say about forests and trees.

The World Atlas of Trees and Forests seeks to reveal the wonders of forest ecosystems by assessing how they work, where they are, and how they look. What are the advantages of treeness that cause this state to emerge, seemingly independently, in very distantly related plants? How do trees balance the advantages and difficulties of expending energy to both grow large and produce viable offspring? How do growth and regeneration processes at different scales interact to generate quasicrystalline patterns of forests that are visible from an airplane? And how do forests function as working mechanisms? This book answers these questions and more by examining samples of the Earth-spanning

domain of forests and their functioning. By comparing major forest systems across the planet—tropical and subtropical rain forests, temperate forests, cloud forests, boreal forests, and so on—we uncover what scientists currently know about forest function and the responses of trees to different environments.

Forests cover one-third of the Earth's terrestrial surface and are found in a remarkable range of very different climatic conditions. The carbon currently stored in our forests' living plants and soils is crucial to planetary function, so when forests are altered, global systems and climate respond. At the end of this book, we discuss these large-scale issues and illustrate the powerful capabilities of new technologies to "see" forests in ways never before imagined. This time of global change, wrought by the size and associated demands of the human population, makes a more extensive understanding of our planet's forests imperative as never before. Scientists the world over are engaged in this important work. We have provided a Further Reading section (see pages 391-393) for those who are inspired to learn more detail about the topics and source materials included in this book.

1

Seeing the Forest for the Trees

Strange trees

We share a mental image of a tree as a tall, woody plant with a trunk and a leafy canopy, but "tree" is not a taxonomic designation. "Treeness" has evolved independently over very different evolutionary lines of plants. Some closely related plant taxa contain both trees and non-trees.

Pepper plants

Consider the genus *Piper* or pepper plants, with 1,000-2,000 species found across the tropics, mostly in lowland rain forests. Depending on the species, the genus includes plants that grow as herbs, vines, shrubs, and trees. Humans have known *Piper* for a long time as important and potentially valuable plants, and for this reason they are well studied. *Piper* species are significant in medicines, drugs, cooking, and religious and cultural ceremonies.

Across the western Pacific islands, from prehistory and into the modern day, water extracts from pounded roots of the Kava shrub (*Piper methysticum*) are used as a social beverage (also called kava) in cultural settings that range from significant ritual ceremonies to informal, convivial kava clubs. Kava shrubs cannot grow

▼ **Is it a tree?**
A Black Pepper (Piper nigrum) *vine in India. The* Piper *genus contains both trees and non-trees.*

in New Zealand, but when the Māori arrived on the islands they recognized the small native tree *P. excelsum* as a Kava relative, calling it Kawakawa and using it for medical purposes. The high value of the seeds of Black Pepper (*P. nigrum*), a *Piper* vine, as well as other spices, motivated the voyage of Italian explorer Christopher Columbus (1451-1502) to find a new western spice route and his subsequent arrival in the New World in 1492. Similarly, Vasco de Gama (c. 1460-1525) extended a sequence of more and more southerly Portuguese explorations down the west coast of Africa, these led to an alternative sea route around the Cape of Good Hope and on to the sources of the spice trade in 1497.

Tree physiognomy

The shape, size, and form of biological entities is often referred to as physiognomy. What are the boundaries of tree physiognomy in relation to other physiognomies? If a strong, straight, tall single trunk might seem a prerequisite of "treeness," then one might consider tree trunks. Of course, the prerequisite that a tree has such a trunk could be parsed quantitatively: "Just how strong must a tree's trunk be?" or "How straight?" or "How tall?" or "How big around?" A discussion of strength, height, and so on, and the sources of their variation, follow. The immediate objective is to simply celebrate the wonderful variety of plants that are trees, or perhaps are not trees—you can decide.

Tree-like plants

Consider some tree-like plants that relax the attribute of having monopodial (single) trunks. Perhaps the most striking of these is Pando, a male Quaking Aspen (*Populus tremuloides*) located in the Fishlake National Forest in south-central Utah. Quaking Aspen often reproduces by suckering with individual lateral roots, sending up stems that look like an individual tree. The several "trees" growing from a shared root system are actually parts of a single individual plant (termed a clone or a ramet) and are genetically identical. Larger stems die and are replaced by new root suckers. With a Latin name meaning "I spread," Pando is an extreme example. It spreads over an area of 107.7 acres (43.6 ha) and is composed of more than 40,000 stems. With an estimated weight of 6,600 US tons (6,000 tonnes), it is the world's most massive living organism.

▲ **Quaking Aspen**
*"Pando" is an individual male Quaking Aspen (*Populus tremuloides*) and the world's most massive single organism.*

El Árbol del Tule (The Tree of Tule) is a Montezuma Cypress (*Taxodium mucronatum*) with multiple stems emerging from a single gigantic trunk. It grows in the town of Santa María del Tule, Oaxaca, Mexico. Accounting for its deeply furrowed trunk by computing the size of a circle with an equivalent cross section, it has a smoothed diameter of 30¾ ft (9.38 m), the greatest of any tree. Its physiognomy and size were taken to imply that the plant was the product of a small grove of different individual trees that had grown together over time. However, in 1996 it was determined that the various parts of El Árbol all had the same DNA. Like Pando, El Árbol is a genetically identical single plant.

▼ **The Tree of Tule**
A single individual with multiple stems that are merged as a single trunk.

Stranglers and banyans

Two unusual types of woody plants are stranglers and banyans, which both begin life as one type of plant—epiphytes—and then grow into another—large, woody individuals. Epiphytes live on the surfaces of other plants and get their moisture from rain and their nutrients from the surrounding air, rain, or debris. Stranglers, often in the genus *Ficus* (figs), originate from seeds deposited high in the forest by fruit-eating birds. Aerial roots from the epiphytic strangler drop down the trunk of the host tree, eventually reaching the ground. These roots encase the host tree and ultimately kill it. The strangler then continues to grow and can become very large.

Other *Ficus* species use aerial roots to form large, spreading woody plants called banyans. When a banyan's aerial roots drop from branches and make contact with the soil, they form trunks, allowing the plant to spread over a large area. For example, the Great Banyan in the Achariya Jagadish Chandra Bose Botanic Garden, near Kolkata in India, is an Indian Banyan (*F. benghalensis)* with a canopy spreading over an area of 4¾ acres (1.89 ha). The Macedonian king Alexander the Great (356-323 BCE) is said to have camped an army of 7,000 under a single banyan growing near what is now Bharuch in Gujarat, India. Intrinsically impressive, banyans are sacred trees in Hinduism, Buddhism, and Jainism, as well as the mythologies of Guam, Vietnam, and the Philippines. One Indian Banyan is also the national tree of India.

STRANGLER FIG

Strangler figs start their lives as epiphytes in the subcanopy of the tropical rain forest. They wrap their roots around the host tree. Ultimately, the host tree is killed. The strangler continues to grow and eventually establishes itself as a canopy emergent.

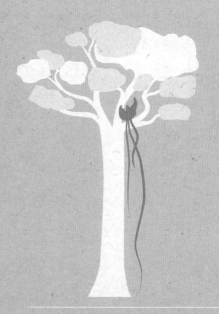  

What is a tree?

The Indigenous inhabitants of El Hierro, the westernmost of the Canary Islands, are said to have resisted the repeated attempts of invasion by European fleets thanks to the protective powers of a holy tree, the Garoé, which provided unlimited water supplies by condensing the clouds above it. Today, the Garoé is many things—a mystical icon, a symbol on the coat of arms of El Hierro, a marvelous legend, and a tree—but what makes it a tree?

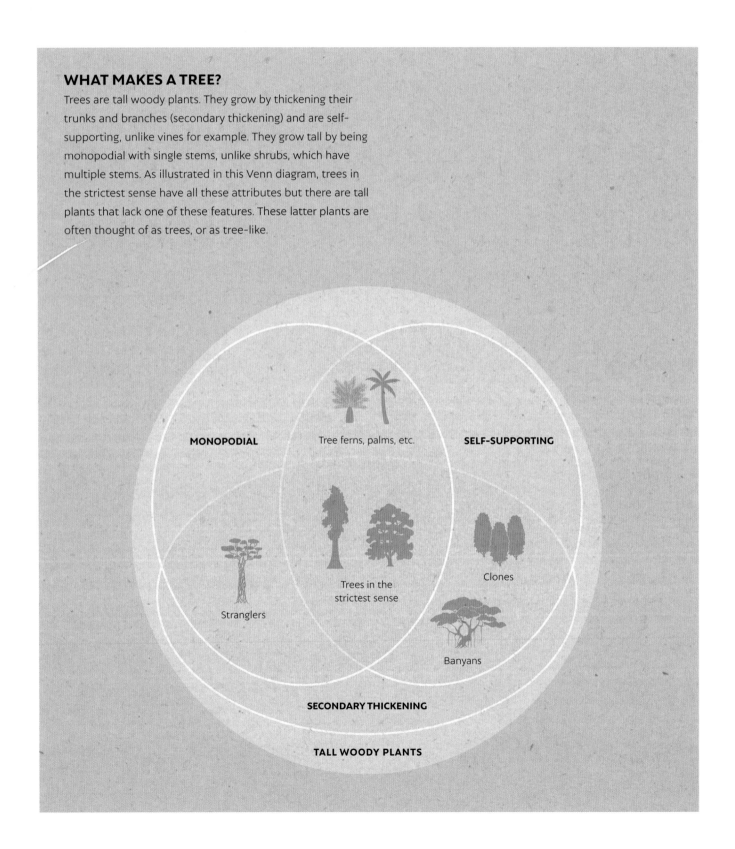

WHAT MAKES A TREE?

Trees are tall woody plants. They grow by thickening their trunks and branches (secondary thickening) and are self-supporting, unlike vines for example. They grow tall by being monopodial with single stems, unlike shrubs, which have multiple stems. As illustrated in this Venn diagram, trees in the strictest sense have all these attributes but there are tall plants that lack one of these features. These latter plants are often thought of as trees, or as tree-like.

MONOPODIAL

Tree ferns, palms, etc.

SELF-SUPPORTING

Clones

Trees in the strictest sense

Stranglers

Banyans

SECONDARY THICKENING

TALL WOODY PLANTS

PRIMARY AND SECONDARY GROWTH

Trees grow in two ways, called primary growth and secondary growth. Primary growth is produced by apical meristems contained in buds at the tips of the youngest stems and roots. Most secondary growth (the thickening of twigs, branches, trunk, and roots) is produced by lateral meristems that are organized into the vascular cambium. The production of bark, produced by the cork cambium, which lies outside the vascular cambium and vascular tissues, is a form of secondary growth. Shoot apical meristems allow trees to grow by stem extension. This produces a key trait of trees—height—but it also can produce the increasing width of tree crowns and allow trees to extend into areas of the crown that have suffered damage.

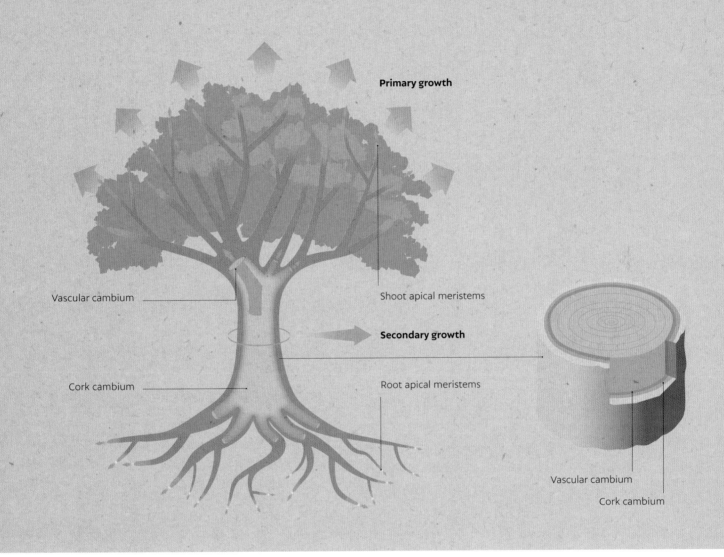

Primary growth

Vascular cambium

Shoot apical meristems

Secondary growth

Cork cambium

Root apical meristems

Vascular cambium

Cork cambium

Defining a tree

Formally, botanists describe trees as perennial vascular plants (tracheophytes—plants with roots, stems, and leaves), with a single stem and perennating (able to survive from one year to the next) tissue at the end of twigs, or as monopodial phanerophytes (with a single stem and buds situated high above the ground). From a functional point of view, the buds (or apical meristems) at the ends of twigs can support reproductive organs (flowers and fruits), grow offshoot branches, or produce leaves. In this way, trees may extend indefinitely. Trees can also be considered as self-supporting plants that typically have a single erect perennial stem that develops branches at some distance above the ground. They are woody, have long-lived organs, and are perennial. Trees grow by becoming taller, referred to as primary growth, but also by thickening their trunk and branches, called secondary growth.

Size

Size is an important criterion when deciding whether a tree is, indeed, a tree. The Greek philosopher Theophrastus (c. 370-287 BCE) recognized the classification of plants into growth habits—the shape, height, appearance, and form of growth of a plant species—such as trees, shrubs, and herbs. In reality, there is no strict limit separating trees from shrubs: some species may grow as shrubs in dry habitats, but they stand upright as trees in more moist habitats. However, overall plant size usually serves as a criterion for defining trees: trees are plants at least 6½ ft (2 m) in stature, and their trunk has a diameter of at least ⅓ in (1 cm). The growth habit is a trait of the species, not of an individual—for example, all members of the same species of pine are considered trees, from seed to adulthood, even though the seedlings and saplings may be much shorter than 6½ ft (2 m).

Inevitably, the definition of trees based on size, being subjective, has a cultural and historical context. Nineteenth-century historians explained the decline of ancient Greece by environmental factors, including an overconsumption of forest resources. However, the environmental historians Alfred Grove and Oliver Rackham suggest that maquis vegetation was the predominant Greek vegetation even before the Bronze Age, as recently revealed in studies of ancient pollen grains from sediment cores in eastern Crete. The Greeks probably considered a lower size threshold for trees and may have considered many of the woody plants of the chaparral vegetation to be trees.

◀ **Tall pine trees**

Pines, especially in crowded conditions, grow tall, with narrow crowns. This is the result of "apical dominance" in which hormones produced at the top of the tree promote height growth and limit lateral branching.

◣ **Shrubs**

Shrubs, here in the Mojave Desert, lack apical dominance, and the abundant branching produces, in a contrast to the pines, a plant that is wider than tall.

Vines

Lianas or vines are not trees: they are not self-supporting plants, but instead require the support of other vegetation to grow from the ground into the canopy. Lianas use attachment devices—hooks, twiners, or tendrils—to climb upon their host. Trees lack such devices. Quite remarkably, many botanical groups of liana species also include tree species. For instance, the Amazonian Monkey Ladder Liana (*Bauhinia guianensis*)—pictured opposite—has close relatives that are among the most common ornamental trees in Asia. Other plant life-forms grow from top to bottom, germinating as epiphytes on treetops and sending their roots toward the ground thereafter. These are called hemiepiphytes by botanists and include the Indian Banyan. Functionally, both lianas and hemiepiphytes are tree parasites, as they use the mechanical support of trees and compete with them for light and nutrients. However, in some cases it may be difficult to distinguish both lianas and hemiepiphytes from trees.

Root systems

A tree not only extends above ground to harvest light resources and disperse its seeds; it also extends greatly below the ground. Tree root systems can be impressive: some roots have been excavated well over 30 ft (10 m) below ground. For a long time, it was thought that trees were capturing water directly from the air. Physics and plant physiology have since taught us that trees take water from the soil, and that deep-rooted trees are found in the driest climates because these deep roots are water-foraging devices. Trees grow below ground much like they do above ground, by extending their apical meristems and occasionally branching off to explore a larger volume of space. Roots also provide trees with essential nutriments, such as nitrogen, phosphorus, and potassium, as well as a range of other micronutrients. Much like leaves above ground, fine roots are specialized organs that absorb water and nutrients. They often function symbiotically with fungi and bacteria, which help them assimilate resources in exchange for shelter and food.

Tree biodiversity

Carefully defining trees is nowhere more important than in documenting threats to biodiversity. The International Union for Conservation of Nature (IUCN) has tasked a global tree specialist group to document the number of tree species worldwide, which they define as "a woody plant with usually a single stem growing to a height of at least 2 meters [6½ ft], or if multi-stemmed, then at least one vertical stem 5 centimeters [2 in] in trunk diameter." Their definition excludes cycads, tree ferns, and tree-like grasses (Poaceae, Bromeliaceae, and Musaceae), which all lack secondary stem growth. This specialist group has so far listed 60,065 species of tree, most of them found in the tropics, with 23,616 in the tropical Americas, 13,029 in the Indo-Malay zone, 9,514 in the Afrotropical zone, 7,470 in Australasia, and 1,415 in Oceania. In contrast, the vast region encompassing all of Europe, temperate Asia, and North Africa harbors only 5,932 species, and North America has just 1,367. Trees are absent from the Antarctic continent.

GLOBAL TREE BIODIVERSITY NUMBERS

Planetary tree biodiversity is largely a tropical story.

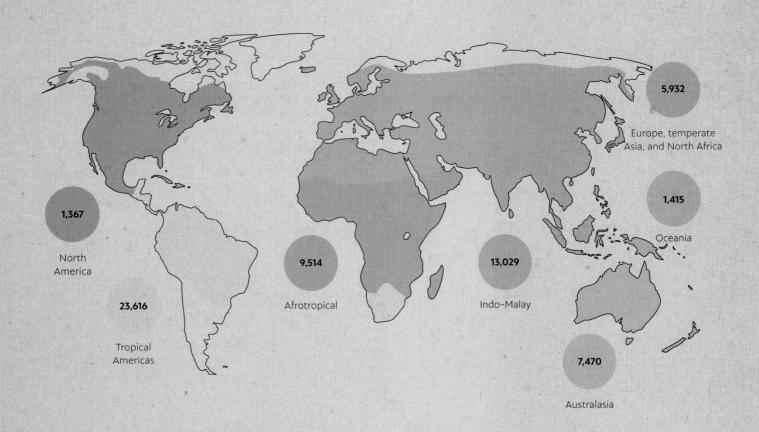

5,932 — Europe, temperate Asia, and North Africa

1,415 — Oceania

1,367 — North America

23,616 — Tropical Americas

9,514 — Afrotropical

13,029 — Indo-Malay

7,470 — Australasia

▲ **Angel Oak tree**

Trees can be identified by their branching "architecture."

Plant woodiness

The woody habit is a condition for perennial plant life, and the long life span of woody species has brought major ecological benefits for land plants, allowing them to reproduce over extended periods. To a large extent, woodiness is what makes a tree a tree. Naturalists have long been puzzled by the fact that some groups of non-woody plant species occasionally have one representative that is woody. In his book on the origin of the species, the English naturalist Charles Darwin (1809-1882) noted that islands often support "trees or bushes belonging to orders which elsewhere include only herbaceous species." He further provided an explanation of this syndrome of secondary insular woodiness as a competitive adaptation against predominantly herbaceous plants of island environments. For example, in the Canary Islands, of the 220 woody species native to the archipelago, no fewer than 38 shifts toward woodiness have been observed. Some species found in the laurel forests of the Canaries, such as *Crambe arborea* (a member of the Brassicaceae, or cabbage family), are examples of secondary insular woodiness, whereas the Garoé tree on El Hierro, which is thought to have been a stinkwood (*Ocotea foetans*), itself a member of the laurel family, Lauraceae (see page 154), is not.

Recent research

The developmental basis for tree shape remains a fundamental scientific question, and one that can now be explored using the sequencing of plant genomes and genome-editing techniques. One major insight came while researchers were comparing the genome of poplars (genus *Populus*) to that of the Thale Cress (*Arabidopsis thaliana*), an herbaceous plant of the cabbage family that is much studied by geneticists. Similar sets of genes expressed during the formation of woody tissue in trees are present in herbaceous plants, which explains how the development of secondary woodiness on remote islands is possible. The potential for an herb species to evolve into a tree species occurs in many plants. However, in herbs the wood-formation genomes are expressed only in the shoot apical meristem.

Researchers have also uncovered the roles of other genes in the overall architecture of trees. For example, changes in a gene of Peach (*Prunus persica*) trees can alter branch growth direction by enhancing the tendency to grow in the direction of gravity (gravitropic response), much as seen in weeping willows (genus *Salix*). Modification of a second gene produces a tree that grows with more upward shoot orientations. Such changes can now be genetically engineered in orchard trees to improve the yield of fruit and nut crops.

Tree branching

In general, non-domesticated trees have evolved similar adaptive geometries—so much so, in fact, that silhouettes of tree branching are used in guidebooks to identify species, even those that are closely related. In "Tree architecture" (page 43), we introduce the work of three botanists, Francis Hallé, Roelof Oldeman, and Philip Tomlinson, who classified architectural types (or models) based on the manner in which branches replicate: terminally (at the ends of twigs) or axially (from the sides of twigs); along a plane—horizontally or vertically; or, one at a time or in whorls.

Importantly, combinations of these different patterns produce architectural types for idealized trees and not their actual realizations. Real trees grow with additional constraints, such as the need to bend for light or for stability, or the risk of shedding a branch.

Tree architecture is also constrained by biophysics, as discussed in "Building tall trees" (pages 46–49). Trees cannot grow taller and taller without limit. They must balance physiological constraints of pulling water to height through conduits in the stem, which is a complex piping engineering challenge. They simultaneously must avoid buckling under their own weight from gravity, a familiar challenge for building engineers.

▼ **Under strain**
The Crooked Forest—a grove of oddly shaped pine trees located near the town of Gryfino, West Pomerania, Poland.

Tree trunk organization

In forestry, trees are either softwoods or hardwoods. Incongruously, not all hardwoods have hard wood, and nor do all softwoods have soft wood. For example, Balsa (*Ochroma pyramidale*) is termed a hardwood even though its wood is very soft and light. To make sense of the term, one must realize that Balsa and the other hardwoods are all angiosperms (flowering plants). Softwood trees correspond to the gymnosperms, or conifers—cone-bearing plants.

Secondary growth

Foresters define trees as perennial woody plants that produce secondary growth, meaning that the stem not only expands in length, but it also thickens radially (outward). Tall woody herbs, ferns, and cycads lack secondary stem growth. While they are tree-like, they are generally excluded from the group that is defined as trees. The process of secondary wood formation is made possible by the activity of living cells under the bark, called cambial cells, which form young woody tissue toward the inner part of the stem, called sapwood. Sapwood cells are organized into a network of conduits that efficiently transport water and nutrients from the roots to the leaves. Through time, sapwood ages, darkens, and loses its sap-transport function through chemical reactions, and is thereby converted to heartwood. In both hardwoods and softwoods, the heartwood is denser and stronger, giving the trunk mechanical strength, whereas the sapwood is less dense and provides the trunk with "plumbing" to move water up to the leaves.

▶ **Sequoia trunk**

*Among the largest trees on Earth, Coast Redwoods (*Sequoia sempervirens*) can live for multiple millennia in very wildfire-prone locations. They attain exceptional sizes— diameters near 30 ft (9 m) and heights over 330 ft (100 m). Their thick bark (up to 1 ft/ 30 cm thick) resists insects, fungus, and fire damage, which is essential to growing old in a dangerous fire-prone environment.*

Softwood and hardwood structure

At the microscopic level and in the most general sense, wood is lignified tissue. However, the cellular structure of the wood of hardwoods and softwoods differs considerably. The wood of softwoods is composed of tubular structures called tracheids. Thin-walled tracheids move water up the tree, while thick-walled tracheids provide strength. Over time, the tracheids fill in, converting from sapwood to heartwood. In hardwoods, support and plumbing functions are strongly divided among the types of cells making up the wood. Special complexes of cells called pit vessels move water upward much more effectively than tracheids; wood fibers in the wood provide mechanical strength. Diffuse-porous hardwoods have pit vessels dispersed through the wood, while ring-porous hardwoods have pit vessels arranged in rings. Ring-porous hardwoods can move water upward about three or more times faster than diffuse-porous hardwoods, which themselves transport water three times faster than softwoods.

Growth rings

In seasonal climates, woody tissue forms during the growing season, and this seasonality is manifest as growth rings in stem cross sections. Within an annual tree ring, the tree initially grows outward by producing "early wood" in spring, which is more vascular than the "late wood" produced in summer. A long, favorable spring produces more early wood, while a favorable summer produces a wider late-wood tree ring. Larger overall ring widths occur in favorable growth years. By piecing together tree-ring measurements for subfossil, historical, and recent tree logs, scientists have been able to produce continuous timelines of environmental variables over the past 13,000 years.

CROSS SECTION OF A TRUNK

A tree is defined by its secondary growth—cambial cells form woody tissue and expand outward.

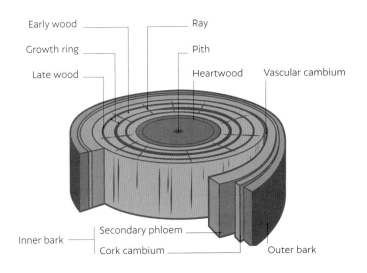

Early wood · Ray · Growth ring · Pith · Late wood · Heartwood · Vascular cambium · Secondary phloem · Inner bark · Cork cambium · Outer bark

Geological history of the tree life-form

The rise of land plants led to a radical transformation of the Earth's atmosphere, carbon dioxide being replaced by oxygen owing to the ability of the plants to carry out photosynthesis. Plant life likely began on land some 450 million years ago, during a geological period known as the Ordovician.

Evidence for the origins of land plants is based on the discovery of microscopic spores with four faces, or a tetrahedral arrangement. Spores are characteristic of a life cycle outside of a permanently wet environment, and the ability of a tetrahedral spore to split into four suggests that the cell was diploid (with two sets of chromosomes) and underwent a meiotic division (with two rounds of division), as do modern land plants. However, the first true land-plant fossil dates from around 430 million years ago, after the Earth's first recorded major extinction event, which marked the end of the Ordovician period. These early land plants were simple life-forms, similar to present-day liverworts, hornworts, and mosses, a group collectively called embryophytes.

The discovery at Rhynie

In 1910, William Mackie (1856-1932), a Scottish physician and amateur geologist, made a surprising discovery in the village of Rhynie in Scotland. There, he discovered strange shapes in microcrystalline quartz rocks, or chert, that had been used to fence a garden. The structures he discovered were later revealed to be an exquisitely preserved soil ecosystem, coated in silica derived from hot springs some 410 million years ago. The Rhynie chert harbored several land-plant life-forms, some of which were lignified, with cell walls thickened with a layer of lignin to provide structural support even though they were all less than 3 ft (1 m) tall. Lignified tissue is characteristic of plants that need to transport water and nutrients through tracheids and is still found today in conifers. The major lesson learned from the Rhynie chert fossils is that lignified plants, or tracheophytes, were present early on in the history of land plants.

Plant genomes provide complementary information to the fossil record. This is because genomes slowly accumulate silent, or neutral, mutations, which do not change the expression of the genomic material. Neutral mutations are like the tick of a clock: the more mutations between two species, the older their common ancestor. Using this technique, paleobotanist Jennifer Morris and her colleagues recently dated the origin of embryophytes to 515-470 million years ago, and of tracheophytes to 472-419 million years ago. One hypothesis suggested by this work is that lignified plants may be older than the Rhynie chert, but the discovery of a suitable site to demonstrate this is still wanting.

▲ **Evolution**

Early land plants were simple life-forms, similar to present-day liverworts, hornworts, and mosses (above and right—artistic rendition from 1890), a group collectively called embryophytes.

PLATE IX.

MOSSES AND LIVERWORTS.

First trees

So we know for sure that lignified plants were present on land 410 million years ago, but how much longer did it take to produce trees? One of the plant fossils recorded in the Rhynie chert was a prostrate life-form called *Baragwanathia longifolia*. This is the earliest representative of the lycopsids, a class of herbaceous vascular plants still present today in the form of clubmosses (genus *Lycopodium*) and an important group in terms of the emergence of trees. Some 370 million years ago, tree lycopsids became abundant. The most typical form of these was *Lepidodendron*, with a beautiful snakeskin pattern on its bark, reaching some 160 ft (50 m) in height, and with small leaves growing directly out of its branches. Its long, thick roots burrowed deep down into the soil layer. Although *Lepidodendron* came to fame as one of the earliest tree forms on Earth, other tree lycopsids have since been discovered. In 2007, the fossil stumps at Gilboa, which have been known since the 1870s, were reinterpreted as being parts of the lycopsid tree genus *Wattieza*, dating back 385 million years. This discovery has significance as the oldest occurrence of a tree life-form in the fossil record.

First forests

A major step in the geological history of the tree life-form began after the end of the Devonian and continued throughout the Carboniferous period, 354–290 million years ago. During this long period of time, the concentration of carbon dioxide in the atmosphere fell precipitously, from ten times the values present in the atmosphere today to roughly modern-day concentrations. Carbon was removed from the atmosphere and stored in the trees and soils of the largest forests ever seen on Earth. However, these forests were very different from the ones we are used to walking through today. Lycopsid trees such as *Lepidodendron* were the dominant species, while another significant component was a tree-like relative of modern horsetails (genus *Equisetum*) called *Calamites*, which grew more than 30 ft (10 m) in height. The forests also harbored plenty of tree ferns. The plants from this period are the origin of the majority of coal, the primary fossil fuel of the Industrial Revolution.

A paleobotanical puzzle

It has not always been easy to unravel the geological history of the tree life-form. One paleobotanical puzzle in particular gave rise to a long-lasting controversy. In 1871, a wood structure attributed to a tree stem was discovered in a geological layer dating back as much as 380 million years. Later, in 1911, fern-like fronds were discovered in the coal-rich Donbas region of Ukraine, and were dated from roughly the same period. It is not until the 1960s that these two elements were found to belong to the same tree-like plant, *Archaeopteris* (right). This genus belongs to a group called progymnosperms, the precursors of seed plants. Their stem anatomy displays remarkable similarities to classic seed plants such as conifers, yet they reproduced by spores rather than seeds.

Archaeopteris

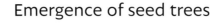

Emergence of seed trees

True seed plants mark another key innovation in the evolution of trees. Two tree-like seed plants were present, although rare, from the Early Carboniferous 354 million years ago: the seed tree ferns; and a genus called *Cordaites*, whose members bear morphological similarities to the modern-day monkey-puzzle trees (genus *Araucaria*). However, it was only around 300 million years ago that seed trees rose to ecological dominance, slowly overtaking the lycopsids. This major emergence of seed trees included groups of modern plants such as the cycads and the Ginkgoales. The latter are astounding trees: their fossil record dates back 280 million years and they are still present today. The Maidenhair Tree (*Ginkgo biloba*) is planted in cities across the world because it is resistant to pollution and pests, and the fruit (borne by female trees) has an unmistakable smell. Many Maidenhair Trees are considered sacred in Japan, including the individual that grows through the roof of Anraku-ji Temple, Hiroshima, which survived the blast of the atomic bomb on August 6, 1945.

▲ **Early trees**
Early carboniferous pine and Cordaites *(right), an early seed tree.*

▶ **Early conifer**
Petrified wood of Araucarioxylon arizonicum *from the Late Triassic, found in the Petrified Forest National Park in Arizona.*

Conifer dominance

After the Permian-Triassic extinction event some 250 million years ago, the largest catastrophe for biodiversity ever documented on Earth, another group of seed plants rose to dominance: the conifers. They slowly emerged to become the main tree life-form during the Triassic and especially through the Jurassic, 248-144 million years ago. The Early Triassic is thought to have been less favorable to land plants compared to the end of the Carboniferous, with an atmospheric carbon dioxide level of around 300 parts per million, close to that found in modern pre-industrial times. The level rose again in the Late Triassic, reaching four times the present-day value. During this era of conifer dominance, forests were probably scarcer than they are today. However, magnificent expanses did exist, as testified by the Late Triassic Petrified Forest National Park in Arizona, dominated by the extinct conifer *Araucarioxylon arizonicum*.

Coniferous forests are pervasive today in temperate and boreal zones, where they can surpass all other trees in stature and in number (the Giant Redwood, *Sequoiadendron giganteum*, is a conifer). There are an estimated 588 extant conifer species, some of them among the most economically valuable trees—for example, it is estimated that about 85 million Christmas trees are produced every year in North America and Europe, often Norway Spruce (*Picea abies*) and Douglas Fir (*Pseudotsuga menziesii*). The earliest representatives of the conifers in the geological history are the yellowwoods (genus *Podocarpus*). The largest known yellowwood tree is Pouakani in the North Island of New Zealand, a 138 ft-tall (42 m) Tōtara (*Podocarpus totara*) that is considered a heritage tree by Māori.

▲ **Heritage trees**
A giant Tōtara (Podocarpus totara) *tree in New Zealand (left) and a Ginkgo* (Ginkgo biloba) *tree (right).*

Flowering plants

The last stage in the history of trees was the appearance of flowering plants, or angiosperms. The explosion of plant life-forms in "recent geological times" was famously called an "abominable mystery" by Charles Darwin in a letter in 1879. While the ancestral forms of flowering plants did not differ dramatically from conifers, they did give rise to the most extraordinary diversification, with well over 370,000 flowering plant species documented today, of which some 60,000 are trees.

The first solid evidence for flowering plants is a pollen form found in both Israel and England and dated around 135 million years ago. The oldest fossil flower dates back around 125 million years. Remarkably, no flowering plant fossil record has been discovered prior to the Cretaceous, which began 144 million years ago. By 100 million years ago, the major groups of flowering plants were already present. Flowers looking a lot like those found in genus *Magnolia* today were among the early flowering plants, together with a strange shrub called *Amborella trichopoda*, located today only on the Pacific island of New Caledonia. This is a flowering woody plant, but its wood structure resembles that of conifers, the sap being transported by tracheids (see page 30). In contrast, most flowering trees today transport sap through shorter, larger, and more complex multicellular conduits called vessels. Later on, but probably around 120-110 million years ago, the three large groups of flowering plants emerged: the monocotyledons (grasses and grass-like plants, such as palms), the rosids (including roses, legumes, mallows, and cabbages), and the asterids (including sunflowers, lavenders, and carrots). By the end of the Cretaceous period, 66 million years ago, half of the 416 flowering plant families were already present.

During the past 140 million years, flowering plants have diversified further, and their flowers, seeds, roots, leaves, trunks, and bark have evolved in response to myriad interactions with insects, mammals, fungi, and bacteria. These evolutionary trends have generated exquisitely complex life-forms and strange organs. While much of this book reflects on today's wonders of nature, a look deep into the past unveils how complex and long the geological history of trees has been, from the early *Lepidodendron* trees to present-day oaks.

TREE EVOLUTION

Trees evolved from land plants as a result of the lignification of plant tissue early on, and the need for plants to grow tall so as to outcompete their neighbors and harvest light. The tree life-form arose as early as 370 million years ago, but it took more than 200 million years before flowering plant trees rose to dominance.

430 million years ago  First land plant fossil found

410 million years ago  Lignified plants present on land

370 million years ago  Tree lycopsids—the first trees

300 million years ago  Seed trees

248–144 million years ago  Conifers become a dominant tree life-form

135 million years ago  First flowering plants (angiosperms)

100 million years ago  Major groups of flowering plants emerge

Tree architecture

The complex form of an individual tree develops over decades, centuries, or even millennia as a consequence of its genetic blueprint and the influence of environmental conditions and episodic forces such as windstorms and insect damage. The study of tree forms and the way these develop is called tree architecture. Here, we touch on four insights into the remarkable diversity of tree forms, even within a single environmental setting.

▼ **Spreading branches**
The Giant Raintree (Samanea saman) is a highly branched, spreading tree in the Pea family (Fabaceae). The species is widely planted outside its native range from Central America to Brazil. This individual is from Thailand.

A tree's four critical tasks

Functionally, the tree's "body" must accomplish four critical tasks: movement of water and nutrients from the roots to the leaves; movement of sugars (the products of photosynthesis) from the leaves to the roots and other non-photosynthetic tissues; mechanical support, with resistance to gravitational forces and wind; and the display of leaves, like so many small solar panels, arranged in a way that efficiently intercepts solar radiation. In addition, the tree must integrate the solutions for these four tasks. For instance, the size of leaves and the complexities of leaf shape have consequences for the branching pattern of the tree crown, while investment in mechanical strength limits the rate of height and crown expansion but lengthens life span—fast-expanding, light-wooded species are also relatively short-lived. Tree species vary in the way they accomplish the four tasks, so that many tree species can be recognized just from their silhouette.

Corner's rules

Edred Corner (1906-1996), a British botanist working in the tropics in the 1940s, made two simple observations that became known as Corner's rules: axial conformity and diminution of ramification. The first of these establishes that the thicker the axis, the larger the "appendage" (leaf or inflorescence) that is borne on that axis, and the second establishes that the greater the number of individual divisions (branches), the smaller the appendage. In other words, for a given total leaf area, trees vary from large-leaved species with thick twigs and few branches, to small-leaved species with thin twigs and many branches. This makes sense: all else being equal, larger leaves should require the support of stouter twigs, and they should also require less branching, because larger leaves can span the resulting gaps.

CORNER'S RULES APPLIED TO TREES

At constant leaf area, trees vary from small-leaved, thin-stemmed, and many-branched (left) to large-leaved, thick-stemmed, and minimally branched (right).

▶ **Da Vinci trees**

Leonardo da Vinci became fascinated about rules that determine the branching patterns of trees. The far right sketch makes a critical prediction that the cross-sectional area of a tree trunk (the lowest line that crosses the trunk) is equal to the summed cross-sectional area at any distance from the base (that is, at the semicircles that represent successive distance from the trunk).

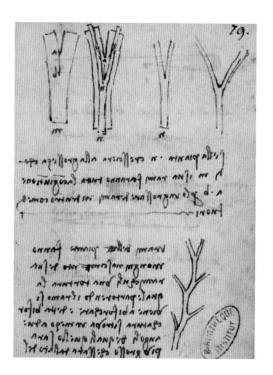
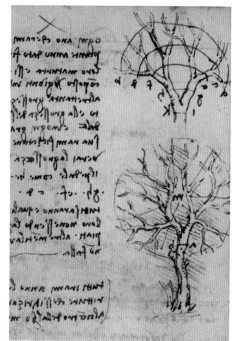

Variations

Leaf sizes also vary with environment: the mean and range of leaf sizes decrease from the tropics to the boreal zone, and from moist to dry forests. However, at any point on these environmental gradients there are usually tree species that vary along the architectural spectrum predicted by Corner's rules. Why does this variation occur? The answer to this is not clear. One theory suggests that because leaves represent a cheaper investment than stems, creating a crown of large leaves and/or a greater leaf area per annual increment of wood can allow such species to be faster in height growth and crown expansion, and thus ideal for the high light levels created by the death of canopy trees.

Leonardo's prediction

The Italian polymath Leonardo da Vinci (1452–1519) made a related prediction, saying that the cross-sectional area of a tree at its base is equal to its cross-sectional area at any distance from the base. In other words, if you gather all the twigs at the edge of a tree crown together as a bundle, the summed cross-sectional area of all the twigs will be the same as the cross-sectional area of the trunk at the base of the tree. To demonstrate this, imagine a set of 100 garden hoses, each 100 ft (30 m) long, gathered at one end as a round bundle. Moving along the bundle, at 30 ft (10 m) from the base, divide the 100 hoses into two sets of 50. Then at 50 ft (15 m) from the base, divide each of the two bundles into two sets (four in total) of 25. Continue this process until you are left, in each final "branch," with a single hose. Thus, we have Leonardo's prediction: the cross-sectional area of the hoses at the base is equal to the combined cross-sectional area of the individual hoses at the tips of the branching.

This simple model echoes one of Corner's rules: the more you divide the branches, the thinner those branches become. In reality, trees deviate somewhat from Leonardo's prediction, because they are not just made up of hollow tubes for water conduction, but also have structures for mechanical support that may vary from tree base to twig tip. It also seems that trees "overproduce" twigs, such that the summed cross-sectional area at the twig level is somewhat greater than the trunk diameter, although there are few direct observations from which to draw a conclusion.

Nonetheless, Leonardo's general idea is implicit in one of ecology's rules of thumb: the cross-sectional area of a tree trunk predicts the total leaf area of the crown. It being much easier to measure diameter than leaf area, field ecologists often take the diameter of the trunk as predictive of the tree's role (total leaf area being tied to total productivity). Because tree trunks often swell near the ground, this diameter is usually measured at "breast height," taken as 4½ ft (1.4 m) above the ground.

FAST AND SLOW CROWN GROWTH

Fast and slow crown growth are represented by height growth among four trees in the high-elevation spruce-fir forests in Great Smoky Mountains National Park (see Chapter 2, pages 70–71, for additional description of the disturbance dynamics of this ecosystem). The size of the disturbance patches (x-axis) is used as a surrogate for light availability.

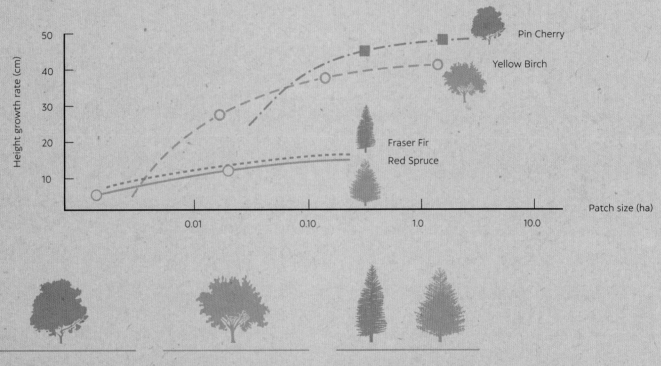

Pin Cherry
A species with high leaf area per annual increment of stem growth and fast growth. This species requires high light (large disturbance patch size) and does not survive under shady conditions. It reaches 20 in (50 cm) extension growth per year in larger patches.

Yellow Birch
A species with intermediate leaf area per annual increment of stem growth. This species requires some disturbance for long survival. It reaches 12–16 in (30–40 cm) extension growth per year.

Fraser Fir and Red Spruce
These two species have low leaf area per annual increment of stem growth. Fir and spruce persist in the deepest shade in these forests, but grow in height only about 2 in (5 cm) per year. They grow faster (up to 6 in/15 cm per year) in disturbed patches but are outcompeted in the largest patches.

MONOLAYERS AND MULTILAYERS

Multilayers distribute leaves in a larger volume, monolayers
tend to make fewer layers and, in extreme, just one.

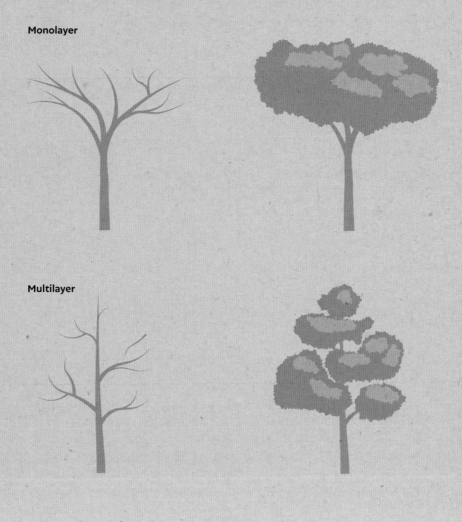

Monolayer

Multilayer

Henry Horn's monolayers and multilayers

The second insight comes from the work of American ecologist Henry Horn, who
in his 1971 book *The Adaptive Geometry of Trees* argued that the light environment
predicts leaf arrangement. More specifically, he said that in low light tree branching
should create less leaf overlap and, in the extreme, what he called monolayers of
leaves, whereas in greater light trees can benefit from greater leaf overlap, creating
what Horn called multilayers. For example, in the interior of a dense forest, with
low light levels, seedlings and saplings are more like the monolayer extreme, and in
patches created by windstorms, fields, and sunlit gardens, with higher light levels,
trees should develop as multilayers. However, individual trees display plasticity and
tree species also differ genetically. Early successional species (see pages 94–97) depend
on high light levels and tend to be multilayers wherever they are found, whereas late
successional species tend to be monolayers, except if they are large and old enough
to dominate the sunlit forest canopy. Interestingly, a 2020 paper by Thomas Givnish
pointed out that there may be other benefits to multilayered leaves, including a
reduction in water loss in sunny environments, that may outweigh the importance
of light interception per se.

The 23 models of Hallé, Oldeman, and Tomlinson

A third insight into tree forms comes from the work of Hallé, Oldeman, and Tomlinson. Their scheme overlaps with some features of Corner's rules in that it is particularly concerned with the pattern of branching. It is distinctive, though, in its emphasis on dynamics of development from seed to adult plant, its emphasis on the spatial position of growing points that produce branching, and its inclusion of where and how reproductive structures are produced. The authors described 23 models for the development of tree forms, naming each for a prominent botanist. Taking the palm form (single unbranched, thick stems and many large leaves) as an extreme in Corner's rules, they named it Corner's model.

Wood density

Our last insight is that, even within one set of environmental conditions, tree species vary greatly in wood density, creating, among other things, a great range of materials fit for different kinds of human use—the Balsa wood of gliding aircraft to wood so dense that it sinks in water. By definition, low-density wood is less costly in terms of the use of carbon products from photosynthesis. One possible consequence of this is that, for a given amount of carbon fixed, low-density woods can create faster volumetric growth rates—faster growth in height and in crown expansion. Indeed, in full sunlight the annual height growth of Balsa trees is ten or more times the height growth of ebony trees (genus *Diospyros*), which have high-density wood. But there's a trade-off: ebony trees, with their slow-growing, densely wooded strategy, are more durable and the lifespan difference between the two species is probably about the same, being ten or more times longer in ebony trees than in Balsa.

▲ **Ebony**
Ebony is a slow-growing, long-lived tree with very dense wood.

▼ **Balsa wood**
In contrast to ebony trees, Balsa is a fast-growing, short-lived tree with light wood with specialty uses such as building model airplanes.

Dragon Blood Tree

The Dragon Blood Tree (*Dracaena cinnabari*) is a striking tree with bright red sap found only on the Socotra Islands (Yemen) of the Indian Ocean—155 miles (250 km) east of the Somali coast and 235 miles (380 km) south of the Yemen on the Arabian Peninsula. Of the vascular plant species on the Socotras 37 percent are found only there (endemic), which is comparable to other oceanic islands such as Mauritius, the Galápagos, and the Canary Islands. The flora of the Socotras have been evolving independently for the past 35 million years when they separated from the Arabian Peninsula. The trees are potentially vulnerable to an extinction under a climatic warming.

The Dragon Blood Tree has a striking umbrella shape and complies to one of Hallé, Oldeman, and Tomlinson's tree architectural models discussed on page 43. It is a great example of what they called Leeuwenberg's model, in which the dominant bud at the end of a twig first flowers and then new twigs are produced that grow around the former flower bud. The stems are a joined assemblage of Y-shaped elements and the trees are made of Y-shaped twigs, which show up well in these photos as well as in the da Vinci tree diagrams on page 40.

Building tall trees

Human architectural wonders pale in comparison to the tallest *Eucalyptus* trees of Australia or *Sequoiadendron* trees of California. From an engineering standpoint, one can only marvel at the fact that a living organism can reach heights of more than 380 ft (115 m). We understand that trees grow tall in order to outcompete their neighbors and harvest as much light as possible, but why is the limit slightly over 380 ft (115 m)? Why is no tree 500 ft (150 m) tall? Why is the limit not 150 ft (45 m)?

One explanation for the cap on tree height is that it is constrained by the mechanics of building tall structures from wood. Tree trunks are tall, slender, vertical wooden columns anchored to the ground. As with any other slender, vertical object, like a tower of wooden blocks, any small displacement may cause it to collapse by buckling. In 1757, Swiss mathematician Leonhard Euler (1707-1783) found that the maximum height a vertical column can reach before buckling under its own weight is related to the column diameter raised to the power of $2/3$. So, if the base diameter of a column doubles, the column's maximum height is multiplied by only a factor of 1.587. However, trees are generally not columnar, instead mostly have a conical, tapered shape, and they are not all made of a homogeneous material. Trunk shape and structure both slightly modify the coefficient of Euler's buckling formula, but they do not change the way maximum height scales with trunk diameter.

Environmental factors

So long as the base of a tree is large enough, Euler's formula does not set a maximum limit on its height. Two other processes must be considered: the risks of being damaged by wind, and the physiological constraints of the tree's hydraulic system. In many parts of the world, strong wind gusts are a major threat to trees; so long as they are sheltered by other trees, the risks of breakage are limited. Yet, the towering giants of the forest are fully exposed to wind, which is therefore a potent selective force against tall trees.

▶ **General Sherman**
A Giant Sequoia
(Sequoiadendron
giganteum*) tree located*
in the Giant Forest
of Sequoia National
Park, California.

Tree hydraulics

The other explanation for the cap on tree height involves water. For a long time, observers thought that trees acquired their water through the condensation of air vapor at the surface of their leaves. However, it was later found that trees lift water from the soil. The control in lifting water upward is the difference in water density in the air relative to that in the leaf. This difference creates a water potential, which the plant tries to balance by transpiring water. The process creates a surface tension in the slender conduits in the tree, and by capillarity the water column is pulled upward from the roots. This theory was first formulated in 1914 by plant biologist Henry Dixon (1869-1953).

Drought stress

Taller trees must compensate for a greater gravitational force, and the pulling force for the ascent of sap should therefore be higher. However, if the tension of the water column is too high, this may create a phenomenon called cavitation, similar to the breakage of a rope under high tension. Water does not "break," but it does undergo a phase transition from a liquid to a gas, and this generates small water vapor bubbles in the otherwise liquid water column. Cavitation under tension produces a major alteration of the inner sap transportation conduits, leading to tissue death and even potentially the death of the entire tree. During extreme droughts, when the air surrounding leaves is very dry, plants lose large amounts of water through their leaf stomata (microscopic openings; see page 213) when they open these to let in carbon dioxide for photosynthesis. Under these conditions, the resultant tension on the water column is high enough to cause cavitation and eventually drought-induced death. Plants are adapted to their climate, and thin water conduits are much less likely to cavitate than wide water conduits, so it usually takes an exceptional drought to result in an actual increased mortality in trees.

As trees grow taller, they are more exposed to dry air and to gravitational forces. In 2004, ecosystem scientist George Koch and his colleagues climbed a tall Coast Redwood (*Sequoia sempervirens*) and measured leaf water tension at different heights during the driest hour of the day. They found that water tension increased linearly from the ground to the treetop, and the highest values were close to values where cavitation occurs. One could imagine that taller trees could avoid cavitation risks by having thin water conduits, but these would make it difficult for them to transport the large amounts of water they need. According to plant physiologist Ian Woodward, the plant hydraulic system should cavitate without other adaptations at an absolute limit at around 330 ft (100 m). Several physiological adaptations can push this limit to a maximum height of 400-425 ft (122-130 m).

WATER TRANSPORT AND CAVITATION

Trees must move water through the xylem in a continuous stream from the roots below to the leaves above. This movement is driven by the evaporation of water from the leaves, called transpiration, which produces tension in the water column. Under drought conditions, the tension becomes so negative, that bubbles of water vapor form, leading to a complete break in the water column—a phenomenon called cavitation.

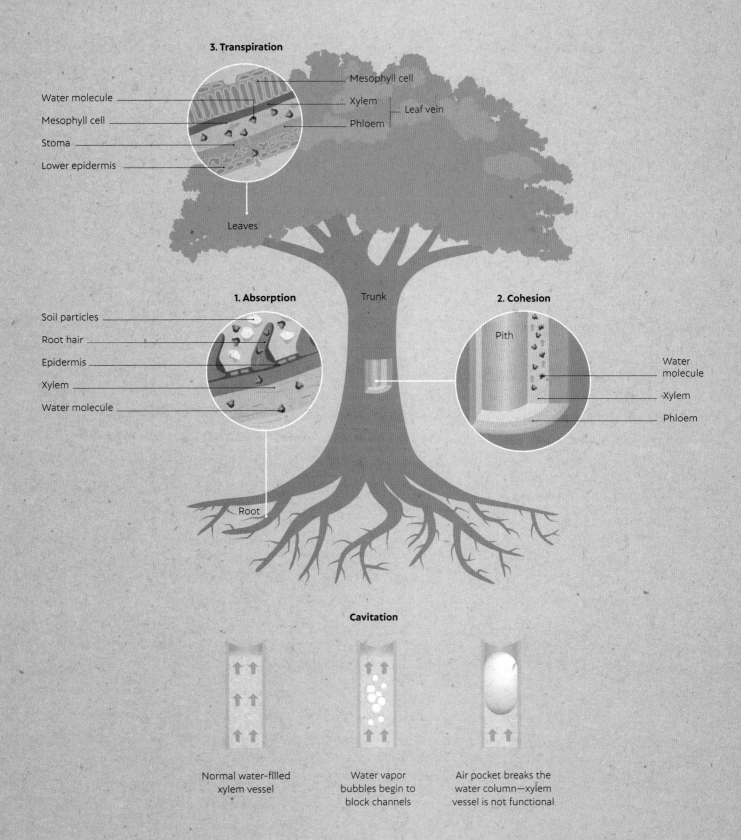

3. Transpiration

Mesophyll cell

Water molecule

Mesophyll cell

Xylem

Stoma

Phloem

Leaf vein

Lower epidermis

Leaves

1. Absorption

Trunk

2. Cohesion

Soil particles

Root hair

Pith

Epidermis

Xylem

Water molecule

Water molecule

Xylem

Root

Phloem

Cavitation

Normal water-filled xylem vessel

Water vapor bubbles begin to block channels

Air pocket breaks the water column—xylem vessel is not functional

Reaching for the sky

The height of forests is an essential measurement, as forest vegetation is typified by verticality. The striving of trees to dominate the canopy, to gain the light they need to drive photosynthesis in their leaves and to gain control of local resources, drive the processes that ultimately produce forest patterns.

GLOBAL FOREST CANOPY HEIGHTS

In 2010, the ICESat satellite provided the first global lidar reconnaissance of the heights of the world's forests measured as height of the tallest 10 percent of the trees.

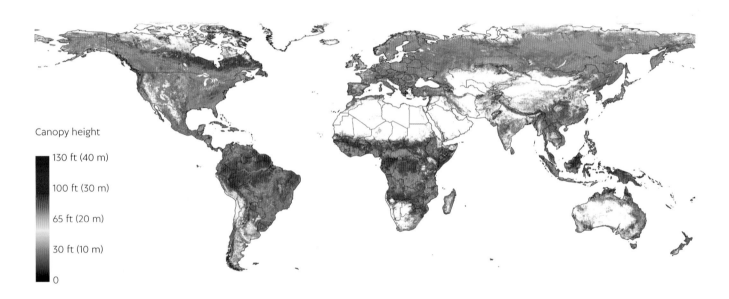

Canopy height

130 ft (40 m)

100 ft (30 m)

65 ft (20 m)

30 ft (10 m)

0

Often a tree's primary allocation to its growth of sugars derived from photosynthesis is to activate the top bud(s) and prioritize their elongation to add height. For ecologists, height reveals much about the status and future of each of the trees comprising a forest. For foresters, the height that a single-species forest of trees of equal age can reach at a given time is called the "site index" and it reveals the value of land for forest management. Site index tells a forester when to thin a forest, when to harvest it, and how densely the seedlings should be replanted in the regenerating forest after harvesting.

The use of lidar (light detection and ranging) instruments from ground, airplane, or satellite platforms has revolutionized local, and now global, capacity to measure forest height and its change. The map above shows the average heights of the tallest 10 percent of the trees in forests as seen from space using a 1,650 ft (500 m) spatial resolution. In this study, scientists used the Geoscience Laser Altimeter System on

board NASA's ICESat satellite to collect and calibrate 1,058,380 forest patches. ICESat was originally designed to measure the amount of ice in the Earth's polar ice sheets; that it has also proved able to measure forest heights is very fortuitous.

The temperate conifer forests were the tallest forests measured by ICESat, but globally they were also the most variable in height. The boreal forests were the shortest forests, and among these the shortest were the extensive deciduous larch (genus *Larix*) forests of northern Asia. The Indo-Malayan region has notably tall tropical and subtropical coniferous forests. Menara, the Yellow Meranti (*Shorea faguetiana*) tree, is a record height for a tropical tree and is from this region. The African tropics has taller temperate broad-leaved and mixed forests, but shorter tropical forests than other regions.

▲ **Lidar search**

Mountain Ash (Eucalyptus regnans, left) and Yellow Meranti (Shorea faguetiana, right). Scientists continue to seek out the tallest trees. New discoveries are on the increase with the availability of remote sensing to survey the heights of forest canopies.

WORLD'S TALLEST TREES

Species of extremely tall trees and the locations where they
can be found on a map of observed maximum tree heights.

1 *Picea sitchensis*
(Sitka Spruce)
230–330 ft/70–100 m

2 *Abies procera*
(Noble Fir)
195–295 ft/60–90 m

3 *Liriodendron tulipifera*
(Yellow Poplar)
80–160 ft/25–50 m

4 *Pinus strobus*
(Eastern White Pine)
130–195 ft/40–60 m

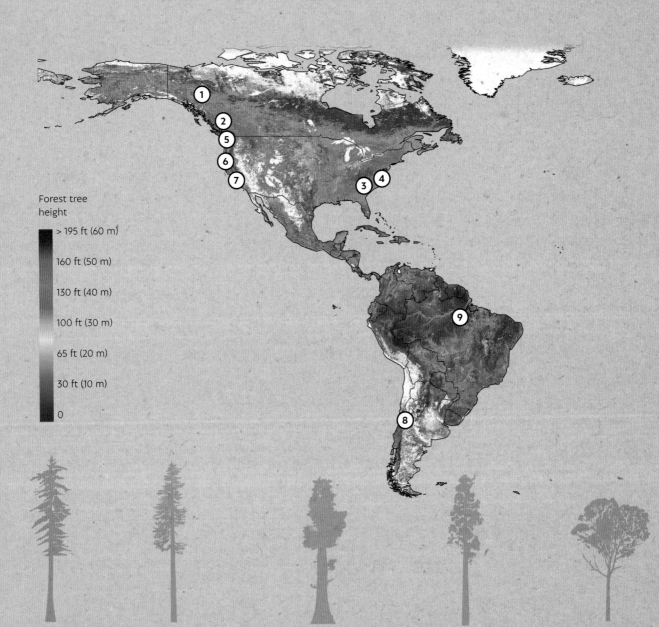

Forest tree
height

> 195 ft (60 m)

160 ft (50 m)

130 ft (40 m)

100 ft (30 m)

65 ft (20 m)

30 ft (10 m)

0

5 *Sequoia sempervirens*
(Coast Redwood)
230–375 ft/70–115 m

6 *Pseudotsuga menziesii*
(Douglas Fir)
160–330 ft/50–100 m

7 *Sequoiadendron giganteum*
(Giant Sequoia)
195–330 ft/60–100 m

8 *Fitzroya cupressoides*
(Patagonian Cypress)
160–230 ft/50–70 m

9 *Diniza excelsa*
(Angelim Vermelho)
160–280 ft/50–85 m

10 *Picea abies*
(Norway Spruce)
130–160 ft/40–50 m

11 *Abies normandiana*
(Nordman Fir)
160–195 ft/50–60 m

12 *Koompassia excelsa*
(Tualang Tree)
160–230 ft/50–70 m

13 *Shorea faguetiana*
(Yellow Meranti)
230–330 ft/70–100 m

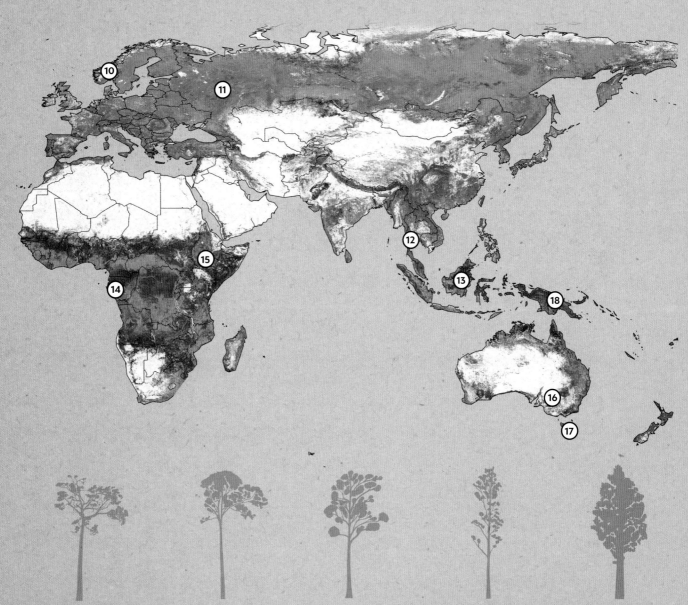

14 *Baillonella toxisperma*
(Moabi)
130–230 ft/40–70 m

15 *Entandrophragma excelsum*
(Tiama)
160–260 ft/50–80 m

16 *Eucalyptus globulus*
(Blue Gum)
195–295 ft/60–90 m

17 *Eucalyptus regnans*
(Mountain Ash)
260–330 ft/80–100 m

18 *Araucaria hunsteinii*
(Klink-Pine)
160–295 ft/50–90 m

2

Scale and the Forest Ecosystem

What is a forest?

As we saw in Chapter 1, "tree" is a biologically complicated term. It follows that if a forest is composed of trees, then its definition could inherit some of that complexity as well. However, dictionary definitions that a forest is "an area dominated by trees" seem straightforward enough. For the sake of simplicity, this is the definition we will use in this book.

▼ **Medieval forest**

In medieval Europe, forests were defined as any uncultivated land, which by law belonged to the Crown and were used as game preserves for royal hunts.

In this simple definition, the one tricky word is "dominated." In forests, trees usually dominate with respect to being the tallest, largest in mass, or most effectual in changing the local environment, but they are not necessarily dominant in terms of having the greatest number of individuals or the most species relative to other structural categories. Forests are structurally complex, and this complexity may be incorporated into one forest definition but not another. One reason a simpler definition for forest is preferred is that the term has hundreds of nuanced meanings, mainly because forests are important to people in so many ways and at so many scales.

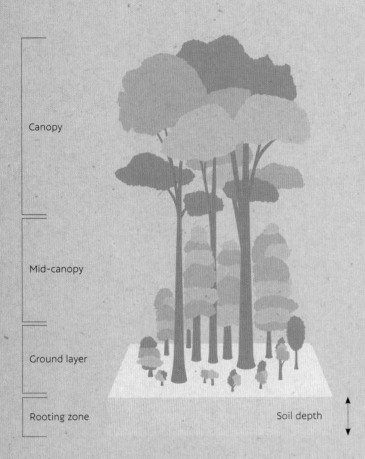

Canopy

Mid-canopy

Ground layer

Rooting zone

Soil depth

COMPONENTS OF A FOREST

In this case a survey plot in a forest is used for simplicity. The canopy is the top of the forest, the mid-canopy refers to trees below the canopy trees, and the ground layer is the vegetation near the ground. The leaf area of the forest is the total area of leaves per area of ground. The rooting zone is the depth into the soil that the roots can access. While tree roots can grow to great depths, in most forests 90 percent or more of the active roots are in the top meter of soil. Survey plots are arranged across an area. Sample systems of survey plots are averaged to obtain a measure of forests over a given area.

The word "forest"

"Forest" as a word derives from ancient law and more precise definitions are important in modern law and environmental policy. Etymologically, it originates from the Latin *foris*, meaning "outside." The Latin root *for(s)* carries this meaning in several European languages—for example, in the English word foreigner, meaning "one from the outside." In medieval England, forests were land outside cultivation and by law belonged to the Crown, typically for use as royal hunting reserves. In Europe, the same concept appears for the first time in the laws of the Lombards, who ruled the Italian Peninsula in 568-774 CE, and in the capitularies of the Frankish emperor Charlemagne (724-814 CE), with forest (*foresta* in medieval Latin) again referring not to the nature of the land cover but to royal game reserves.

Forest legislation

Law and ecology still come together in defining a forest. Increasing the growth and expansion of forests can reduce greenhouse gas concentrations in the atmosphere and ameliorate global climate change, and this drives a significant focus on forests today. We are now deeply involved with policy and legislation of forests of trees at every scale, from patches of trees to forest parks, to state and national forest reserves, and to forests over the national and global levels. Forest consultant H. Gyde Lund has compiled a running list of 1,713 words that might be translated as "forest" in more than 500 languages, along with more than a thousand other definitions developed for use at international, national, state, provincial, or local levels. In these, a forest is defined as an area of land covered to some degree by trees, or at least potentially so.

TREE CANOPY COVER

The amount of forest cover depends on how forests are defined. The maps shown here show the global extent of forest under the requirement that 75 percent of the surface is covered by tree canopies (top), and 10 percent of the surface (bottom). (Sources: Hansen et al. 2003; Kirkup 2001.)

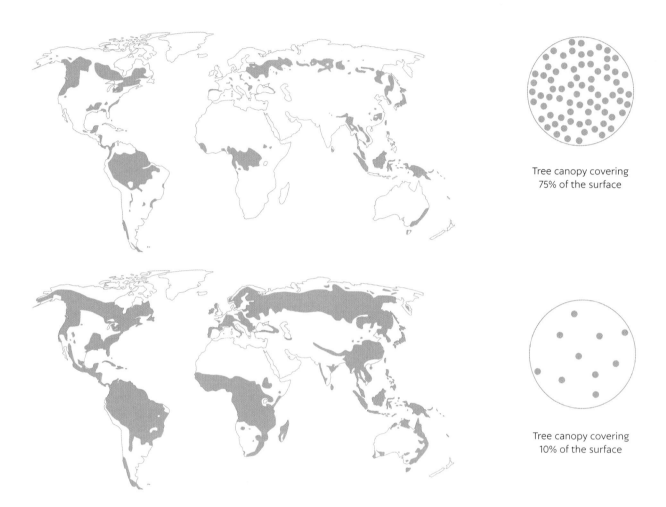

Tree canopy covering
75% of the surface

Tree canopy covering
10% of the surface

Defining forest lands

National laws and policies often attempt to bound forest definitions quantitatively by asking a set of questions. What is the minimum area a forest must occupy? What is the minimum tree cover in a forest? How tall must the trees in a forest be? In countries in which trees are planted in strips for erosion control, for shelter from the wind, for shade, or for aesthetics, how wide must these strips be to be called forests?

Minimum tree cover (the area of the sky blocked by leaves, stems, and branches) is sometimes not considered a necessary criterion in the definitions included among Lund's many terms. If it is considered at all, it ranges from as little as 10 percent up to 80 percent. It is important to note that the greater the lower limit of tree cover used to define a forest, the less "forest" there is in a particular area, region, or nation. The Food and Agriculture Organization of the United Nations defines a forest as an area of more than 1¼ acres (0.5 ha) with trees taller than 16 ft (5 m) and with the tree canopies covering at least 10 percent of the area. This definition is often used in international data compilations of forest cover and is the usual legal descriptor for a range of international forest issues, including storage of carbon or biomass (weight of organic matter per unit area), national inventories of forest cover, and rates of forest clearing or reforestation.

AUSTRALIAN CLASSIFICATION

The Australian government has a long tradition of systematically classifying its unique vegetation types using a combination of cover and height. Some examples of forests categories include the following:

- Tall closed forests (rain forests)—closed forests with tree heights above 100 ft (30 m) and reaching to 330 ft (100 m) in height; cover greater than 70 percent

- Tall open forests—tree heights above 100 ft (30 m) and reaching to 330 ft (100 m); cover 30–70 percent

- Open forests—tree heights above 30 ft (10 m) and reaching to 100 ft (30 m); cover 30–70 percent

- Low open forests—tree heights to 30 ft (10 m); cover 30–70 percent

- Woodlands—tree heights to 100 ft (30 m); cover 10–30 percent

- Open woodlands—tree heights to 100 ft (30 m); cover less than 10 percent

- Low closed forests—tree heights less than 30 ft (10 m); cover greater than 70 percent.

Height

100–330 ft (30–100 m)			Tall open forests	Tall closed forests (rain forests)
30–100 ft (10–30 m)		Woodlands	Open forests	
0–30 ft (0–10 m)	Open woodlands	Low closed forests	Low open forests	
% Cover	0–10%	10–30%	30–70%	70–100%

The ecosystem concept

The mid-1930s was a time of great challenge for ecologists. A horrific drought and poor farming methods in the North American Prairies combined to create the Dust Bowl, amplifying the effects of the Great Depression and leaving the nation and the world reeling from the consequences of past abuses of the land and natural systems.

Amid this worldwide turmoil, the Ecological Society of America produced a pivotal publication, the 1935 issue number 4 of the journal *Ecology*, dedicated to Henry Chandler Cowles (1869-1939), whose work on long-term change in ecosystems is discussed in Chapter 3. This publication was a kaleidoscopic interweaving of topics in an ecologically changed and still changing United States. At the start of the issue is a remarkable paper by the Cambridge professor Sir Arthur G. Tansley (1871-1955) entitled "The use and abuse of vegetational concepts and terms." This contained the first printed use of the word "ecosystem."

Tansley defined the term with the intent of transforming ecology beyond a mere description of nature and toward a scientific understanding of dynamic change in nature. Since the first usage of the word was in its definition, one might think this would make its meaning clear. However, the botanist's text is somewhat opaque to the modern reader:

▲ **Dust bowl**

Drought acerbated widespread land abuse across North America in the 1930s. In this setting, the ecosystem concept originated from attempts to predict dynamic systems of ecological/environmental change.

▶ **Ecosystem components**

An ecosystem is a specifically defined, interactive ecological/environment system. It is defined to understand and predict change.

It is these systems so formed which, from the point of view of the ecologist, are the basic units of nature on the face of the earth. Our natural human prejudices force us to consider the organisms (in the sense of the biologist) as the most important parts of these systems, but certainly the inorganic "factors" are also parts—there could be no systems without them, and there is constant interchange of the most various kinds within each system, not only between the organisms but between the organic and the inorganic. These ecosystems, as we may call them, are of the most various kinds and sizes. They form one category of the multitudinous physical systems from the universe as a whole down to the atom.

What Tansley referred to as an ecosystem would nowadays be called a system of definition, a clearly defined abstraction that includes the important parts of systems and their interactions but excludes irrelevant things. Forming abstractions is an essential procedure for progress in modern science in general, and is no less so in forest ecology. One isolates system components and interactions to gain understanding. The ecosystem is formulated in this same manner—identifying the components needed for understanding a given question at a given time and at a given scale.

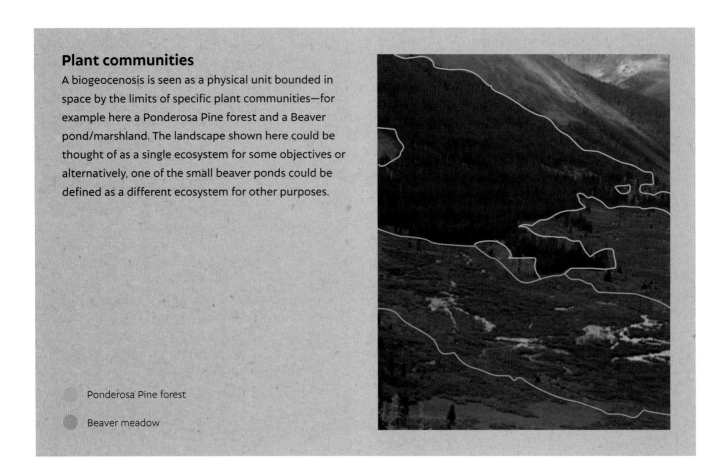

Plant communities

A biogeocenosis is seen as a physical unit bounded in space by the limits of specific plant communities—for example here a Ponderosa Pine forest and a Beaver pond/marshland. The landscape shown here could be thought of as a single ecosystem for some objectives or alternatively, one of the small beaver ponds could be defined as a different ecosystem for other purposes.

- Ponderosa Pine forest
- Beaver meadow

Forest ecosystems

Since the term ecosystem is a concept, ecologists study an ecosystem not *the* ecosystem. Research objectives determine an ecosystem's case-specific definition. However, there are many ecological studies that have similar objectives and hence use similar ecosystem definitions. For example, an older but similar concept to ecosystem is biogeocenosis. This is defined as a community of plants and animals, along with their associated abiotic environment. A community in this case is an area with a similar assemblage of plants and animals across its extent or compared to other areas, and abiotic refers to inanimate components such as geology, the non-living parts of soils, and weather variables. Biogeocenosis is often applied by ecologists in central Europe somewhat analogously to the use of ecosystem. However, it differs from ecosystem as a definition by its reference to a specific area defined by the plant or animal community. It is a special case of an ecosystem—one in which its size or location size is defined by a community.

Ecosystem services models

Ecosystem services models are often based on the flows of commodities that people receive from properly functioning forests, including clean water, flood and erosion control, and wildlife populations. They are often constructed to determine the value forests have for people and/or indicate the risks if the forests producing these services were taken away. In this context, forest ecosystems are defined as environmental services delivery systems. As with food webs, transfers of valuable services of commodities coming from a forest are shown in diagram format, with the various services sometimes quantified as dollar values. Models based on these ecosystems are often developed to incentivize the offset of environmentally detrimental aspects of human activities.

Food webs

Another commonly used subset of ecosystems are food webs. These often emphasize plants and animals, and the transfer of food energy among them through predation. They are generally represented as "who eats whom" diagrams, with arrows indicating energy transfer and boxes indicating food energy stored in a particular population. This energy transfer is sometimes abstracted as a positive or negative effect of one species on another, and the complexity of the pathways varies under different conditions, which has implications for the maintenance of species diversity at a given location. One important issue concerns whether there are species in a location whose removal might cause a collapse in the total number of species there. Similar questions arise in assessing the effects on food web patterns of the introduction of exotic species. The current rate of extinction of species across the planet is high, and food web models are valuable tools for exploring the potential knock-on effects of one species' extinction on others.

Ecosystems that emphasize element cycling resemble food webs, but they trace the movement of elements through an ecosystem (see pages 100-105). Food energy is dissipated as it moves through food webs, but chemical elements are conserved in transfers within forests. Forest ecosystems often include large recycling loops, particularly with respect to essential elements for plant nutrition (see pages 92-93).

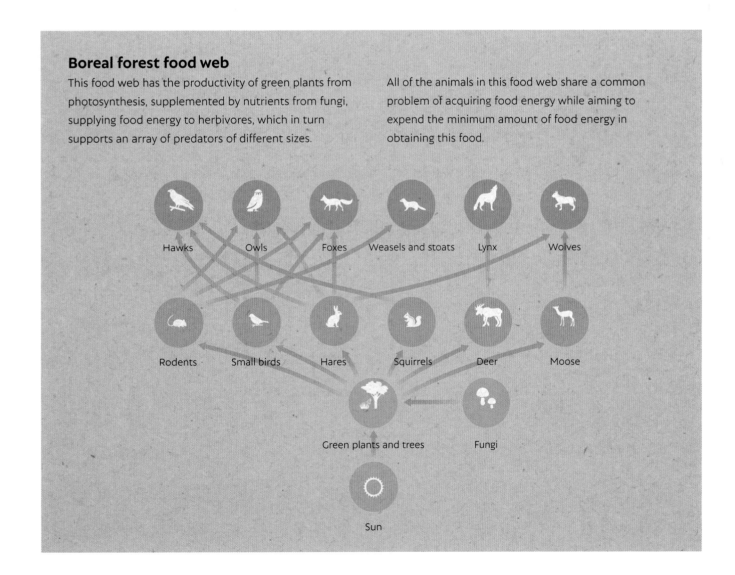

Boreal forest food web

This food web has the productivity of green plants from photosynthesis, supplemented by nutrients from fungi, supplying food energy to herbivores, which in turn supports an array of predators of different sizes.

All of the animals in this food web share a common problem of acquiring food energy while aiming to expend the minimum amount of food energy in obtaining this food.

Hawks   Owls   Foxes   Weasels and stoats   Lynx   Wolves

Rodents   Small birds   Hares   Squirrels   Deer   Moose

Green plants and trees   Fungi

Sun

The tiles of a mosaic

When one flies over a mature forest or views it from a high lookout point, a graininess of the canopy arises from the average size of a large tree. Depending on the forest and its age, this is in the order of 30-100 ft (10-30 m) in diameter. The grains or tiles, which are the crowns of large individual trees, tessellate to form the mosaic that is the forest canopy.

▼ **Crown shyness**
Crown shyness is the tendency of tree canopy crowns to have open space between them.

Because buds often grow at or near the ends of tree limbs, the branches of adjacent trees knock them off when they are whipped about by the wind. This creates a phenomenon called crown shyness, in which the crowns of trees do not touch and there is space between them. Lie on your back on the floor of a forest and look straight up through the canopy, or look at the same view taken with the fish-eye lens of a camera. The pattern of light streaming through the canopy has a beauty that resembles the rose window of a Gothic cathedral, and much of that light comes from center (directly overhead), through openings created by crown shyness. Much less light comes through oblique side-view angles.

Crown shyness and the forest floor

The regularity of forest canopies, combined with crown shyness, implies that the forest floor is mostly shaded by the dominant canopy trees—a photograph taken at midday in a forest displays speckles of light. It is not surprising that many small forest animals, particularly young mammals, have light or white spots as camouflage in their light-speckled habitats. Spots of the brightest forest-floor illumination derive from shafts of light shining through direct, open paths from the sky to the ground, which are created by crown shyness. When the canopies of the trees are deep, crown shyness generates openings from the top of the canopy to the forest floor. If the angle of incoming sunlight matches the orientation of these openings, then shafts of sunlight shine through the canopy to the ground. Because the sun's angle changes with the time of day and time of year, these sun flecks blink on or off at locations through the canopy and on the forest floor. On the forest floor, green plants rely on the light provided by sun flecks and light shafts for their photosynthesis.

▲ **Blending in**
Juvenile mammals, such as fawns, often have white spots to help them blend with forest floor sunspots.

Yoda's law

When viewed from above, crown shyness sharpens the boundaries among the individual tree crowns and increases the apparency of the mosaic nature of forests. This is especially easy to see in conifer forests, such as Douglas Fir (*Pseudotsuga menziesii*) forests. Crown shyness among encroaching, adjacent trees causes the trees to carve away the edges of their neighbors, a phenomenon called crown-pruning by foresters. Tree-to-tree competition in closed forests generally favors the larger, "dominant" trees, with subordinate trees growing more slowly and suffering, leading to increased death. This drives a reduction in the overall number of subordinate trees (thinning) in a growing forest, a phenomenon called Yoda's law for the Japanese ecologist, Kyoji Yoda (1931-1996), who first described it. Thinning laws originated when Japanese forest ecologists were looking to predict the numbers and sizes of trees growing in regenerating stands from a theoretical basis because they did not have the extremely long records of forest yield that form the empirical basis for European forestry. Some important statistical issues vex the derivation of the relation between

the average size of trees and the total number of trees. Nevertheless, Yoda's law indicates a semi-crystalline regularity in the organization of forest canopies. In nature, this regularity may be one of the sources of the beauty of forests as an object of contemplation.

Granularity and self-organization

With modern remote-sensing technologies, one can detect the graininess of forest canopies, as well as quantify the rates of photosynthesis according to tree-scale granularity across entire landscapes. This is in no small part due to the many ways in which trees alter their local environments. A theoretical basis has developed for understanding the manner in which the forest mosaic self-organizes through predictable interactions into regular patterns and spacing. Further, the death of an individual canopy-level tree is a locally significant event in a closed forest, initiating a more-or-less predictable chain of responses over time that repair the holes in the ventilated canopy. The sections that follow discuss these essential forest processes in more detail.

▼ **Crown shyness from above**
Aerial view of a coniferous forest canopy in the Carpathian Mountains, Ivano-Frankivsk Oblast, Ukraine.

Pattern and process in forests

Alex S. Watt (1892-1985), a professor at Cambridge University, England, published a highly influential paper in 1947 entitled "Pattern and process in the plant community." The key insight of this paper is that all vegetation, whether grassland, heathland, or forest, consists of patches that differ in age—that is, time since the last disturbance (sudden destruction of living biomass) or mortality event (see pages 80-81).

▼ **Natural firebreak**

Firebreaks, whether man-made or natural, are areas with reduced burnable fuels and/ or areas in which the potential fuels have a high moisture content. River channels have both low fuel and high moisture.

Watt stated that some patches are young due to recent disturbance or species decline, while others are old because they have been free of recent disturbances or deaths. He argued that a vegetation pattern is a snapshot of an ongoing dynamic process. Prior to this, vegetation ecologists had often focused only on the patterns themselves and, within these, usually only on the oldest patches. Watt's revolutionary "pattern and process" perspective links all patch types with the dynamic process—in other words, vegetation has to be understood as both pattern and process. While process creates pattern, the converse is also true. For instance, a flammable patch of forest may be surrounded by natural "firebreaks" like wetlands, such that a fire is unable to spread to that patch, thereby lowering fire frequency there.

Age and process

We can take this a step further: the processes themselves can be correlated with patch age. One of the vegetation types Watt described in his paper is English deciduous woodland. With time, the dominant trees here become larger, but they also become more vulnerable to wind and insects. Thus, the probability of disturbance increases with patch age. In other words, regardless of whether wind and insects increase or fall over time for other reasons, there is a natural rhythm of forest disturbance that is a function of time since last disturbance. As time goes by, short-lived species that colonize disturbance patches are replaced by longer-lived species that are more tolerant of low-resource conditions. And so the cycle repeats— as long as all other conditions, such as external factors, remain constant.

PATTERN AND PROCESS

The concept of pattern and process was initially developed by Alex S. Watt in his doctoral work in 1924 on ancient beech forests on the Sussex Downs in southern England. Watt had the insight that the patchwork patterns of small areas occupied by trees of different sizes in a mature European

Beech (*Fagus sylvatica*) forest that he studied arose from an ecological process filling the openings left in the forest canopy by the death of a large canopy tree. The patches of the forests could be resolved by reassembling them into a coherent sequence of regular underlying change.

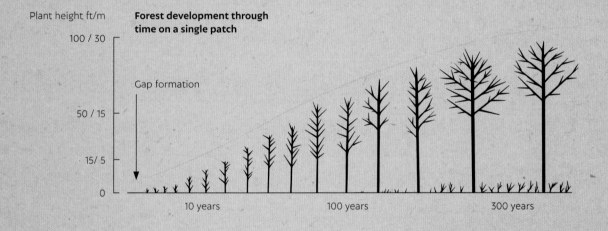

Plant height ft/m

Forest development through time on a single patch

100 / 30

Gap formation

50 / 15

15/ 5

0

10 years 100 years 300 years

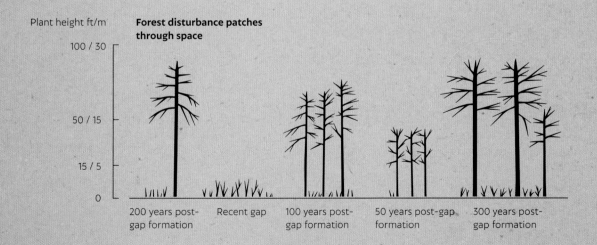

Plant height ft/m

Forest disturbance patches through space

100 / 30

50 / 15

15 / 5

0

200 years post-gap formation Recent gap 100 years post-gap formation 50 years post-gap formation 300 years post-gap formation

Dominant species after disturbance

To further illustrate the importance of pattern and process, consider the high-elevation spruce- and fir-dominated forests of the southern Appalachians in Great Smoky Mountains National Park, North Carolina and Tennessee. There are four potential dominants of the forest, depending on disturbance characteristics: Pin Cherry (*Prunus pensylvanica*), Yellow Birch (*Betula alleghaniensis*), Red Spruce (*Picea rubens*), and Fraser Fir (*Abies fraseri*).

Trees that dominate large patches

Disturbances that cause the loss of tens to hundreds of canopy trees result in colonization by Pin Cherry, a species with a persistent pool of dormant seeds in the soil. These high-magnitude disturbances, causing the upheaval of many trees and exposing mineral soil, are rare. Pin Cherry seeds are capable of long dormancy (100 years or more) and the species is the fastest grower of the four species considered here. It soon dominates large disturbance patches but lives only 40-60 years. It reproduces at 5-10 years of age and goes on producing seeds, replenishing the dormant soil seed pool. Without disturbance, Pin Cherry declines and ultimately is represented by only the dormant seeds below ground.

▶ **Pin Cherry**

*Pin Cherry (*Prunus pensylvanica*) is a rapidly growing but short-lived tree that colonizes large disturbance patches, usually from a buried pool of dormant seeds that accumulate in high elevation soils through bird dispersal.*

▶ **Yellow Birch**

*The seedlings of Yellow Birch (*Betula alleghaniensis*) have a low survival rate in the shade but can colonize gaps resulting from the fall of three to five or more canopy trees.*

Trees that dominate small patches

At the other end of the disturbance spectrum are windstorms that cause the loss of 1-5 canopy trees. It is rare that Pin Cherry dominates in these small patches. Instead, the three other species compete here, and they each have an interesting contrast in their life histories. Yellow Birch is intolerant of deep shade and its small, abundant seeds do not have long dormancy. Seedlings from these seeds rarely survive for five years in the shade, but where there is more sun, many germinate and survivorship is high. Yellow Birch does especially well on mineral soils produced by tree uprooting and on the moist, moss-covered trunks of fallen trees. Its roots often grow over the trunks and down into the soil (when the trunk is gone, the trees can appear to be "up on stilts"). Yellow Birch starts competing for new disturbance patches at a very small size since germination occurs just after colonization.

By contrast, the two other main species, Red Spruce and Fraser Fir, are shade-tolerant. Their seeds do not have long dormancy, and their seedlings and saplings persist and grow slowly in the shade for decades prior to disturbance. When the disturbance occurs, they may be from 3 ft to tens of feet tall, as contrasted with the very young (and small) seedlings of the Yellow Birch. There is a risk to these understory stems in that they may be damaged by falling trees during the disturbance event. If they avoid this damage, they grow faster than they did before the disturbance because they are "released" from the limiting conditions, including low light, that they experienced prior to the disturbance. However, they do not grow as fast as Yellow Birch, which in turn does not grow as fast as Pin Cherry in the largest disturbance patches.

Contrasting strategies

Thus, the various species have contrasting strategies. Pin Cherry is a specialist of the largest disturbance patches. In the small disturbance patches, spruce and fir have the head start in terms of initial size, but they may suffer damage from falling trees, while the birch grows faster once it has germinated. In some new disturbance patches, it may be a toss-up as to which succeeds! Finally, there is an interesting difference between the spruce and fir: both are shade-tolerant, but the spruce has fewer seeds and saplings than the fir, and lives about twice long as the fir (250 years vs. 120 years). In other words, the fir is more able to take over canopy spots, but the spruce hangs on to those it acquires twice as long as the fir. The fir has to have a higher rate of reproduction because, like Alice in Wonderland, it has to run twice as fast to stay in the same place.

▲ **Red Spruce**
As a deeply shade-tolerant species, Red Spruce (Picea rubens) increases through successional time.

▼ **Fraser Fir**
Fraser Fir (Abies fraseri) is also deeply shade-tolerant. While it does increase through successional time, its maximum lifespan is less than one-half that of Red Spruce and Yellow Birch. Hence, it must produce many more successful seedlings to remain a codominant of these forests.

Gap colonization and fir waves

Alex S. Watt's gap-filling paradigm (see pages 68-69) has underpinned the formulation of modern computer models that simulate the interactions among trees by predicting the growth, death, and regeneration of each tree on a small area of land about the size of the canopy gap left by the death of a large tree.

▶ **Exposed hillside slopes**

On exposed hillsides in the northeastern US and in similar settings in Japan, long, white, evenly spaced strips of trees move slowly across the landscape.

Probably not entirely coincidentally, forests are often sampled using small survey plots of about the same size. One can sample a forest landscape with such plots to get an inventory of the trees there and then resample it some years later to detect changes. Models of the changes of the individual trees on small plots can then be compared to resurvey data and applied to predict expected forest change over time. Simulating thousands of small plots inhabited by millions of trees of multiple species is light work for a modern computer.

Fir waves

One does not expect vegetation to arrange itself into patterns, but in some cases "self-organizing" vegetation does just that. For example, fir waves occur naturally in Balsam Fir (*Abies balsamea*) forests on exposed, windswept mountain slopes in the northeastern United States. At a distance, these appear in the landscape as white stripes. The stripes are, in fact, the white trunks of standing dead and downed trees; the green sections in between are the green crowns of regenerating fir trees following the "crest" of the fir wave. A spatially synchronized pattern in dying trees forms as mature trees die from exposure to winds and rime ice. In cross section, a wave of death and regeneration moves in the direction of the prevailing winds. Fir waves also form under similar climatic conditions on windy slopes in Japan, notably on Mt. Shimagare (meaning "Stripes of Dead Trees"), but involve two different fir species, Maries' Fir (*A. mariesii*) and Veitch's Fir (*A. veitchii*).

Fir waves are more than ecological curiosities; they are significant as natural examples of the pattern and process paradigm. In forests, pattern and process predict the recovery of a local area following changes resulting from the death of a large canopy-dominant tree. The resultant opening in the forest canopy lets in more light and potentially provides additional resources. Seedlings and small saplings begin to grow and compete with one another to become the next dominant tree. A mature forest arises as a mosaic, comprised of the locations at which the death of a big tree at some time or another has initiated this sequential recovery process. Putting the landscape mosaic pieces together is like assembling an ecological jigsaw, the puzzle being resolved by identifying patterns of individual small patches covered with different temporal vegetation stages of this small-scale quasi-cyclical process. In fir waves, the recovery process is clearly seen, displayed across an exposed hillside.

PROGRESSIVE DIE OFF

In cross section, a fir wave reveals a sequenced recovery
following the death of a large tree. This affords opportunities
for the regeneration and growth of small trees windward
of the dead tree. The death wave continues to move leeward,
the new tree grows and eventually becomes the large tree
that falls victim to the next traveling wave.

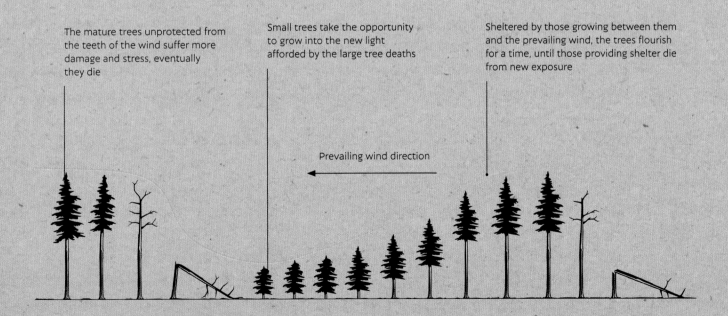

The mature trees unprotected from
the teeth of the wind suffer more
damage and stress, eventually
they die

Small trees take the opportunity
to grow into the new light
afforded by the large tree deaths

Sheltered by those growing between them
and the prevailing wind, the trees flourish
for a time, until those providing shelter die
from new exposure

Prevailing wind direction

The roles of different trees

Since the pattern and process concept of ecosystems was initially developed to explain the process through which canopy gaps are filled following the deaths of large trees, it is useful to consider the different ways a tree might survive and prosper in a closed forest. Differences in regeneration, tree maturation, growth, and longevity all conspire to make one species "win" under one set of conditions but another species win under another set.

▼ **Evapotranspiration**
This combines the evaporation of water from leaf tissues and water from all other sources, such as soils, water bodies, and plant surfaces.

One factor often mentioned is shade tolerance. We have already touched on this in discussing the interactions among trees vying for dominance following disturbance in the Great Smoky Mountains National Park (see pages 70-71). Some shade-tolerant species are capable of growing slowly in lower light conditions, while light-demanding species grow more rapidly under conditions of high levels of light. Often after a large disturbance, the light-demanding species initially prosper but then subsequently fail to regenerate in their own shade, losing dominance in the next generation to more shade-tolerant trees.

Trade-offs

There are trade-offs involved in these differences among trees. For example, a tree with a large volume of tissue that is biochemically capable of high rates of photosynthesis under high light conditions suffers the costs of maintaining this volume when light conditions are lower. In the case of Ponderosa Pine (*Pinus ponderosa*), its seedlings must have at least 30.6 percent of full sunlight to break even on the costs of their photosynthetic "machinery" versus the gains from maintaining high levels of net photosynthesis when unshaded. In contrast, Sugar Maple (*Acer saccharum*) needs only 3.4 percent full sunlight to meet its costs and can lurk on the forest floor waiting for the death of an overhead tree. There are also high costs associated with having many layers of leaves (multilayers; see page 42), but these offer greater productive capability in high light conditions. In contrast, monolayer trees with a single leaf layer have lower costs but cannot profit as much when there is more light.

There are other similar trade-offs for trees: trees that capture a lot of incoming light need more water to cool their leaves by evapotranspiration; trees with high photosynthesis rates need more plant nutrients to produce leaves; and trees in low nutrient settings are more likely to be evergreen and hold their leaves longer, but new leaves often have higher photosynthesis rates. There is no single best way to be a tree—the best strategy depends on the environment. However, trees can have a powerful effect on their microenvironment. They alter the shading, the evapotranspiration of water, the uptake of nutrients, and the micro-conditions for seed germination.

▲ **Sugar maple**
*Sugar maple (*Acer saccharum*) seeds possess a "wing" for stabilized descent to the ground. The species is shade tolerant, so the seedlings produced by these seeds can be prevalent in forest understories.*

◤ **Ponderosa Pine**
*Ponderosa pine (*Pinus ponderosa*) seedlings are shade intolerant and compete with dense grasses. They can benefit from low intensity fires that reduce grass cover.*

How to be a tree

It is through the trade-offs trees make that they give richness to the dynamics of forests. Roelof Oldeman (who has long been involved in developing geometric models of tree architecture; see page 43) defines two basic strategies on how to be a tree. Trees could take the strategy of being "gamblers," producing many seeds that sprout and, if they are in relative sunny, favorable places, grow rapidly to become canopy trees. Or they might be "strugglers," which can persist in shady environments even though they have low growth rates. As trees around them die, the strugglers inch upward and through their tenacity can eventually become a canopy dominant.

Upon their deaths, large trees produce large gaps; smaller trees produce small gaps or may hardly produce canopy gaps at all. Strugglers regenerate relatively well in smaller gaps because they are more tolerant of shading, while gamblers regenerate in large gaps because they can take advantage of the higher light levels found there. In the case of many gamblers, tree regeneration is triggered by the change in the microenvironment created when a tree falls to produce a large gap (more light, hotter and perhaps drier conditions, exposed mineral soil uprooted by the falling tree, and so on). Trees can therefore be categorized as producing gaps when they die (or not) and requiring gaps to regenerate (or not). These two dichotomies taken together produce four different combinations of how to be a tree, and their interrelationships span all the standard types of ecological interactions.

Species that require gaps to regenerate and create gaps when they die, called large gamblers, are self-reinforcing. The death of a mature large gambler in the canopy is likely to lead to its replacement by another larger gambler species. The death of a large gambler also promotes the success of small gambler species, because these require gaps. However, small gamblers do not create large canopy gaps when they die, so their presence diminishes the number of future potential gaps needed by both large and small gamblers. Taken as a whole, large and small gamblers in an ecosystem have a positive-negative or, in ecological terms, a prey-predator relationship. Considering other pairings of simple tree roles: large gamblers and large strugglers are mutualistic and create a forest with large gaps; small strugglers and both large and small gamblers have a strong competitive relationship that favors small strugglers in the battle to control the size of the gaps; large and small strugglers are mutualistic and create conditions that help one another's regeneration. The interactions involved in holding canopy area in a forest have the complexity and intrigue of conspiracies for the throne in a medieval castle.

STRUGGLERS AND GAMBLERS

Large gambler species require gaps to regenerate and create gaps when they die; large struggler species do not require gaps to regenerate but create gaps when they die; small gambler species require gaps to regenerate but create gaps when they die; small struggler species do not require gaps to regenerate and do not create gaps when they die. Arrows indicate the effect of the death of a tree of one category on the category of the replacement in the next generation. The straight arrows indicate the positive or negative effect of the current presence of a given type of tree to the success of another type of tree in the next generation of canopy trees. The curved arrows indicate the effect of a given type of tree being replaced by the same type in the next generation. For example, large gamblers on their death create large gaps and are likely to be replaced as a canopy tree by another large gambler. Not the case for small gamblers, which do not produce the large gaps that they would need to replace themselves.

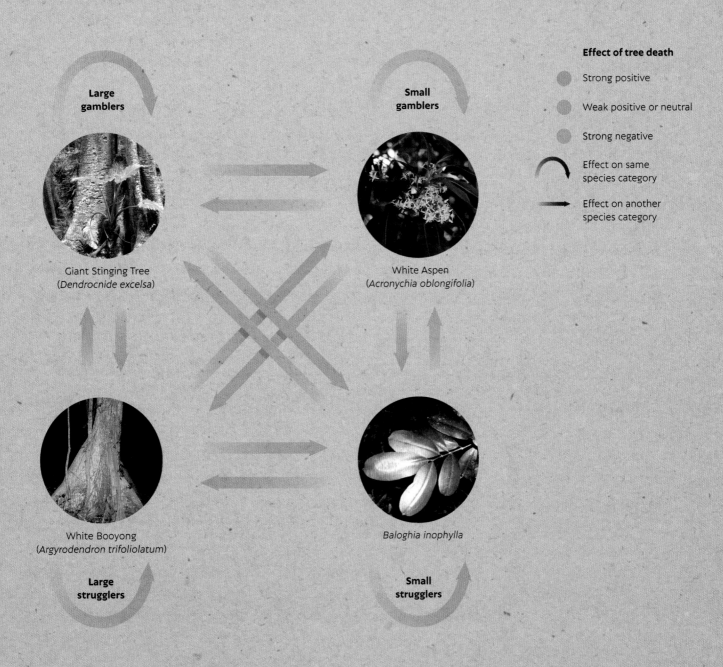

Large gamblers

Giant Stinging Tree
(*Dendrocnide excelsa*)

Small gamblers

White Aspen
(*Acronychia oblongifolia*)

White Booyong
(*Argyrodendron trifoliolatum*)

Large strugglers

Baloghia inophylla

Small strugglers

Effect of tree death

Strong positive

Weak positive or neutral

Strong negative

Effect on same species category

Effect on another species category

3

The Forest as a Dynamic Mosaic

Forest dynamics

Trees grow slowly from a human perspective and, in the absence of any sudden-acting human or natural disturbances, they can seem to be unchanging. If we examine them more closely, however, we can see evidence that forests are actually made up of dynamic patches that form a mosaic in which each patch has a different age, history, and trajectory. As defined in Chapter 2, this mosaic can also be described by pattern and process—a pattern of forest types and ages, and the processes that drive future changes.

▶ **Dynamic patchwork**
From an aerial view, mixed forests display a striking autumnal patchwork of green conifers interspersed with red, orange, and yellow broad-leaved deciduous trees.

In this chapter we explore the ways in which different tree species have dramatically differing roles in this dynamic patchwork. Forest dynamics also play an important role in the ecological health of the planet and in our own relation to the environment. This is because the patchwork affects how forests take up carbon from the atmosphere (acting as a carbon sink), how they release it after a disturbance (acting as a carbon source), and how they represent great storage vaults of carbon withheld from the atmosphere in their leaves, twigs, branches, boles, and root systems. Developing our understanding of forest dynamics has been one of the great achievements in ecological science over the last few decades.

Agents of forest change

At a landscape scale, forests are shaped by the slow-acting forces of growth and accumulation of living material (biomass), and by the fast-acting forces of natural and human disturbances such as felling and deforestation, which rapidly reduce biomass. Natural disturbances occurred even in pre-human times, but today their frequency and intensity are much influenced by anthropogenic environmental changes and patterns of land-use change.

Natural disturbances

Natural disturbances include windstorms, ice storms, avalanches, soil instability, droughts, floods, fires, volcanic eruptions, disease and pest outbreaks, and patterns of erosion and deposition along coasts and rivers. Characteristic disturbances vary across topographic positions and environmental gradients of temperature and moisture. For instance, fire requires sufficient moisture to allow the buildup of woody biomass between events and dry periods that dehydrate the biomass to carry a fire. Climate change is altering these events through variations in temperature, rainfall, and wind. Disturbance can also hasten the response of forests to climate change, in the sense that undisturbed vegetation cover presents a kind of inertial resistance to environmental change if the long-lived trees are viable as adults but no longer living in their ideal environmental setting. When disturbance to the existing canopy occurs, regeneration may then be rapid in response to the changed environmental conditions.

▼ **Wind**
The force of windstorms can overcome the structural resistance of trees, resulting in snapping of tree stems or the uprooting of whole trees. Here, the force of the wind exceeded the tensile strength of the tree stems, resulting in snapping.

The disturbance regime

The summed characteristics of natural disturbances in a particular region is called the disturbance regime. It includes not just the kind of disturbance, but also the disturbance frequency and magnitude. These two characteristics are usually inversely correlated: large and severe disturbances are rare, while small and mild ones are more common. Disturbances also vary in their specificity. For instance, some forest disturbances primarily affect the overstory (for example, large trees take the brunt of windstorms and are more likely to be hit by lightning), while others primarily affect the understory (for example, flooding and low-intensity fires that sweep through the forest at ground level but do not affect the canopy trees). In addition, pest species, whether natural or human-introduced, are usually specific to particular kinds of trees. Forest stands—areas with forests that are relatively similar with respect to tree age, size, and species composition—are often delineated by disturbances.

Disturbance magnitude also has consequences for forest age structure and patterns of forest stands. When disturbance affects large blocks of forest, the resulting pulse of forest regeneration results in a stand with canopy trees that are all close to one another in age. Disturbances that affect individual trees or small patches of trees result in a stand that is "all-aged," meaning that there is a greater age range among the dominant canopy trees.

▲ **Flooding**

Flooding can be a significant source of mortality in trees. Tree species vary in terms of the duration of flooding they can withstand.

▲ **Serotiny**

Like many other trees, Australian Banksia *store and protect their seeds in fire-resistant seedpods. These open after being roasted by wildfire to release viable seeds and regenerate new seedlings.*

◤ **Australian Grass Trees**

Grass Trees (Xanthorrhoea australis) *have resin that resists the heat blast from fire.*

Resistance adaptations

Disturbances have also been important evolutionary forces. Adaptations to disturbance include traits that allow some species to resist disturbance mortality, or different traits that allow other species to respond quickly to the conditions that occur after a disturbance has passed.

One of the most dramatic adaptations is cone serotiny, whereby species produce cones that are sealed shut by resins and require exposure to the heat of fire before they can open. This occurs in many species of trees worldwide—a good example is seen in some pines (genus *Pinus*). The fire must be both hot enough (in terms of the temperature experienced by a cone) to open the cone, and of short enough duration that the seeds fall onto the forest floor after the fire has passed. Because the cones do not open every year, a tree "stores" a decade or more of seed production in its crown, with a large number of seeds then being dispersed after fire. The seeds also often benefit if the fire has removed dense leaf litter on the soil surface and has reduced competition from pre-fire vegetation. In some pines, there is genetic variability in serotiny, such that some cones open without fire whereas others stay shut. Having multiple strategies in a variable and uncertain world is called bet hedging by evolutionary ecologists.

An interesting, but more subtle, adaptation to fire is tree bark. Species that occur where there are frequent fires often have thicker bark at a given tree size compared to "thin-barked" species that are more sensitive to fire. Thick bark insulates the cambium from exposure to high temperatures, which can kill living cells.

Strikingly, fire-resistant species often have their thickest bark growth within 6-9 ft (2-3 m) of the ground, the zone in which flames are more likely to be present. These species allocate less bark growth to canopy branches, where fire exposure is rarer.

Fires can heat the trunk of a tree enough to kill the cambial tissue all the way around the trunk, a process called girdling. This prevents the tree from growing continuous new vascular tissue that is needed to connect its roots to its canopy and eventually kills it. The temperature of some fires may be such that only patches of the cambial tissue are destroyed. In this case the wounds are manifested as fire scars. These are entry points for disease and pests, and increase the chance of tree mortality. If a tree survives and continues to grow, the trunk grows around the fire scar and eventually covers it. Fire scars are embedded in a tree's concentric growth rings (see pages 294-295 and 306-307) and document fire history and fire frequency.

Thick bark

Ponderosa Pine (Pinus ponderosa) trees have bark that is thickest near the ground to resist wildfire damage.

Serotinous cones

Table Mountain Pine (Pinus pungens) has serotinous cones that open to release their seeds after being heated by wildfires.

**Epicormic
sprouting**

Pitch Pine (Pinus
rigida) *is an example
of a species that
sprouts after a fire.*

Recovery adaptations

Another suite of disturbance adaptations includes those that affect recovery after
disturbance, rather than resistance to disturbance. Some species are adapted to the
high light levels and increased resources of recent disturbance patches, whereas
other species are adapted to the deep shade that occurs in undisturbed forest (see
pages 74–75). In addition to higher light levels, sites with a recent disturbance
have higher available nutrient levels because of the organic debris caused by the
disturbance, the increased decomposition rates due to higher temperatures at the
soil surface, and the reduction in inter-tree competition due to the felling of canopy
trees. The species that have evolved to take advantage of the sudden increases in
these resources therefore benefit from these conditions. Adaptations for rapid
colonization include frequent and large seed crops of light, wind-dispersed seeds
that are ready to germinate when shed from the tree (see pages 70–71).

Rapid colonization can also result from a contrasting strategy: the long
accumulation of a dormant seed pool in the soil, called the seedbank. Soil seedbank
species accumulate seeds over decades while "waiting" for the next disturbance
to trigger their germination. Such seeds have thick coats that restrict the entry of
moisture, nutrients, and oxygen. We do not have data on all seedbank species, but

some tree seeds have been documented to remain dormant in the soil for more than a hundred years. Forest soils are preloaded with species waiting for the opportunity that occurs right after a disturbance affecting the formerly dominant trees.

Shade

As explained on pages 70-71 and 74-75, trees whose seedlings can survive undisturbed in forest understories are called shade-tolerant species, whereas those that wait for disturbances to create higher light levels are called shade-intolerant species. Between these extremes are species that have intermediate light requirements. Thus, where there has been an appropriate alternation of disturbances and disturbance-free periods, and where this disturbance creates different patches of forest with different light levels, there is a higher diversity of tree species than when the forest is either homogeneously shady or has homogenously high light levels.

Other traits are correlated with shade tolerance. Shade-tolerant species are longer-lived and come into reproductive maturity later in life than shade-intolerant species. They may produce fewer but heavier seeds, because the parent tree stores energy sources (carbohydrates and oils) in the seeds as a "parental investment" to allow the young seedling to become established in a shady and competitive forest. By contrast, shade-intolerant species are relatively short-lived, with maximum ages usually measured in decades rather than centuries, and reach reproductive stages earlier (often within the first decade of growth). Suites of traits related to life span and reproduction are called life history strategies. A mix of disturbances and times without disturbance allows species with different life histories to evolve and persist in a forested landscape.

▲ **Fire resistance and recovery**

*Canary Pine (*Pinus canariensis*) has traits for both fire resistance and recovery. The trees' stems are resistant in the sense of surviving fires through the protection afforded by tree bark. They also show a recovery response in the sprouting of new stems from tree boles and branches.*

Gap dynamics as a source of habitat diversity

A mature forest is a mosaic of tree canopies at different stages of recovery. The cycles of canopy gap generation and the subsequent filling of gaps promote a diversity of microenvironments. Across a forest, this heterogeneity provides niches for different plants, animals, and microorganisms. Just as IDH links disturbance frequency with the diversity of species in a landscape (see box on page 85), so the local gap-generation/gap-recovery cycles similarly enhance diversity of species.

▼ **Treefall**
Toppled tree after a hurricane—the gap left by a dead tree can be a driver for an increased richness of species.

The Chablis concept

The Chablis concept posits that the death of a large tree produces microsites for the regeneration of several tree and plant species. The diversity of animal species inhabiting the forest is related to the diversity of tree heights and the patchiness of the landscape. The concept was developed by Roelof Oldeman and Francis Hallé, whose architectural models of tree form were discussed in "Tree architecture" (see page 43). They defined it as the consequences of a large treefall and the effects of this fall on the immediate environment. An observer walking up to the base of

a windfall tree would encounter a great heap of exposed, upturned soil from the ripped-out roots. Behind this tip-up mound, there would be a soil pit, perhaps filled with water or perhaps exposing the bedrock and subsoil that normally remains unseen below the upper soil layers. And there would be a hole in the forest canopy directly overhead.

Depending on the forest and the crown width of the fallen tree, there might be direct sunlight streaming onto the forest floor through this canopy opening, or there might be an increased level of indirect light, which is very efficient at driving the photosynthesis process. Some of the small trees directly below the fallen tree would grow faster in this improved light regime. Looking from the root base, the straight trunk of the tree would be lying on the forest floor. If the trunk has missed knocking over any other large trees, the soil along the length of the fallen trunk would be relatively undisturbed and the light level here would be relatively unaffected. Further down the trunk would be a zone of great destruction, where the tree's crown, full of heavy branches, has crashed. Here, there will be upturned soil and a large hole in the canopy caused by the felling of many smaller trees by the fallen crown. The environmental conditions close to the location of the fallen tree's crown will usually be hotter, drier, and sunnier than in the surrounding forest.

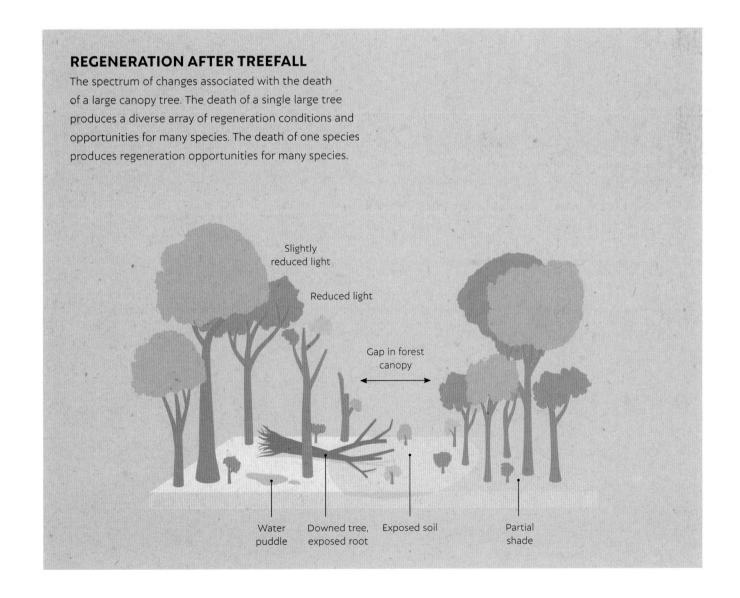

REGENERATION AFTER TREEFALL

The spectrum of changes associated with the death of a large canopy tree. The death of a single large tree produces a diverse array of regeneration conditions and opportunities for many species. The death of one species produces regeneration opportunities for many species.

Slightly reduced light

Reduced light

Gap in forest canopy

Water puddle

Downed tree, exposed root

Exposed soil

Partial shade

Regeneration

A Chablis as just described would offer regeneration sites for trees and other plants that otherwise might be quite rare in a particular forest. One can see the process of the Chablis on the ground by hiking in a mature forest and observing the species regenerating in association with treefalls of different ages. In a truly ancient forest, one finds hill-and-hummock surfaces. These comprise flattened rises in the soil surface that are the remains of tip-up mounds from which the wood and roots have long decayed away, and small dips, the partially filled-in holes in the back of the tip-ups. Occasionally, one sees a tree with stilt roots that originally germinated on the top of a downed tree trunk, now long decayed away, or a straight line of such trees, all of which regenerated long ago on the same large dead tree trunk.

Micro-habitat hotspots

A second example of micro-habitat diversity involves the relationship between horizontal and vertical heterogeneity in a forest mosaic landscape. There is a dependable correlation between the numbers of bird species in a forest and the presence of leaves in the vertical profile at all levels of the forest. This relationship between bird species diversity and foliage height diversity is normally applied over an area of 250 acres (100 ha) or more. The micro-heterogeneity seen in the spectrum of plant-regeneration sites also applies to animal niches. The standing but dead trunks or "snags" of trees that have died and decayed in place become micro hotspots for the nesting and feeding activities of birds and other animals.

Following on from this, one would expect a single-species forest plantation with trees evenly spaced to have much less diversity than a similar-sized tract of natural forest. Even though the plantation may be of similar area, have a similar mass of leaves, branches, trunks, and so on, and equivalent (or higher) rates of productivity, the diversity of the plantation measured as the total number of species it supports can be as much as a tenth lower.

▲ **Regeneration**
Yellow Staghorn Fungus
(Calocera viscosa)
growing on a dead tree.

Fundamental biomass dynamics

What are the larger-scale changes averaged over time for a mosaic landscape? The dynamics of tree biomass in a canopy-sized patch of forest over generations of trees is cyclical. Over time, a graph of tree biomass at one of these patches resembles a saw's teeth—it increases when trees are growing to fill a canopy gap and drops abruptly with the death of the dominant tree. The summation of these cycles is the fundamental response expected for a forest.

Following a disturbance over a large area, summed biomass changes of each patch in a forest mosaic increase as all patches have young growing trees. The trees of this initial generation grow old together, and eventually the deaths of some are balanced by the continued growth of other old trees, or of young trees in gaps at other locations, and the accumulation of biomass is constant over the landscape. If the dominant trees have similar longevities, there can be a subsequent period when several (perhaps the majority) of the forest mosaic patches have synchronized deaths among their canopy-dominant trees and the landscape biomass drops. Over time, patch-scale biomass dynamics become desynchronized, and the biomass curve varies around some overall average. In the case of reafforesting areas to store carbon and ameliorate global climate change, the expectation is that new forests should take up more carbon than they emit and be a "sink" for atmospheric carbon. Over time, however, this landscape could become a carbon "source" as the initial trees die and decay. Eventually, the forest land would store considerable carbon but on average would be neutral (neither a source nor a sink). To be effective in the long term as a carbon sink, the forest would need to be protected from any change that would make it a carbon source.

A fluctuating composition

What is the structure of a mature forest system at the end of this process? In the case of a mature forest covering many acres, one would expect to see a heterogeneous mixture of patches, each at different phases of gap replacement. The proportions of each of these gap phases should reflect the proportional duration of the different gap-replacement stages.

Such patterns have been documented for several different mature forest systems. The presence of shade-intolerant trees in patches in undisturbed mature forest is one observation consistent with the mosaic dynamics of mature forests. The mosaic elements in many natural forests is somewhat larger than one would expect from the filling of single tree gaps, indicating an importance of phenomena that cause multiple-tree replacements. Longer records for forest mosaics indicate tree species may fluctuate in abundance. Variations in local weather, such as a series of droughts causing synchronized large tree deaths, followed by a run of cooler, wetter years, could promote the regeneration of large numbers of species that require cool conditions for regeneration. The resultant forest would not be the same had those cool, wet years been hot, dry years instead.

CARBON DISTURBANCE RECOVERY

Over time, as a forest matures, the forest mosaic would have patches with all stages of development and recovery. As the forest matures, the variation in plant biomass is the average of all the mosaic patches and becomes relatively constant. At time A (blue) the forest is storing biomass or carbon, at B (brown) carbon gain from growth is balanced by loss from death; at C (pink) death exceeds growth and the forest is a source of carbon to the atmosphere; at D (green) continuing through E (purple) growth and death balance and the forest is carbon neutral.

Successional patches synchronously recovering from disturbance

Mature forest is a mosaic

Time

Expected biomass change recovery from disturbance

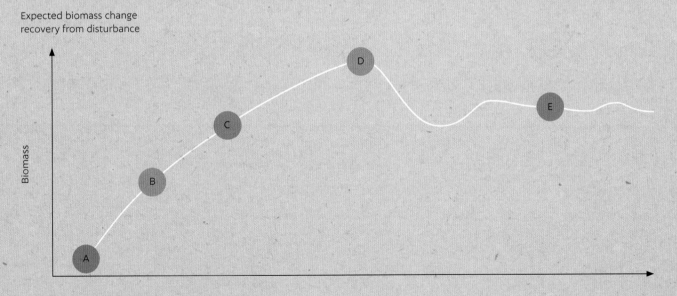

Biomass

Time

Forest succession

In 1860, the American naturalist and philosopher Henry David Thoreau (1817-1862) published an essay, "The succession of forest trees." In it he stated that a field once abandoned would likely become colonized by pines; that the pines, if left alone, would eventually be colonized by oaks and other hardwoods; and that the hardwood forest, consisting of long-lived species that could continue to reproduce in place, would then dominate the site for hundreds of years.

▼ **Thoreau's notes**

Thoreau's Walden Pond, through a forest. One of his key observations concerned successional changes that occurred when farm fields were abandoned, with composition shifting from fast-growing early colonists, including pines and birches, to longer-lived hardwoods, including oaks and beeches.

While the word "succession" and the analogy to the succession of kings (here forest dominants) had been used some decades earlier, Thoreau's essay was influential in that he stressed the mechanisms that lead to successional change. Even in this simple example, we can see that the central mechanisms are competition among the species available at the site and changing environmental conditions caused by the developing ecosystem itself, including the increase in shade and organic matter in the soil.

Observing successional change

Projecting successional changes into the future, studies suggested that there was, at least in theory, a predictable and stable endpoint of this development. The qualifier "at least in theory" is needed here, because over the centuries required for succession to run its course, there would also likely be disturbances that would reset the successional clock to earlier stages of development changes and changes to the environment, which would alter the competitive relations of species.

Documenting change

Because successional change may take place over centuries, how do ecologists document these changes? Seven approaches have been used, each with its advantages and limitations.

1. Direct observation of change on permanently marked sample plots.

2. Experiments, in which forests are characterized and then subjected to various magnitudes and frequencies of disturbance, whether direct human disturbance or "natural experiments" that result from natural disturbances to study plots.

3. Comparison of historical photographs with modern ones taken at identical locations ("repeat photography").

4. Space-for-time substitutions, in which forests of different ages but all in a common environmental setting and sampled within the same time period are used to infer a successional sequence.

5. The presence in current vegetation of legacy features from the past, such as fire scars and population decline for species characteristic of early successional stages.

6. Fossils and subfossils in layered deposits that can be dated, such as pollen grains that accumulate in the sediments of lakes and bogs, and which reflect thousands of years of vegetation change.

7. Simulation modeling, in which species life history traits (dispersal rates, growth rates, competitive abilities, and longevities) and changing environmental conditions are used to project successional dynamics over time.

◀ **Observing change**
A rain forest researcher studies tree growth in the Rio Macho Forest Reserve, Costa Rica.

PRIMARY SUCCESSION

Early on, ecologists distinguished two kinds of
succession: primary and secondary. In primary
succession, the ecosystem development starts with a
sterile substrate such as bedrock, lava flows, volcanic
ash deposits, or extensive sand deposits. The key is that
no soils exist and there is no remnant of any previous
ecosystem that might have occurred on the site. Over
time, plants colonize the area, adding organic matter
and starting the process of soil development, and
causing other environmental changes through increasing
biomass and shade. Newly formed waterbodies can also
be considered a starting point for primary succession—
with the accumulation of sediments at last elevating
the substrate and allowing soil development. Of course,
not all primary successions proceed very far toward soil
development. Some open rock surfaces are so steep that
organic matter and soil simply wash downhill, and some
waterbodies may be so deep and wide that the influence
of sedimentation never produces a substrate on which
soils can form. Repeat disturbances also interrupt the
long-term process of soil development.

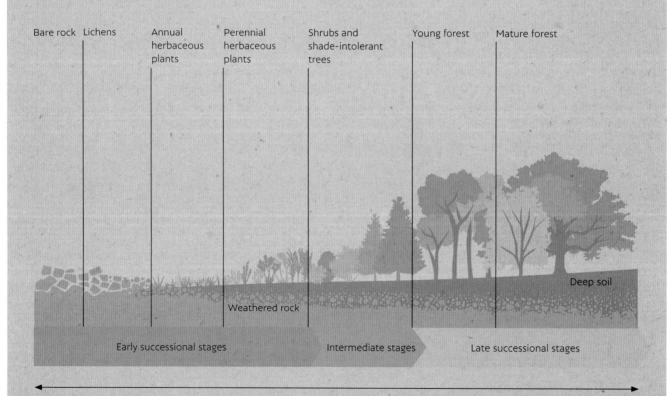

Bare rock Lichens   Annual   Perennial   Shrubs and   Young forest   Mature forest
                      herbaceous   herbaceous   shade-intolerant
                      plants   plants   trees

Deep soil

Weathered rock

Early successional stages   Intermediate stages   Late successional stages

Hundreds to thousands of years

SECONDARY SUCCESSION

By contrast, secondary succession begins with soils remaining from a previous ecosystem, which are not sterile but harbor remnant biota—various plant, animal, and microbe species. Thus, succession after agriculture and after forest cutting are examples of secondary succession. Whether left over after human or natural disturbance, the remnants of the previous ecosystem— such as soils, downed logs and branches, and biota— are called the ecosystem legacy. In this sense, primary successions have no ecosystem legacy, while secondary successions do. However, ecosystem legacy can vary tremendously in secondary successions, ranging from low amounts of soil, organic debris, seeds, insects, fungi, or other species, either due to severe disturbance or erosion after disturbance, to high amounts after mild disturbances unaccompanied by erosion. This variation in legacy produces a family of potential secondary successions, each with its own starting point.

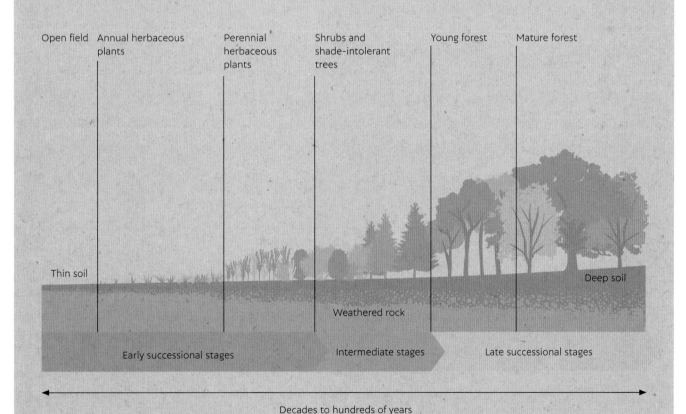

Open field | Annual herbaceous plants | Perennial herbaceous plants | Shrubs and shade-intolerant trees | Young forest | Mature forest

Thin soil

Deep soil

Weathered rock

Early successional stages | Intermediate stages | Late successional stages

Decades to hundreds of years

*Twisted ancient oaks
in Wistman's Wood,
Dartmoor National
Park, UK.*

Rates of successional change

Because of their "head start" in terms of ecosystem legacy, secondary successions are usually faster than primary successions. By projection of observed changes, the rate of change becomes low, or even zero, at the endpoint of both primary and secondary successions. In the absence of disturbance and environmental change, succession should produce stable ecosystems.

Forest successions produce structural changes. Early in the successions, perhaps within several decades if seed sources are available and the soil has not been severely eroded, seedlings and then saplings densely cover the surface. Although these stems are small, their summed leaf area usually attains levels near those pre-disturbance. This leaf-area increase drives greater rates of biomass accumulation. Often, total forest biomass reaches a maximum before the successional endpoint is reached, perhaps in the first century or two. As a forest accumulates biomass, it thins to become less dense in the numbers of trees, but dominant trees reach large sizes.

As the life spans of the first colonizers are reached, within the first century, composition shifts toward longer-lived species. Increasing tree sizes also means we begin to see standing dead trees and, finally, large logs on the forest floor, which are important aspects of habitat structure. Since later successional species may live for centuries, this production of large woody debris may take 500 years or more. Some pre-disturbance species, such as forest understory wildflowers, have low reproductive output and slow dispersal, and may recover from disturbance at a similar time span as the production of large woody debris. At the endpoint of succession, the deaths of large trees produces persistent age-patchiness in the forest. In turn, this can contribute to a late successional decline of total forest biomass, but also to the maintenance of tree species diversity.

Old-growth forests

When natural disturbances occur at long intervals, constituent trees reach their maximum sizes and ages between disturbances. Such forests are valuable in research and are called old-growth forests and ancient woodlands. They are also termed primary forests to distinguish them from secondary forests, which develop after human removal of the original forests. Old-growth forests can be "old" in three interesting ways. First, and most obviously, the canopy trees of old-growth forests are old. Keeping in mind that the trees of a forest can be all-aged if the pattern of disturbance is of small patches, then not all canopy trees will be old in an old-growth forest. For that reason, this criterion for the label "old-growth" often uses a set formulation, such as that old-growth forests must have at least 75 percent of canopy trees that exceed 75 percent of maximum life span.

A second way that forests can be old is that they have remained uninfluenced by humans—they have been shaped only by natural forces. Very few forests meet this criterion today, if for no other reason than that global air pollution and climate change now permeate our world. The third way that a forest can be "old" involves shifting our perspective from the age of individual trees to that of the forest itself. If the ecosystem was never harvested or converted to agriculture, but rather has been a forest through multiple generations of trees dating back to an era when humans had low influence, we can say that the ecosystem, if not the trees, is old. And this would be true even if the current tree canopy is relatively young due to a recent disturbance, such as a windstorm or fire. An old forest ecosystem can be, in some patches and at some times, dominated by young tree stems.

▼ **New forest growth**
A young tree among the Sequoias, Mariposa Grove, Yosemite National Park, California.

Element cycles

Mature trees are immense organisms that impinge mightily on their immediate environment. Forests recycle matter internally, and their capacity to change the chemistry of their soils and drainage waters gives them a metaphorical resemblance to individual organisms. Studies of the movement of materials into, inside, and out of forest ecosystems spring from interactions among three major "carrier" systems: water and atmospheric transfers, organic matter, and acidity.

▼ **Salty nutrients**

Salt is highly soluble and rapidly washed out of forest ecosystems. Sodium is an essential nutrient for animals and large herbivores with high rates of salt excretion feeding on low-sodium plants are strongly attracted to salt. One striking example is the Gaur, found in moist forests of South and Southeastern Asia.

Water and atmospheric transfers

Precipitation (rainwater, ice, or snowfall) delivers material from the atmosphere to the forest (wet-fall). When there is no precipitation, atmospheric dust (dry-fall) similarly serves to transport material into forests from the outside. The mass of different input elements varies with the geology of the areas upwind of the forests. Calcium, potassium, and magnesium—all significant plant nutrients—are generally high in areas adjacent to oceans. Forests are generally found in climatic conditions of ample water supply, at least seasonally so, and elements that are more soluble preferentially dissolve and drain from forests into the groundwater and streams. Sodium—an element essential to animals but less to plants—is also strongly transported into forests near oceans, but its input to forests is much smaller in the interiors of landmasses away from the coastal zone. The solubility of most sodium compounds means that they are often washed into streams and out of the forests. This results in a sodium shortage and the strong attraction of large herbivores living in wetter forest systems, such as the Gaur (*Bos gaurus*) to sources of salt.

MAJOR COMPONENTS IN FOREST ELEMENT CYCLES

These are transfers involving organic carbon uptake and release; transfers involving water; and generation of acidity and the release of elements dissolved from minerals by this acidity.

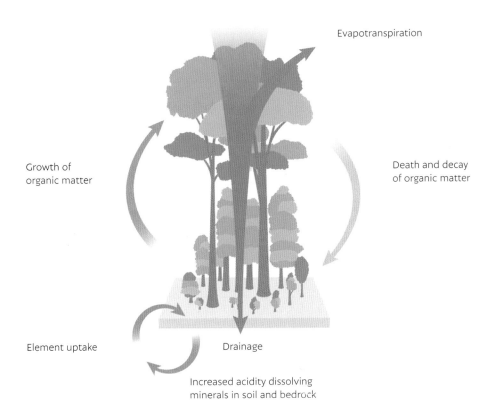

Input of material in precipitation (wet-fall)

Evapotranspiration

Growth of organic matter

Death and decay of organic matter

Element uptake

Drainage

Increased acidity dissolving minerals in soil and bedrock

Organic matter

A second transport system in forests recycles elements associated with plant tissues and is driven by tree growth and death. Tree growth takes up nutrients from the soil and incorporates them into new plant tissue. This uptake arm of the recycling system is coupled with an eventual release of these elements (mineralization) through the decomposition of litterfall—mostly shed leaves, but also parts of flowers, seeds, small twigs, and so on. Dead tree trunks and large branches also decompose, albeit more slowly, and are additionally important in the release arm of this recycling system. In tropical forests decomposition occurs rapidly and litterfall is gone within a matter of a month or two, resulting in relatively little organic material on the forest floor. In contrast, the rates of decomposition in temperate forests are slower, and two years (more or less) of annual litterfall lie in various stages of decay on the forest floor. Boreal forests have deep, peaty layers of decomposing litter, with ten, 20, or even more years of annual litter production beneath the trees. When conditions are less favorable for litter decomposition, its breakdown slows and peaty deposits store nutrient elements, such that the recycling of organic matter recycling grinds to a halt. This occurs in colder forests, in dry forests, and in forests lacking sufficient available nutrients to support the microbes that are the agents of the decomposition/mineralization processes.

Chemical signature

Differences in element transfers within forest ecosystems they inhabit, are reflected in the chemistry of animals. Blue-winged Warblers are common in North Carolina (above Cullasaja Falls in the Nantahala National Forest), but their feathers can identify the breeding locations of these birds wintering on Caribbean Islands.

SOIL PH

The availability of nutritional elements within soil varies with pH. The light blue represents the ideal range for most plants.

4.0 pH	4.5	5.0	5.5	6.0	6.5	7.0	7.5	8.0	8.5	9.0	9.5	10.0

Acidic						Alkaline						
Strongly			Slightly	Very slightly	Very slightly	Slightly	Medium		Strongly			

NITROGEN

PHOSPHORUS

POTASSIUM

SULFUR

CALCIUM

MAGNESIUM

IRON

MANGANESE

BORON

COPPER AND ZINC

MOLYBDENUM

Acidity

Many forest processes generate acidity. The standard measurement of acidity, pH, involves the concentration of hydrogen ions (denoted H+) in a solution. A solution with a pH of 7 is neutral, one with a pH greater than 7 is alkali, and one with a pH less than 7 is acidic. The scale is logarithmic, so that an acidic solution with pH 2 has ten times the H+ of a less acidic solution with pH 3. Plants generally grow better in soils with pH values between 6 and 6.5 (slightly acidic), and the availability of essential plant nutrients declines in more acidic soils. Tree growth demands an uptake of the positively charged ions (cations) of plant essential elements (such as calcium, potassium, and magnesium). The emission of cations, mostly hydrogen ions, balances the cation uptake at the root surface. Decomposition of organic materials also forms mild organic acids, and the respiration of living roots releases carbon dioxide, which interacts with soil moisture to form carbonic acid. This forest-generated acidity dissolves minerals in the bedrock and the soil. With the depletion of these mineral sources, the acidity of the soil increases and a series of elements change their solubility. Essential elements can be carried from the forest ecosystem soil water by the water-transport system into streams and lakes. The role of acidity and atmospheric transport in the long-term development of forests and forest soils over long periods of time is illustrated by the examples given in the "Long chronosequences" section on pages 106–109. In these cases, forests increase mass, followed by decrease over hundreds or thousands of years. The three transport systems bring together the climate, the soils and surface geology, and the geographic proximity to oceans, geologies, and landforms, to produce a regional signature from the ratios of different elements and their isotopes in water, plants, and animals.

Watershed studies

The study of forested watersheds has greatly increased our understanding of the forest as a working mechanism, particularly in terms of forest element cycles. A watershed is an area of landscape that contributes water from precipitation to a given point in space. In many watershed studies, this "point in space" is a weir, a small dam on a stream that impounds a small pond. The input of the material to the watershed is collected from precipitation and dust, and its output is measured by determining volume of streamflow over the weir and concentrations of chemicals in the water. Many watershed studies have manipulated the forest landscape as an experiment, observing the balance between incoming and outgoing amounts of different elements or the loss of water to evapotranspiration from different vegetation in replicate watersheds.

▲ Water flow

A simple V-shaped notch for measuring water flow in a stream. The height of water flow over the V-notch embedded in a small dam or weir gauges the volume of water flowing in the stream.

◥ Old-growth Douglas Fir forest

*These are magnificent forests with towering evergreen conifers. The species' regeneration is adapted to fire and after 400 years of stand development old-growth Douglas Fir (*Pseudotsuga menziesii*) forests demonstrate the powerful verticality of a Gothic cathedral.*

More recently, watershed studies have been actively extended beyond the measurement of landscape inputs and outputs. As discussed on pages 60-63, forest ecosystems can be conceptualized using diagrams with boxes to represent the storage of different elements (in terms of mass per unit area) in system components and arrows implying the transfers among boxes over time. The same modeling paradigm underlies computations of the transfer of atoms of different elements through natural ecosystems. These "compartment models" have their origins in pharmacological studies in the 1930s, which used similar abstractions to trace pathways of medicines or other materials through the human body.

A compartment model developed by forest ecologist Phillip Sollins and colleagues in 1980 to investigate the movement of elements through the H. J. Andrews Experimental Forest in the Cascade Mountains of western Oregon has become a classic study. This watershed study investigated the effects of different methods of harvesting Douglas Fir (*Pseudotsuga menziesii*) forests at a vast scale. The forest's rainfall is from clouds produced in air transported across the Pacific Ocean and is low in calcium and many other elements, and was among the cleanest in North America. The Oregon study was developed at a time when rainfall in the eastern United States and Europe had very low pH values due to air pollution—indeed, it was acidic enough to dissolve outdoor statues in Europe and tombstones in the United States.

The Oregon study considered the cycling of elements and the production of hydrogen ions in a relatively natural setting with no significant input of pollution from humans. Calcium, for example, is strongly recycled by the organic matter transports, and much of the input of the element is from weathering rocks—aided by the forest's acid production. Other essential elements—including potassium, magnesium, nitrogen, and phosphorus—are also recycled and held in the forest by the organic matter transport system. Significantly, the study was the first to determine the movement of hydrogen ions through a forest ecosystem. In this case the acidity was largely on dissolving minerals in the soil and bedrock of this ecosystem.

CALCIUM RECYCLING IN DOUGLAS FIR FOREST

Transfers of calcium as measured by Phillip Sollins and his colleagues in a classic study in old-growth forest in the Cascade Mountains, western Oregon.

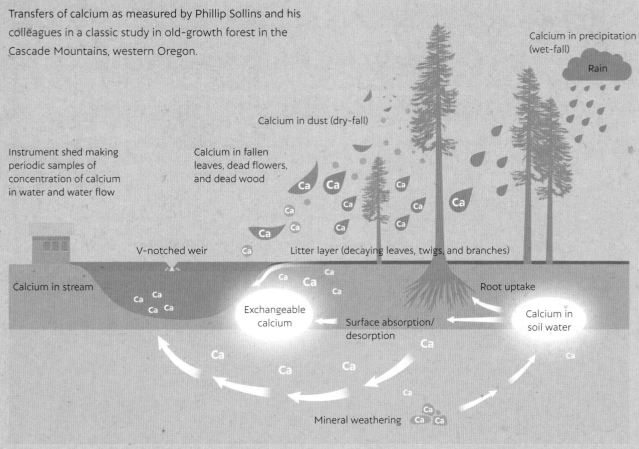

Calcium in precipitation (wet-fall)

Rain

Calcium in dust (dry-fall)

Instrument shed making periodic samples of concentration of calcium in water and water flow

Calcium in fallen leaves, dead flowers, and dead wood

Ca Ca Ca Ca Ca Ca Ca Ca Ca Ca

V-notched weir

Litter layer (decaying leaves, twigs, and branches)

Calcium in stream

Ca Ca Ca Ca Ca Ca Ca Ca Ca

Exchangeable calcium

Surface absorption/ desorption

Root uptake

Calcium in soil water

Ca Ca Ca Ca Ca Ca Ca

Mineral weathering Ca Ca Ca

Long chronosequences

"The ecosystem concept" on page 60 defines an ecosystem as an interacting system of processes responding to external drivers to produce ecological patterns, all of these occurring over similar scales of time and space. This implies that if one conducted a scientific study at a particular spatial scale over a given time interval, the collected observations would relate to general forest patterns seen at these scales.

Many ecological studies are at the scale of 250 acres (100 ha) over a few years. While it is logistically impossible to conduct direct 1,000-year studies over large areas, there are significant things researchers want to know at longer and larger scales. For example, what are the modern consequences of the slow and probably ongoing spread of tree ranges displaced by, and still recovering from, the melting of massive continental glaciers 12,000 years ago? How long will it take for forests to recover and adjust from exotic pests and diseases introduced 100 or more years ago? What are the forest responses to climatic variations? What is the influence of the slow development of the soil? The answers to all these questions and more could be invisible in the results of short-term, local studies.

Darwin's dust

On January 16, 1832, Charles Darwin was on board HMS *Beagle* off the coast of the Cape Verde Islands, about 750 miles (1,200 km) from the nearest land, when a storm from Africa deposited fine dust on the ship, which the young scientist collected. This contained the shells of freshwater diatoms (single-celled algae with silica casings) and phytoliths (solid bodies of silica in the surface cells of plants). A century and a half of scientific detective work has identified the sources of Darwin's dust and the many deposits recorded there since: the freshwater diatoms come from Lake Chad, a large lake in central Africa; and the phytoliths originate from fires in the Sahel, a semiarid region in western and north-central Africa extending eastward from Senegal.

Similar transport of dust and smoke feeds into the southern Amazon Basin from fires in southern Africa. This raises the question: "Does the Sahara fertilize the Amazon?" This may indeed be the case with phosphorus and iron, which can be in short supply in forests, particularly those in which most of the nutrients are held in the living trees. Deep ocean sediments reveal that this process has been taking place for millions of years, with the "fertilization" turning off when the Sahara is in a wet phase and turning on when the desert is in a drier phase. So, does the Sahara even partially drive the Amazon? Calculations and measurements by atmospheric scientist Robert Swap and colleagues, which have been corroborated by other scientists working in the atmospheric transport of materials, would indicate that it does.

▶ **African markers in the dust**
Dust storm from the Sahara Desert off the coast of West Africa— fine dust transported from Africa may play a role in fertilizing the Amazon Basin.

▼ **Diatoms**
Microscopic diatoms in drops of water.

Chronosequences

Modern advances in remote sensing have provided novel information on the patterns of ecosystems over extensive areas. We present some of this in Chapter 12 and elsewhere. However, the observation times are relatively short—on the scale of years to decades. Understanding longer-term responses has been a persistent challenge for ecologists for well over a century and remains so.

Some special cases of space-for-time substitutions (see page 103), known as chronosequences, do provide insight into the long timescale changes in forests. Chronosequences are naturally ordered by some underlying large-scale processes, often involving the progression of change of soils. While ideally they are a collocated set of study locations for understanding forest change that differ only by their age, each chronosequence has experienced a different weather history at a given age. This is because a 25-year-old plot would reflect the weather history of the last 25 years, but the weather history for a 100-year-old plot's first 25 years would have occurred between 100 and 75 years ago. This may or may not be a significant problem.

The Indiana Dunes study

The classic Indiana Dunes chronosequence study was developed by Henry Chandler Cowles in 1899. The Indiana Dunes (an Illinois state park at the time, and now a national park) are sand dunes that formed from Lake Michigan at the end of the last ice age, 12,000 years ago. The youngest dunes start nearest

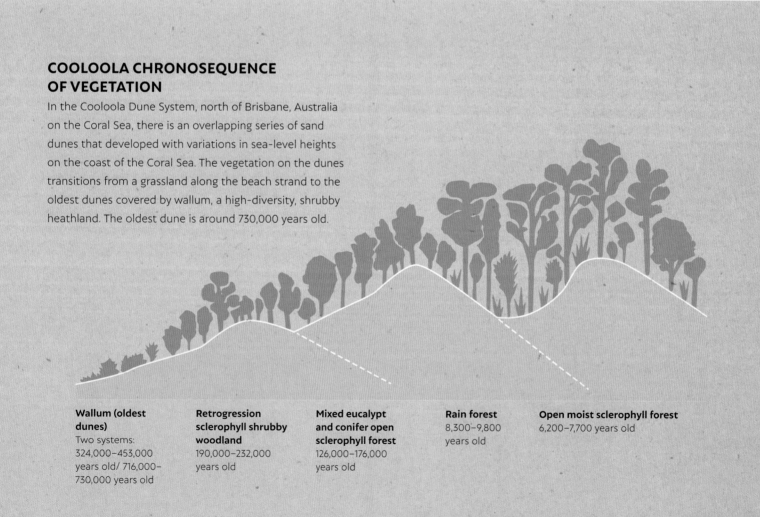

COOLOOLA CHRONOSEQUENCE OF VEGETATION

In the Cooloola Dune System, north of Brisbane, Australia on the Coral Sea, there is an overlapping series of sand dunes that developed with variations in sea-level heights on the coast of the Coral Sea. The vegetation on the dunes transitions from a grassland along the beach strand to the oldest dunes covered by wallum, a high-diversity, shrubby heathland. The oldest dune is around 730,000 years old.

Wallum (oldest dunes)
Two systems:
324,000–453,000 years old/ 716,000–730,000 years old

Retrogression sclerophyll shrubby woodland
190,000–232,000 years old

Mixed eucalypt and conifer open sclerophyll forest
126,000–176,000 years old

Rain forest
8,300–9,800 years old

Open moist sclerophyll forest
6,200–7,700 years old

the lakeshore. Away from the shore lies a progression of older and older dunes. The soils on the different dunes also have progressively more organic matter and more nitrogen with increasing age. The last of these dunes is forested. Combining these observations with other old dunes in Indiana, Cowles proposed a primary successional sequence with an American Basswood-Northern Red Oak-Sugar Maple (*Tilia americana, Quercus rubra*, and *Acer saccharum*) forest developing on sheltered dune slopes and in protected dune pockets. Well-drained, moderately exposed dunes were drier and had an associated tendency for wildfires, and they developed forests of Black Oak (*Quercus velutina*). Cowles opined that change in vegetation over time was directed not toward a constant mature vegetation type, but was controlled by another variable—the improvement and change in soils over a long period of time.

In 1958, Jerry Olson documented the chemical and physical processes working to produce fertile forest soil from sand at the Indiana Dunes site. Olson noted, "Probably Cowles assumed that, after the early rapid changes of succession were over, there would be a slow but certain improvement in soil conditions and hence the potentialities of future succession ... But it is necessary to consider the possibility that the limit for some variables might even decline in time." This decline, sometimes called retrogressive succession, can also be seen in the 750,000-year sequence of sand-dune ecosystem change at Great Sandy National Park in southern Queensland, Australia. We might add to this that chronosequences may forever pursue an ever-changing climate.

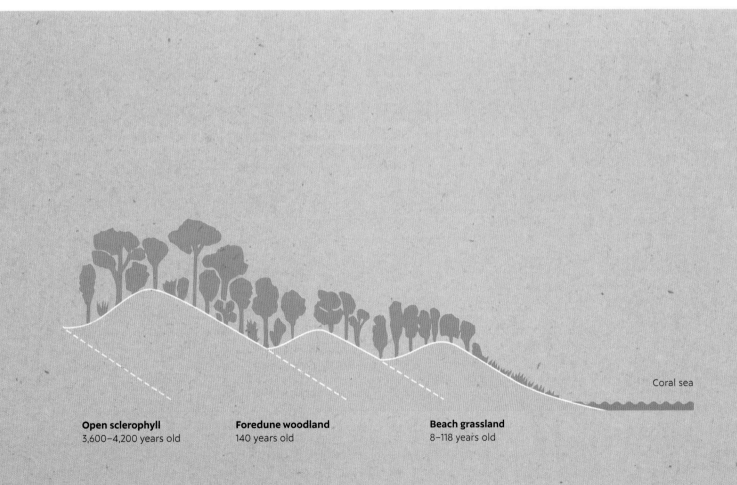

Open sclerophyll
3,600–4,200 years old

Foredune woodland
140 years old

Beach grassland
8–118 years old

Coral sea

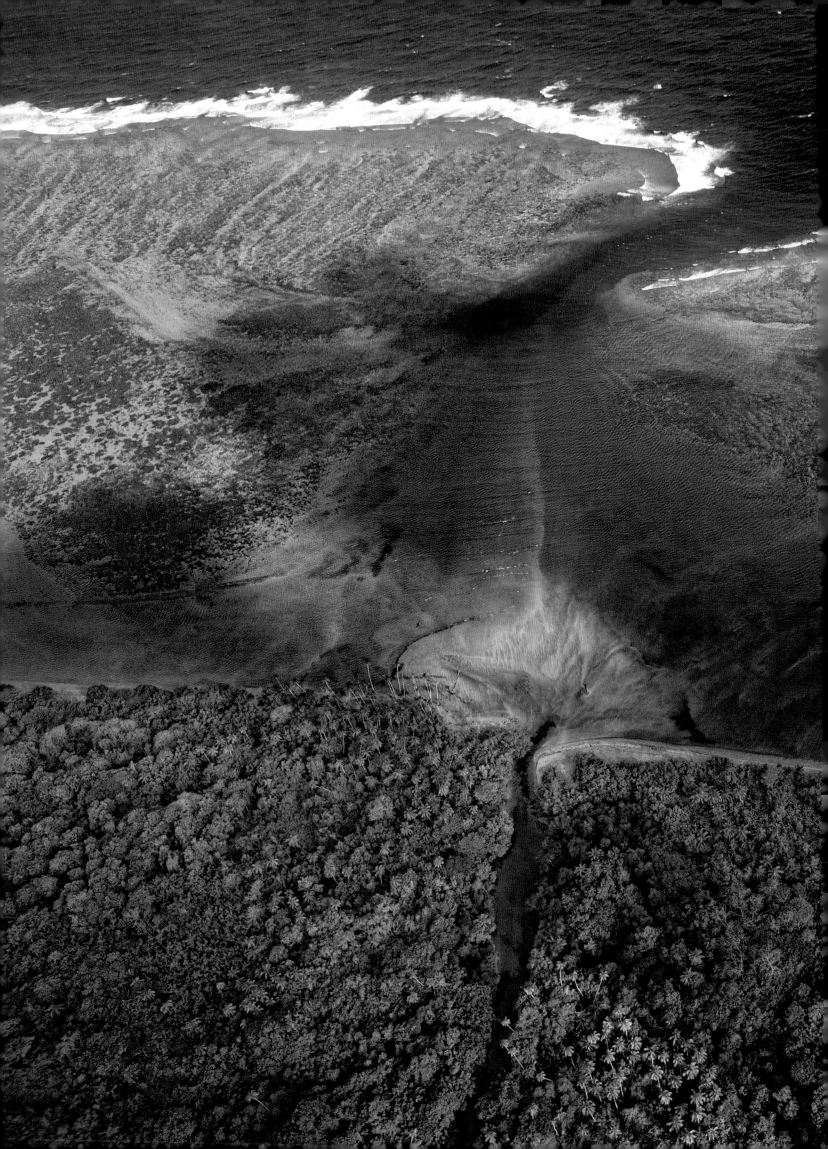

4

Mapping the Forests of the World

Early vegetation maps

The origins of cartography have been lost in history and the exact purpose of maps in their earliest iterations is unknown. It appears that mapmaking may have evolved concurrently among many peoples and in various parts of the world.

Thus far, the earliest maps discovered are portrayals of land features on Babylonian tablets and drawings inside Egyptian tombs. Both civilizations were interested in fertile areas and made surveys along river valleys to arrange plans for their crops and to develop canals, roads, temples, and even entire settlements. Similar land drawings have been found in cave paintings in Europe, pre-Columbian sketches in Mexico, Inuit ivory carvings, Marshall Islands stick charts, Tahitian drawings of South Pacific geography that helped the English explorer Captain James Cook in his navigations in the eighteenth century, and precise scaled maps of Chinese Zhou dynasty (c. 800 BCE) royal geographers. The Latin word *mappa* means "flat cloth," which early mapmakers are thought to have drawn on and used to represent a single region or the entire Earth—*mappa mundi*. To draw features in proportion, geographers and cartographers have developed legends and rules through the millennia, transforming mapmaking from an art to a science.

Ptolemy

In his eight-volume magnum opus *Geographia*, the mathematician and geographer Claudius Ptolemaeus (or Ptolemy, c. 100–c. 170 CE) succeeded in systematizing the art of drawing on a plane surface by using geographical projections and thus established the fundamental tenet of modern cartography. He was the first cartographer to discuss the challenges of representing the spherical Earth on a flat sheet of paper. Ptolemy used coordinates based on the mathematics of a circle and curved parallels in order to develop map projections, and he invented a system of parallels, known as latitudinal and longitudinal lines, based on observations and measurements of zenith angles developed in his earlier book on astronomy, *Almagest*. Ptolemy designed the parallel lines so that the length of the longest day of the year differs from one line to the next by a quarter of an hour. He was able to place the same grid system on either a local map or the entire planet to achieve a projection system that is closest to what is now known as the equal-area projection. He also introduced the concept of just proportions, or drawing maps to scale, thus allowing the incorporation of survey data.

"Geography," Ptolemy wrote, is "a representation in pictures of the whole known world together with the phenomena which are contained therein." He limited the issues and challenges of mapmaking of the known world to exploration, discovery, and data collection, which preceded the work of cartography. This description withstood the test of time and was instrumental in subsequent achievements in the science of geography until the late twentieth century, when technology considerably expanded our knowledge and allowed for mapping to precede human excursions and explorations. Ptolemy extended his concept of mapping general features by incorporating climate and topographical information into maps and their legends. Today, this is considered his most important contribution to the discipline of physical geography.

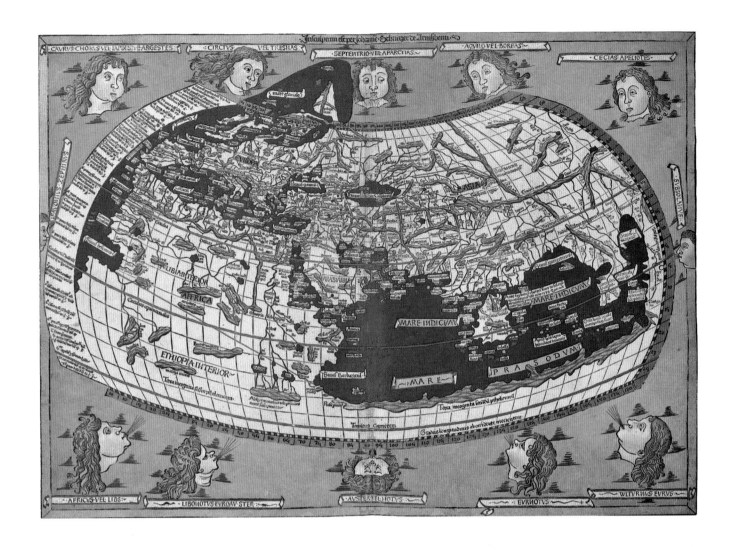

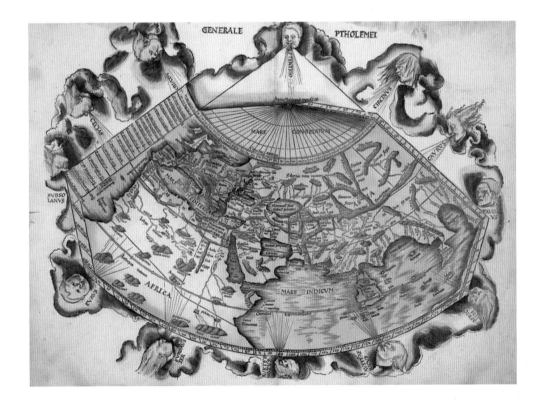

Ptolemy maps

Map of the ancient world reconstructed from Ptolemy's Geographia *(c. 150 CE) in 1482 by Lienhart Holle (top) and lithographed in Strasbourg (1513) (left) with different colors for continents and natural features.*

▼ Vegetation mapping

Cartographer César-François Cassini produced the first topographic and geometric map of France with vegetation cover.

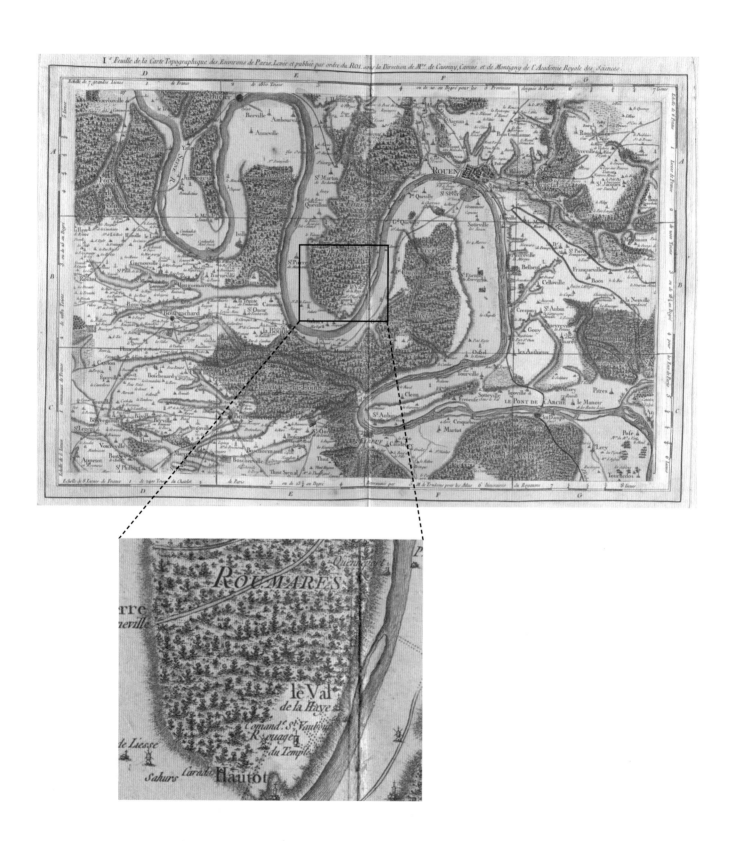

Mapping the natural environment

Ptolemy's illuminations have had a profound effect on explorers and their travels throughout history, and Byzantine scholars and Muslim cartographers continued his geographical traditions throughout the medieval period. However, after the rediscovery of Ptolemy's maps in the fifteenth and sixteenth centuries and the translation of *Geographia* into Latin, the impact of his work on the geographical understanding of the world became much more visible. During the Renaissance, the rules and techniques of map projection, spatial scales, and patterns of climate and topography outlined in *Geographia* prompted explorers and scientists to begin a new era in the production of scientific maps of the natural environment at a global scale.

Following the Renaissance, the depiction of vegetation on maps continued with growing frequency and accuracy as forests grew in significance due to their timber resources, hunting reserves, and military importance. As topographic accuracy developed in maps, so too did vegetational representations. The first relatively modern map of vegetation was commissioned by King Louis XV of France in 1744, who tasked the cartographer César-François Cassini de Thury (1714-1784) with producing an exact topographic map of France. Cassini used the shortest possible line between two points on the curved surface of the Earth to develop a map at a scale of 1:80,000 and included detailed vegetational representations. He was able to distinguish broad-leaved deciduous forests from the evergreen needle-leaved forests on his topographic sheets, and in some regions he delineated even more detailed forest separations based on dominant species groups in wetlands, scrublands, and vineyards.

Although topography and vegetation were integrated into maps early on, cartographers soon realized that topography represents vegetation in only a very limited sense. Independent classification of vegetation based on taxonomic (species), physiognomic (overall structure and physical appearance of the community), or broader ranges of ecological observations started to manifest on maps, establishing the foundation of vegetation science in ensuing years. The exploration literature of the late eighteenth and early nineteenth centuries, particularly in North and South America, included comprehensive studies of plant species and ecosystems in geographical spaces and set the stage for the development of modern biogeography.

Humboldt's pioneering approach

When a young Charles Darwin set sail on his five-year voyage on HMS *Beagle*, he took with him only a few books, among them the Bible, Milton, and an account of travels in Venezuela and the Orinoco Basin by German polymath Alexander von Humboldt (1769-1859). Like Darwin, Humboldt was a giant of the nineteenth century who helped shape our understanding of the world we live in. Unlike Darwin, however, he is little known today.

▲ **Alexander von Humboldt**

Portrait of Alexander von Humboldt painted in 1806 by the German painter Friedrich George Weitsch (1758-1828).

Humboldt died in May 1859, just six months before the publication of Darwin's *On the Origin of Species*. Until the mid-nineteenth century, Humboldt's renown continued to dominate that of Darwin, but today the reverse is true. Humboldt was an international figure, a leading scholar of the day, whose prominent work, *Cosmos* (1845-1862), was translated into 11 languages. His memoir of scientific and adventurous voyages in the Americas, *Relation historique du Voyage aux Regions équinoxiales du Nouveau Continent* (*Personal Narrative of Travels to the Equinoctial Regions of the New Continent*; 1814-1825), became a standard fixture of libraries.

Expedition to South America

Humboldt's *Essai sur la Géographie des Plantes (Essay on the Geography of Plants*; 1805) was considered the most influential scientific document of its time. The publication is based on his five-year voyage to Spanish South America (1799-1804) with his friend the botanist Aimé Bonpland (1773-1858). Their expedition covered four geographic regions. They initially focused on the flora, fauna, and environment of rain forests and mountains of what is now Venezuela, Colombia, and the northern Andes, and later on the human geography in Cuba and Mexico. The pair collected 60,000 plant specimens and discovered about 3,600 new species, including geographic coordinates and descriptions that were later verified by botanists who were able to reconstruct Humboldt's itineraries in Latin America. During the expedition, they encountered indigenous tribes and benefited from their knowledge of the flora and fauna and the landscape.

Using their specimens and environmental measurements, Humboldt and Bonpland experimented with newfound hypotheses on plants and geography, in addition to verifying previous hypotheses by earlier explorers. They also exchanged and compared their findings with those of other scientists they encountered. Among these was José Celestino Mutis (1732-1808), a Spanish physician and botanist based in Bogotá, Colombia, who had a vast herbarium of more than 20,000 plants. Mutis was commissioned by King Carlos III of Spain to study *Cinchona*, the so-called "fever tree," and other medicinal plants, and he was able to treat Bonpland's malaria using *Cinchona* bark. Later, Humboldt and Bonpland met Francisco José de Caldas (1768-1816), a self-taught Colombian naturalist living in Popayán, who had independently discovered a way to determine altitude based on the boiling point temperature of water. Caldas compared notes with Humboldt and found an impressively close agreement in their altitude measurements, and subsequently made his own description of plants of the Andes mountains. These encounters suggest a vibrant historical period in Europe and the Americas, with scientists and explorers engaged in groundbreaking research to understand different environments and the relationships between living and non-living elements.

▲ **Vegetation patterns**

A cross section of Chimborazo and Cotopaxi from Tableau physique. *The plant species are listed according to the altitude at which Humboldt and Bonpland found them during their expedition.*

▲ **Biogeography**

German botanist Karl Friedrich von Martius' biogeography of Brazil overlayed on information from Humboldt and 22 other explorers of South America (1852). The color legends (bottom left) show vegetation

formations with names after Greek nymphs: Naiades, the nymph of waters for Amazonian rain forests; Dryades, the nymph of forests for coastal Mata Atlantica; Oreades, the nymph of hunting fields for Cerrados and savanna of central Brazil;

Napaeae, the nymph of the ravines for Araucaria forests and Campos Sulinos (southern grasslands); and, Hamadryades, a nymph that dies and resurrects referring to Caatinga and semi-arid vegetation of northeast Brazil.

Tableau physique

When Humboldt returned to Paris in 1804, he spent the next three years reviewing crates of specimens and notes on plant geography, the environment, and human societies to write *Essay on the Geography of Plants* and develop the accompanying *Tableau physique des Régions équinoxiale (Physical Tableau of Equinoctal Regions)*, which together established the foundation of Humboldtian science, based on precise quantitative methodology. *The Tableau physique* includes detailed observations of elevational distributions of plant species in the equatorial Andes, as demonstrated on a cross section of the Chimborazo and Cotopaxi volcanoes in Ecuador. Humboldt extended this cross-sectional approach to map the distributional patterns of vegetation in mountainous areas of the world in the Andes, Himalayas, Alps, Pyrenees, and Tenerife, creating the concept of a vegetation belt to explain geographic patterns of plant species by climate and establishing the foundation of biogeography. He continued to revisit his concept of the vegetation belt for more than 20 years, modifying his model over time in order to understand the complex processes associated with the ecological effects of climate. The influence brought about by Humboldt's *Essay on the Geography of Plants* on his contemporaries was immediate and palpable.

Karl Friedrich von Martius (1794-1868), a German botanist and another intellectual giant of the early nineteenth century, was an early adopter of Humboldtian science. Martius, who is also known as "the father of palms," began *Flora Brasiliensis* in 1840, which contained taxonomic information for more than 20,000 species of mainly angiosperms collected during his expedition throughout Brazil in 1817-1820. He divided Brazil into five floristic regions based on physiognomic formations adopted from Cassini and Humboldt.

Isothermal lines

One of Humboldt's main contributions to mapping vegetation was the theory of isothermal lines, which connect elevations that have similar or equal annual temperatures. Cartographers used isothermal lines to capture the regular variations in snow height on mountains, vegetation features such as treelines (see pages 156-157) and transitions between evergreen and deciduous forests, and subsequently the separation of boreal, temperate, and tropical ecosystems. These theoretical lines provided a general summary of the global pattern of environment and vegetation that would preoccupy biogeographers and ecologists right up to the present day. Indeed, modern data show that the global treeline follows an isotherm of 43 °F (6 °C) mean temperature for the growing season, suggesting a low temperature limit for tree growth everywhere on Earth. The progress in mapping vegetation that followed the Humboldtian approach was made along two distinct but interconnecting efforts: to identify more effectively factors in the environment that seem to control vegetation distribution from local to regional scales; and to improve the representation of different levels of ecological organizations and processes that define vegetation patterns and their changes through time. These efforts eventually led to the methodology that starts with species-level information and from these develops functional groups that reveal climate-vegetation relationships or assemblages. It is the latter that represent recognizable diversity of plant communities and their geographical distributions.

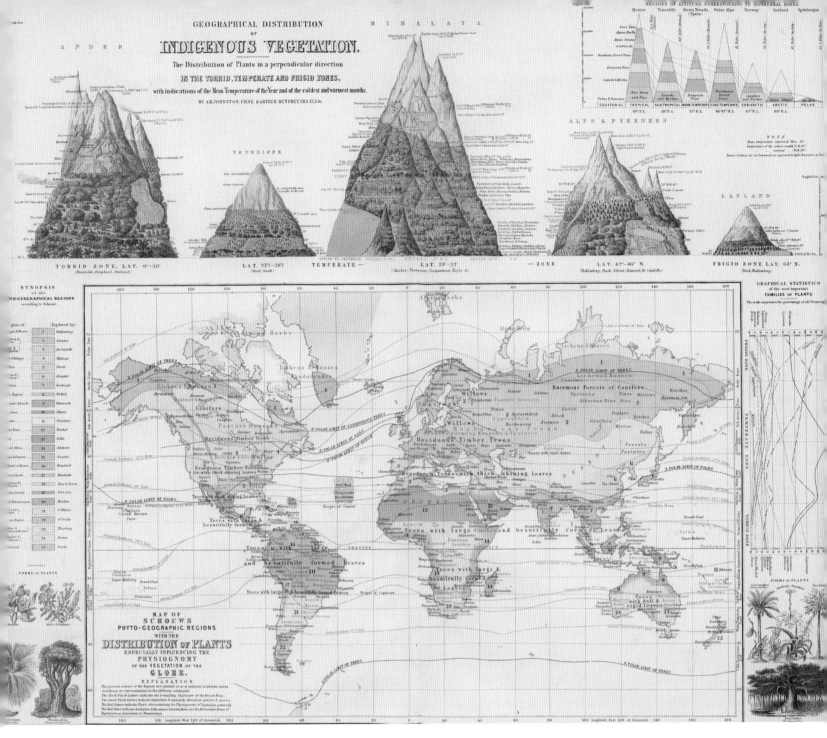

World plant distribution map

An 1854 map of world plant distribution based on Humboldt's information. The top panel shows the Physical Tableau of mountain ranges showing elevation bands in vegetation and characteristics of the physical environment in the Andes, Tenerife, the Himalayas, the Alps, and Lapland. The bottom panel depicts Humboldt's isothermal lines across the globe indicating regions with similar temperatures; these lines laid the groundwork for mapping global vegetation.

Scale in conventional vegetation maps

The amount of detail included in a vegetation map is mostly a function of the scale of the map, which in turn has a strong bearing on the type of material that can be shown. Historically, vegetation maps aimed to portray the geographic patterns of vegetation formations. Paper maps were the only way these patterns could be stored and presented, and most vegetation geography or ecology systems were accommodated using the map scale.

Broad vegetation formations are shown at small scales, while the distribution of small plant communities needs to be shown at large scales. Mapping vegetation on paper is further constrained not only by the size of the paper, but also by the size of area being mapped and the type of vegetation classification used. Classification of vegetation requires a degree of generalization or the abstraction of vegetation formations depending on the scale of the map and direct observations collected in the field. In fact, most conventional maps were developed by first adding the observations on a map and then sorting and organizing the information. This a *posteriori* mode of classifying vegetation is fundamentally different from any preconceived notion or a *priori* characterization of vegetation. It is strongly tied to the data collected in the field, such as physiognomic divisions (forests, grasslands, cultivated fields) or environmental factors (temperature, moisture, topography), as well as the actual purpose of the map.

Optimum scale

The scale of a map has a direct bearing on the size of the area being mapped and the type of vegetation classification selected. The components of spatial scale are grain and extent, which refer to the size of smallest observation or map unit and the total size of the map area, respectively. Map scale is the relationship between a distance on the map and the corresponding distance on the Earth. It can be expressed as the equivalence of different units—for example, the scale 1:100,000 means that 1 inch on paper = 100,000 inch or 1.578 miles on the ground). A map that is classified as small scale (for example, smaller than 1:1,000,000) is used to represent large regions such as the whole world or continents, a medium-scale map (for example, with a scale ranging from 1:100,000 to 1:1,000,000) is used to represent regional or country areas, and a large-scale map (for example, with a scale larger than 1:100,000) is used to represent smaller areas such as landscapes and towns where more detailed information needs to be included. The optimum scale of a vegetation map is determined by considering the size of the area being covered and the kind of detail to be shown. Both the accuracy and the legibility of the map depend, among other things, on the dimension of the smallest area depicted on the paper, such as trees growing along a river.

Maps at any scale are powerful to convey information, but they can also be deceptive. Mapmakers have dealt with this for centuries, while developing projection techniques to display the curved surface of the Earth and its content on a flat surface. Mathematically, it is difficult to preserve variables such as size, shape, direction, and distance of objects simultaneously by flattening the Earth's surface. No map provides true-to-scale distances for any measurements. Depending on map projections, geographic regions may not be objectively presented. Historically, map projections have been the subject of political and territorial disputes.

◀ **Small scale**

Map of the distribution of vegetation on Earth, 1910. Small scale maps are used to represent large regions such as the whole world or continents.

◤ **Medium scale**

Vegetation map of Australia, 1931— medium-scale maps represent regional or country areas.

◤ **Large scale**

Large scale maps represent smaller areas, such as landscapes and towns where more detailed information needs to be included.

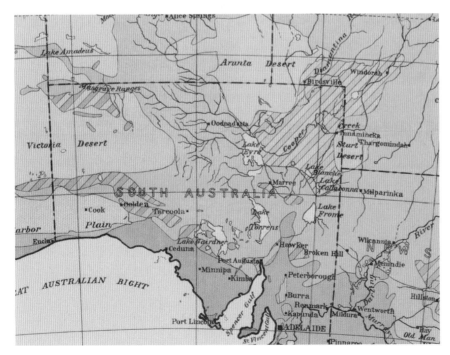

▶ **Mapping vegetation**

Tropical rain forest in the Choco region of the Pacific coast of Ecuador showing degrees of forest succession after clearing for cultivation—throughout the nineteenth and twentieth centuries how to map vegetation boundaries and plant communities was the source of lively debate.

Classifying vegetation to suit map scale

The classification of the vegetation on a map depends on the limitation of the scale. A vegetation stand is often defined as a contiguous area with a similar species composition, physiognomy, and structure, in which structure describes the vertical and horizontal patterns of vegetation, or the distribution of size classes of individuals or above-ground biomass. A vegetation stand is typically the smallest spatial scale used in vegetation maps that focus on landscape-type representation. However, the scale of the map in terms of its grain size and extent can define a hierarchy of vegetation classification. In increasing vegetation grain size, the classification can be arrayed in spatial scales from large to small, starting from individual (plant/gap scale) and ranging up to community (stand scale), vegetation type, and land cover, and to formations varying from landscape to regional scales. It is therefore imperative for the cartographer that the vegetation types used at different scales are studied in the field and are based on quantitative field surveys of the plant communities.

Classification methods and drawbacks

From the early nineteenth century, scientists became interested in studying and mapping vegetation on the basis of the uniformity of its internal characteristics and the distinctiveness of its external characteristics. The distinctiveness of a plant community implies a discontinuity from the surrounding vegetation and has formed the basis of numerous classification schemes. Most early European and American scientists did not make a distinction between an actual stand of vegetation and the abstract concept of a plant community, but this approach gradually gained significance through the nineteenth and twentieth centuries particularly in the classification method developed by Swiss botanist Josias Braun-Blanquet (1884-1980). His approach, called phytosociology, had a strong emphasis on the typology of plant communities based on observation of the species in a plot (*relevé*) within the vegetation stand. Braun-Blanquet paid much attention to how plant communities interact with the environment and with one another, and how they constitute a "social unit" with definite conditions, a concept that was later incorporated into the definition of ecosystems. The latter are considered distinct and bounded communities that can be conveniently studied based on their biotic and abiotic characteristics.

Debates on distinctiveness and mapping vegetation boundaries continued through the early twentieth century. Some American botanists, such as Henry Gleason (1882-1975), advocated that species are individualistically distributed along environmental gradients and cannot be bounded in communities. Others, such as Frederic Clements (1874-1945), who pioneered ecological succession theory, introducing the idea of using "climax" or equilibrium vegetation as a "holistic approach" to separate plant communities. Others, such as Arthur Tansley (1871-1955) never accepted Clements' view that succession is a developmental process whose final stage is the climax formation. Tansley was convinced that in a given region, the variety of environmental factors may produce different climax formations. Their lively debate continued for more than 20 years without any impacts on Clements. Meanwhile, maps based on climax vegetation were incorporated in a number of landscape management applications, although the drawback of this method is that the two-dimensional nature of paper maps makes it difficult to assign more than one climax vegetation in a given location.

CONCEPT OF SUCCESSION
AND CLIMAX VEGETATION

According to botanist Frederic Clements, succession is part of a developmental process in which the plant community undergoes a well-defined series of stages of structure and biomass development resulting in a mature or climax state best suited to local environmental and climate conditions.

| **Plants stage** | **Shrubs stage** | **Young forest** | **Mature forest** | **Climax forest** |
| First 5 years | 6–25 years | 26–50 years | 51–150 years | 150–300 years |

Geographical information system (GIS) maps

Another mid-nineteenth-century story that relates to progress in mapmaking took place in cholera-hit London in 1854. The British physician John Snow (1813-1858) began mapping outbreak locations on roads, property boundaries, and water supply lines. When analyzing his data, Snow noticed that cholera infections were mainly associated with water supplies. His cholera map was a groundbreaking discovery in connecting geography with public health, and it marked the advent of spatial analysis and the concept of the geographic information system (GIS).

Early GIS maps

The history of GIS gradually evolved from static maps on paper to dynamic digital maps, and from basic spatial analysis to a more complex problem-solving approach. Between 1850 and 1950, before the computer age, maps were simple—they were used for planning roads, other transportation routes, and new developments, and for locating points of interest—and they were all still done on paper. From the early 1960s to 1980s, GIS flourished due to advances in three technological arenas: map graphics as outputs using line printers, advances in data storage using mainframe computers, and recording coordinates as data input. With these innovations, all that GIS needed was a brilliant mind to integrate the various methods and approaches. That mind belonged to Roger Tomlinson.

Tomlinson was a British Royal Air Force pilot whose subsequent doctoral thesis was titled "The Application of Electronic Computing Methods and Techniques to the Storage, Compilation, and Assessment of Mapped Data." It was during his

▶ **GIS pioneer**

With his 1855 map of cholera outbreaks in London, John Snow laid the groundwork for spatial analysis techniques that were later used in GIS mapping.

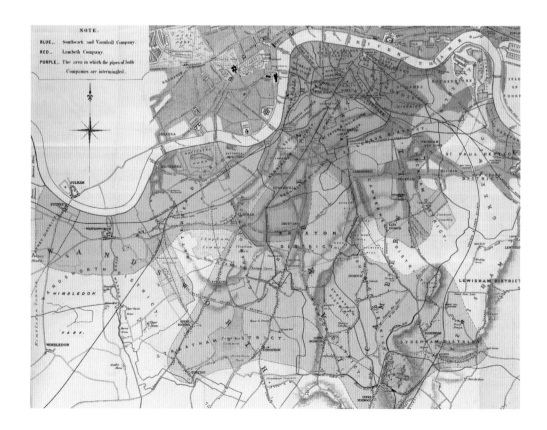

CHOROPLETH MAP

A choropleth map of forest area by country as percentage of total landmass.

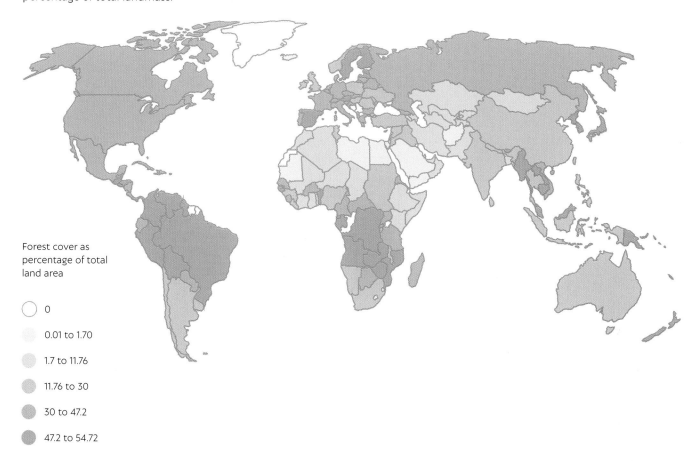

Forest cover as
percentage of total
land area

○ 0

0.01 to 1.70

1.7 to 11.76

11.76 to 30

30 to 47.2

47.2 to 54.72

tenure with the Canadian government in the 1960s and working in an Ottawa-based aerial survey company that he conceptualized the Canada Geographic Information System (CGIS) by adopting a layer approach for mapping land cover and land use with the emerging computer technology. The Canada Land Inventory data that were collated through Tomlinson's CGIS included soil, drainage, and climate characteristics, and were used to determine and map land capacity for crop types and forested areas. It was soon recognized that accurate and relevant data were vital for mapping land cover and helping with decision making around land use, and many groups and agencies around the world consequently started using GIS systems.

Choropleth mapping

It was, however, the pioneering work of the United States Census Bureau that led to the development of geographic base file and dual independent map encoding (GBF-DIME), which was then used in 1970 to store digital census data. GBE-DIME was a file format that supported digital data input, error fixing, and even choropleth mapping to digitize and classify roads, urban areas, census boundaries, and vegetation types. The choropleth mapping technique (from the Greek words *choro*, meaning "region," and *pletho*, meaning "multitude") took off as a new approach to provide thematic information based on statistical data through some predetermined symbols, colors, or shading patterns within defined geographic regions. This inspired different classification methods for separating geographical regions with similar characteristics into the same classes.

Developments in GIS

In its pioneering stage up until the mid-1970s, GIS continued to be fostered by multiple national agencies around the world, in particular the Harvard Laboratory for Computer Graphics and Spatial Analysis, which developed Odyssey GIS, the first vector GIS. The Harvard Laboratory was founded in 1965 by architect and town planner Howard Fisher through a grant from the Ford Foundation to bring together geographers, cartographers, mathematicians, computer scientists, and artists to reconceptualize existing thematic mapping and spatial analysis. Much of the early focus of this laboratory was invested in computer mapping and modeling tools such as SYMAP, yet it offered two main contributions that played a significant role in the development of GIS: environmental and architectural designs, and computer-aided designs

The Delmarva study

While focusing on landscape architecture at the Harvard Laboratory, Carl Steinitz used SYMAP to map the Delmarva Peninsula in Delaware and east Maryland. This included multiple layers of data to characterize the landscape, organized in grid cells by incorporating relevant information such as the percentage of land use and land cover (agriculture, forest, urban), average elevation, and vectors of roads, shorelines, and counties. The Delmarva study was a major breakthrough in what would become GIS. Steinitz and his team of researchers and students improved the map-production capability of SYMAP by introducing a simple interweaving grid-based input system that was named GRID. This system evolved into

▲ **GIS mapping**

A GIS map showing gridded distribution of global vegetation cover (top) along with a fine-scale GIS product (above) showing the vegetation NDVI index (green foliage status of the tree canopy) overlayed on a drone lidar forest-height scan.

a springboard for later innovations in software packages, such as ERDAS, which influenced the grid-based spatial analysis tools in the 1980s and 1990s. GIS entirely transformed the relationship between map scale, data accuracy, and resolution as used in paper maps. A map scale that was fixed and unalterable when printed on paper could now be reduced in size or enlarged on the GIS display or prints. This means that the geographic data in a GIS do not have an actual "map scale," but instead it is the display scale that influences the amount of detail and the size and placement of text and symbols on a map.

Jack Dangermond, who joined the Harvard Laboratory in 1967, took the grid-based analysis a step further. He introduced computer-aided designs into SYMAP and succeeded in printing the first computer-generated map. He later founded the Environmental Systems Research Institute (ESRI), which is now recognized as the most important global venue for the development of GIS tools and analytics. Together, these advances formed a perfect mapmaking toolkit, and one far beyond the imagination of the nineteenth-century pioneers.

GIS DESIGN

Example of Geographic Information System (GIS) database design showing the organization of geographic information into a series of data themes or thematic layers that can be integrated using geographic location. Each GIS contains multiple themes for each location and a series of analysis operations that allow the themes to be combined based on points, lines, polygons, surfaces, or rasters.

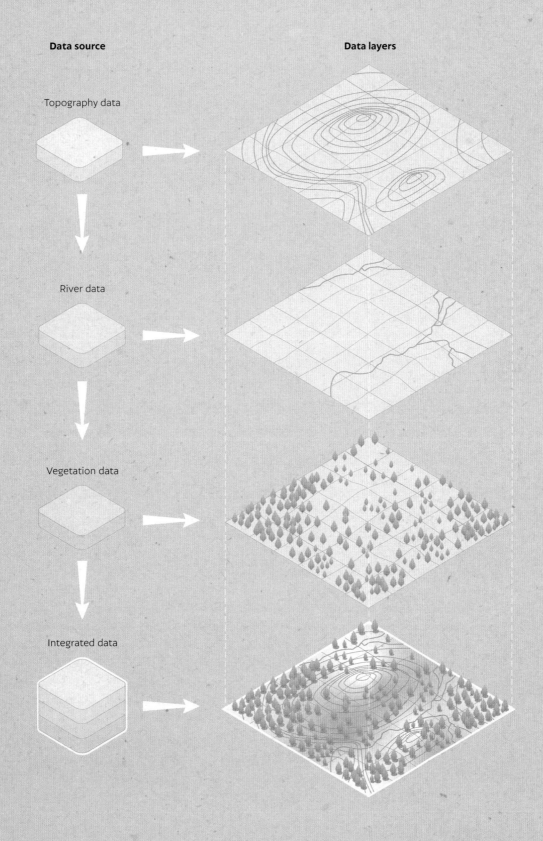

Data source

Topography data

River data

Vegetation data

Integrated data

Data layers

Map legends

A legend is the key to a map. It offers information about the number and variety of vegetation types in a map and reveals how the map content is organized. The organization of a map requires a terminology system that represents the type of vegetation classification and, at the same time, conforms to the purpose of the map. An important element is the "unit of interest," the choice of which affects how vegetation information is organized and effectively represents the patterns and shifts or changes in vegetation.

For von Humboldt, species were the unit of interest for connecting vegetation with the environment. His transverse view of vegetation along elevational gradients in the Andes included hundreds of plant genera and species, combined with environmental factors. Other units of interest, such as those based on the fundamental processes of plants (for example, photosynthesis and respiration) or categorizing species into functional groups, may allow the vegetation–climate relationship to be represented more effectively and extend the mapping to larger regions.

Vegetation classification systems make use of two principal properties: floristic composition and physiognomy. In mapping vegetation, it is desirable to start with a physiognomic-ecological system, which includes criteria such as life-forms (for example, dominant plant type), structure (for example, height and density), seasonal cycle, and other environmental factors. This system allows worldwide comparisons and may be implemented at small, medium, and large scales depending on the chosen criteria. In contrast, classification systems based on floristic composition, adopted by botanists, focus on individual species or a combination of species, with taxonomic information collected in the field and used solely over small areas. This system has limitations when used for mapping vegetation in areas with large numbers of important species, such as tropical and subtropical ecosystems.

Physiognomic categories

Based on physiognomic classification, the entire vegetation of the Earth is divided first into woody and herbaceous plants. Following this pattern and hierarchy, woody vegetation is classified based on leaf characteristic and seasonal habit, such as broad-leaved evergreen, broad-leaved deciduous, needle-leaved evergreen, needle-leaved deciduous, and finally leafless woody vegetation. The leafless types, referred to as aphyllous, are mostly succulents and often have chlorophyll inside their stems, branches, and twigs, such as the *Euphorbia* forest in Ethiopia. Two additional categories are often added to this system: the mixed vegetation type, where multiple structure types are codominant; and the semi-deciduous type, which refers to a combination of broad-leaved evergreen and broad-leaved deciduous trees found in tropical and subtropical regions. Similar categories based on appearance and physiognomy have been developed for non-woody herbaceous vegetation, including graminoilds (different types of grasses), forbs (broad-leaved herbaceous plants such as ferns), and bryoids (lichens and mosses).

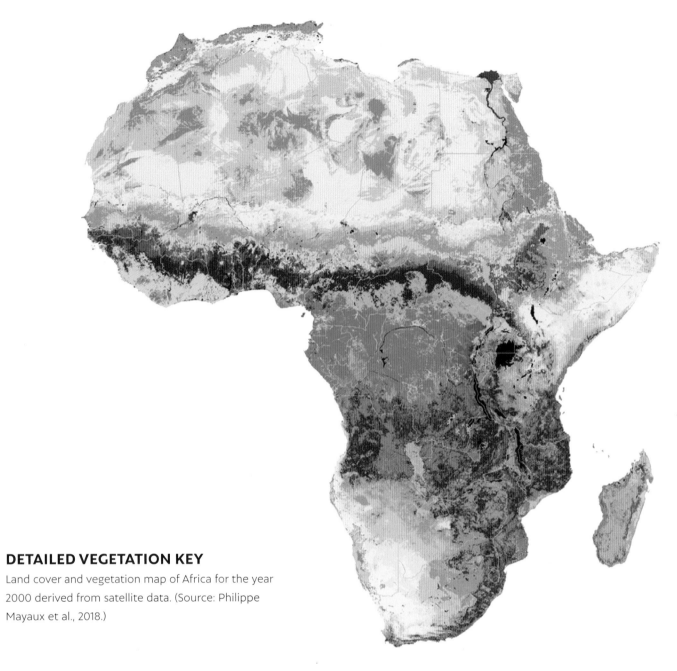

DETAILED VEGETATION KEY

Land cover and vegetation map of Africa for the year 2000 derived from satellite data. (Source: Philippe Mayaux et al., 2018.)

Forest classes

- Closed evergreen lowland forest
- Degraded evergreen lowland forest
- Submontane forest
- Montane forest
- Swamp forest
- Mangrove
- Mosaic forest/croplands
- Mosaic forest/savanna
- Closed deciduous forest

Woodlands and grasslands

- Deciduous woodland
- Deciduous shrubland with sparse trees
- Open deciduous shrubland
- Closed grassland
- Open grassland with sparse shrubs
- Open grassland
- Sparse grassland
- Swamp bushland and grassland

Agriculture

- Croplands
- Croplands with open woody vegetation
- Irrigated croplands
- Tree crops

Bare soil

- Sandy desert and dunes
- Stony desert
- Bare rock
- Salt hardpans

Other

- Waterbodies
- Cities

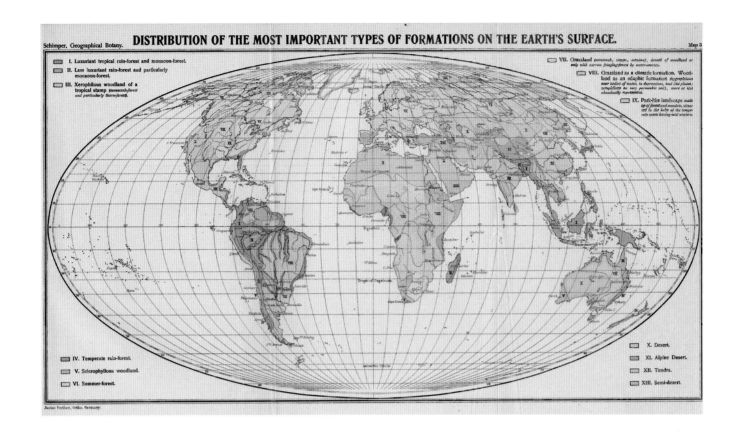

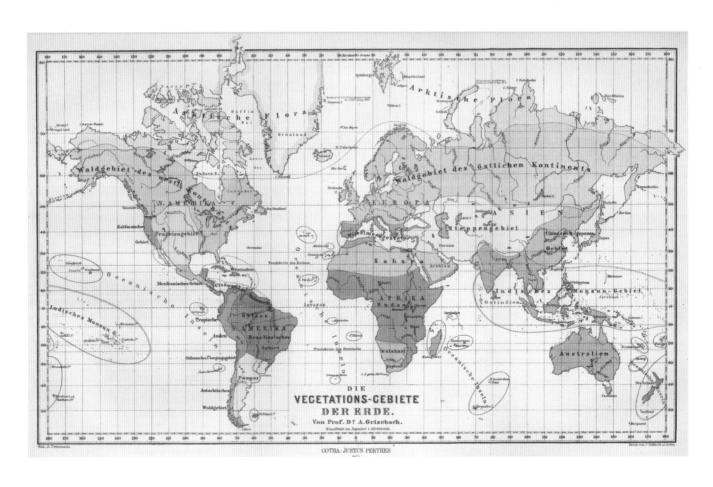

Global vegetation maps

At a broad scale, the global distribution of vegetation has been represented by geographic region and by biome type. A biome is a large vegetation environment characterized by both abiotic factors such as climate and soil, and biotic factors such as plant community and wildlife. The use of biome type to present world vegetation patterns in cartography is apparent in even the earliest maps, which combined physiognomy, ecology, and floristic information. The 1872 global vegetation map by German botanist August Grisebach (1814-1879) and the 1898 world-scale map by Andreas Schimper (1856-1901), another German botanist, are among the most important examples of maps with classification systems that resemble modern biomes. In formulating his map, Grisebach used detailed accounts of species in different regions and combined them with regional climate information to categorize 54 forms according to their appearance. His classification of vegetation varieties had both ecological focus (for example, tropical rain forests and prairies) and taxonomic focus (for example, Australian flora, palms, and ferns). Schimper's biomes were largely based on a physiognomic-ecological classification system, and included tropical, subtropical, and temperate rain forests, broad-leaved and needle-leaved forests, savanna forests and shrublands, steppes, transitions between steppes and deserts, and tundra.

Climate and vegetation

Today, these categories continue to be used extensively, even in modern vegetation maps based on satellite observations and remote-sensing techniques. The explanations for these mapped vegetation patterns have inspired plant ecologists and geographers to postulate on the relationships between climate, physiognomy, and structure. The consistency of vegetation patterns among different global maps and their geographic regularity arise from the geographic regularity of the Earth's main climate regions, driven by global circulation patterns of the Earth's atmosphere. As shown by the Köppen's climate system (devised around 1900 by Russian-German meteorologist Wladimir Köppen), this circulation system divides the climate into zones of low pressure and frequent precipitation near the equator, high pressure and low precipitation of arid regions in the subtropics of each hemisphere, and many other zones in between. Each is associated with broad categories of vegetation and life-forms.

The first attempt to quantify the climatic limits of vegetation types and demonstrate the unity of the global vegetation system was made by Swiss botanist Eduard Rübel in 1930, but the first complete global system of climatically predictable vegetation types was developed by the American botanist and climatologist Leslie Holdridge in 1947 (see page 132). Both approaches led to the development of the concept of climatic envelopes in the early 1970s that established the foundation of biogeography and later the ecological niche theory formulated by the father of modern ecology, George Evelyn Hutchinson (1903-1991). These are the upper and lower limiting values of climate variables that control the geographic range of plant communities, including their species composition and physiognomy.

◀ **Biome mapping**
The 1872 global vegetation map (top) by August Grisebach and the 1898 world-scale map (bottom) by Andreas Schimper. The detailed classification systems developed by these German botanists are similar to biome categories depicted in modern maps.

The Holdridge vegetation map

The Holdridge life zone system solved the main problems of vegetation classification by developing an empirically and objectively based hierarchical system. During the Second World War, Holdridge collaborated with other botanists on a program initiated by the United States Board of Economic Warfare to extract quinine from *Cinchona* bark to treat American troops suffering from malaria in the Pacific. In a series of expeditions to South and Central America, Holdridge followed Humboldt's footsteps in gathering information about climate and vegetation formations and functions.

Life zone ecology

In his now famous paper in *Science* journal in 1947, Holdridge introduced the concept of world plant formations, which he devised after exploring the relationships between mountain vegetation and other surrounding vegetation units in Haiti. He constructed a chart to differentiate dry land vegetation from 100 closely equivalent formations, each separated by temperature, precipitation, and evaporation lines.

Holdridge consolidated all his ideas later in a 1967 publication, *Life Zone Ecology*, which was prepared for the Tropical Science Center in San José, Costa Rica. In this, he delimited life zones using three measurements of temperature and moisture available for plants, including biotemperature as a heat summation index based on monthly air temperature, annual precipitation in millimeters of water, and potential evapotranspiration ratio (the ratio of average annual potential evapotranspiration to average total annual precipitation). He derived potential evapotranspiration figures from the biotemperature multiplied by 58.93, a constant estimated by Holdridge to show millimeters of water evaporated or transpired from the ecosystem. He then converted all three indices to the logarithmic system, to make all life zones equal in significance

The main advantage of Holdridge's system is that anyone having access to the same set of data will be able to classify it in the same fashion, leaving little room for subjectivity. Holdridge ensured this level of precision by drawing three sets of parallel lines to represent the three measurements, each inclined toward the other at an angle of 60 degrees. All lines are equidistant but hold values that progress geometrically in all three measurements. The overall effect is that of a triangle with multiple hexagons, each containing one specific type of vegetation at the intersection of the three given climate values. In drawing the schematics of the life zones, Holdridge added latitudinal zones and altitudinal belts to both sides of the triangle in a harmonized spacing, such that every vegetation type is readily identified with five variables: temperature, precipitation, evapotranspiration, latitude, and altitude. Holdridge's arrangements allow for 38 vegetation types at small map scale (1:1,000,000), but his drawing can be further subdivided depending on local data and vegetation variations. Although his map had legends assigned to vegetation types occurring solely in Guatemala, it had worldwide applications and has since been used to map life zones at national to continental levels.

HOLDRIDGE LIFE ZONE MAP

The Holdridge life zone system is based on a bioclimatic scheme and used for the classification of global ecosystems and vegetation types. The right side of the graph shows precipitation range and altitudinal belts, the left side the potential evapotranspiration ratio and latitudinal regions, the bottom side shows the humidity provinces. The hexagons within the triangular coordinate system represent different life zones found on the Earth.

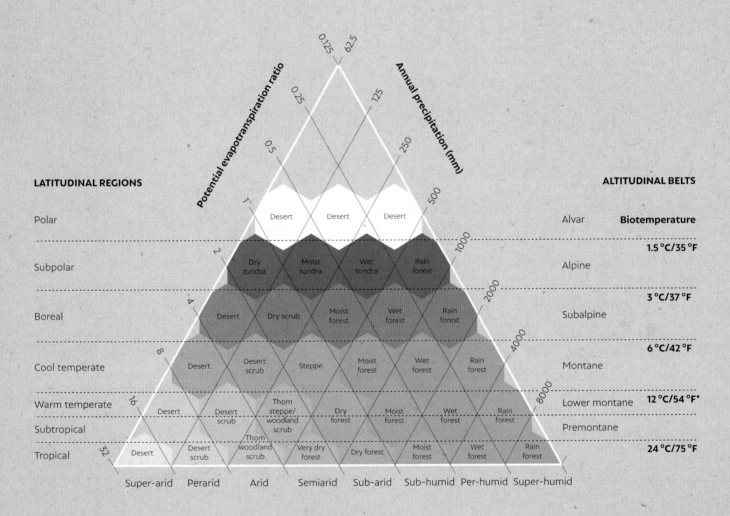

LATITUDINAL REGIONS

Polar

Subpolar

Boreal

Cool temperate

Warm temperate

Subtropical

Tropical

ALTITUDINAL BELTS

Alvar · **Biotemperature**

1.5 °C/35 °F

Alpine

3 °C/37 °F

Subalpine

6 °C/42 °F

Montane

Lower montane · 12 °C/54 °F*

Premontane

24 °C/75 °F

Potential evapotranspiration ratio

Annual precipitation (mm)

Super-arid · Perarid · Arid · Semiarid · Sub-arid · Sub-humid · Per-humid · Super-humid

HUMIDITY PROVINCES

*Critical temperature

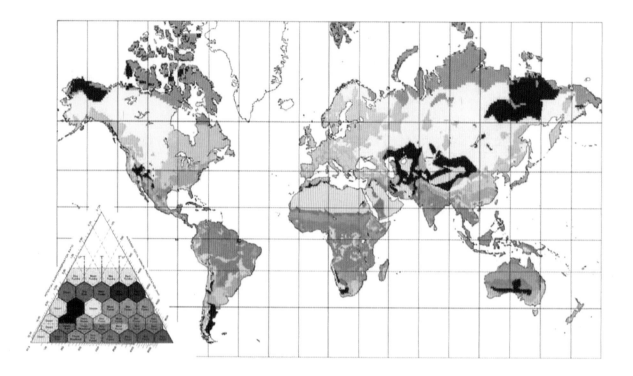

▼ **Global terrestrial ecosystems**
The first global scale vegetation map developed by Emanuel et al. 1985, based on the Holdridge life zone classification system

developed using climate data at resolutions of 0.5° latitude × 0.5° longitude. The color scale is shown in the inset and corresponds to Holdridge's chart shown on page 133.

KÖPPEN CLIMATE ZONES

Köppen climate classification of the state of Montana in the United States identified as cold semiarid steppe continental type climate with warm summers and cold winters.

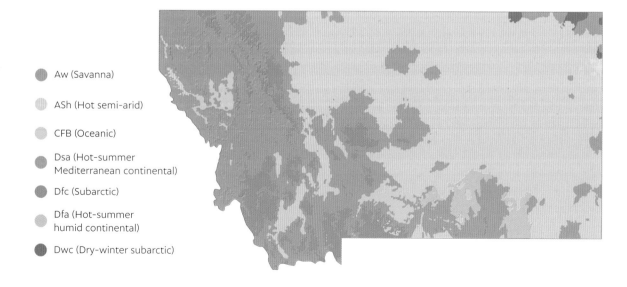

- Aw (Savanna)
- ASh (Hot semi-arid)
- CFB (Oceanic)
- Dsa (Hot-summer Mediterranean continental)
- Dfc (Subarctic)
- Dfa (Hot-summer humid continental)
- Dwc (Dry-winter subarctic)

Climate-based vegetation maps

The appeal of the Holdridge life zone classification is it allows vegetation categories to be overlaid onto corresponding climate envelopes. Holdridge's life zone chart and systematic classification of climate data significantly improved earlier climatic vegetation maps based on Köppen climate zones. He devised a climatic scheme, using quantitative data to predict all potential vegetation distributions globally. This allowed vegetation maps that represent plant communities to be used as a climate record. Many later studies that focused on understanding and modeling climate change implemented the Holdridge life zone approach. In 1985, American environmental scientist William Emanuel and colleagues used life zones to map global terrestrial ecosystems for the first time. They developed the map by applying the life zone algorithm to a globally interpolated world climatology dataset based on weather station data records in grid cells of 0.5° latitude by 0.5° longitude.

Gaussen's approach

At the same time as Holdridge was developing his life zone classification, alternative climatic vegetation maps were being produced elsewhere in the world. The Perpignan sheet of the vegetation map of France at the scale of 1:200,000, developed by Henri Gaussen in 1948, implements a different approach, based on the use and manipulation of color. The biogeographer identified and organized colors according to the spectrum, then used them to describe climate conditions. He chose the red end of the spectrum to correspond to dry and hot conditions, and the blue and violet end to represent cold and humid conditions. Gaussen established his categorization of humidity based on the number of dry and humid months per year, and the definition of each month based on the number of dry and humid days. As with the Holdridge life zone system, Gaussen's approach suggests that given climate conditions correspond to certain types of vegetation or plant community. His method was used by Heinz Ellenberg and Otti Zeller in 1951 to develop a large-scale version of climatic vegetation map at the scale of 1:50,000. Due to the sparseness of weather stations in the relatively small area they were mapping, the pair used data on vegetation phenology, or seasonal changes, instead of climate data. In this case and others like it, the climate information shown is relative rather than absolute because it does not rely on instrumental recordings. However, it is quantitative because it is based on measured seasonal changes of certain plant species.

Analyzing climate change

The potential response of vegetation to climate is considered imperative to understanding and assessing environmental change. These changes are either global in nature, such as increasing atmospheric carbon dioxide concentrations, or local and regional in extent but have global impacts on Earth system processes, such as deforestation, fire, and the loss of biodiversity.

▶ **Glacial erosion**
Coast of the wild Siberian taiga river with mounds of glacial erosion. Scientists use ecological models to analyze changes in global climate patterns.

Ecologists have been challenged by the paramount question of how the plant communities that are being affected by humans in innumerable ways respond to changes in global climate patterns. This relies on the understanding of a wide range of vegetation patterns and processes, including photosynthesis at the leaf level, demography and structure at individual tree to stand levels, disturbance and recovery processes at the landscape level, and changes in species composition at the regional level.

A more direct evaluation of climate change magnitude is achieved by studying the geographic changes of vegetation that are traceable to their interrelationship with climate. This is a viable approach, regardless of the various ways by which the relationship between vegetation and climate is quantified and mapped. Holdridge's life zones (see page 132) and their climate indicators are valuable tools to detect vegetation response to climate change, especially when predicting a new future state of equilibrium between vegetation and climate.

Past, present, and future

Operationally, studying vegetation responses to varying environmental changes requires empirical data from the leaf level up to population and community levels. Vegetation maps or their GIS equivalents can be used to extrapolate the data to higher levels of organization, at larger space scales and timescales. Historically, vegetation scientists have debated whether vegetation responses to environmental change are "organismal" in character and occur across the entirety of the plant community, or are "individualistic" in character and composed of independent species-level changes. Vegetation maps cannot directly quantify the magnitude of climate change because they do not represent the cause or potential timescale of the change. Observations of spatial variations in plant communities gained from botanical data and paleoecological records show the continuous changes of plant species assemblages through time, and are therefore better suited to the individualistic view.

Paleoecological studies, initiated by Kaspar Maria von Sternberg (1761-1838) in the early nineteenth century, have provided insights into past vegetation and climate. Empirical data from plant fossils imply changes in the climate over the past 10,000-15,000 years that are similar in magnitude to changes we may see in the near future. Ecological models compensate for the lack of vegetation response data by using climate predictions from general circulation models (GCMs). GCMs use a conceptual framework to mathematically synthesize our current understanding of the relationship between vegetation patterns and climate to predict potential patterns under novel environmental conditions. These models use terrestrial vegetation patterns as a control on the vast extent of land and atmospheric interactions, such as exchanges of carbon, water, energy, and other trace gases.

GCMs are founded extensively on maps that link vegetation to climate and other environmental conditions such as soil and topography. In their 1985 paper, Emanuel and his colleagues used GCM-based predictions of climate with double the contemporary levels of atmospheric carbon dioxide to assess vegetation responses to climate change. Predicted patterns showed significant changes in northern latitudes across the boreal forests and tundra, where vegetation conditions depend heavily on temperature, and a substantial shift toward drier vegetation across much of the Earth due to a reduction in precipitation.

Detailed analysis

Numerous global applications of ecological modeling suggest that vegetation classification— whether as life zones, biomes, or formations— may influence predictions of vegetation response to climate. Using base maps with detailed vegetation descriptions allows more effects to be predicted. For example, a map with only one class of forest will show either very minimal or no climate change effect compared to a map that separates forests into boreal, temperate, tropical, dry, and wet, or other more precise categories. A study focused on eastern United States tree species carried out by landscape ecologist Louis Iverson and colleagues in 2008 demonstrates this point. They used a distribution map of 134 major tree species under current conditions and computed how the distribution might change in different future climate scenarios with low and high atmospheric carbon dioxide concentrations. Their results show a reduced presence and performance of key species such as Loblolly Pine (*Pinus taeda*) in the southeast, and a shift northward in areas away from their current range. Even at much aggregated levels, the results demonstrated a substantial change in forest types across the eastern United States.

Ecological modeling has improved significantly in the last decades. In early versions, climate was viewed as an influential factor in determining the distribution of vegetation and its characteristics. However, there are other important factors, perhaps the most important of which is the impact of human-induced disturbances. Recent models incorporate changes of vegetation from human land-use activities in predicting vegetation response to climate. The challenge in accurately predicting the response of the planet's vegetation to climatic change, therefore, resides in the demand for fresh observations and new maps to better capture global vegetation patterns, physiognomy, structure, and floristic composition.

▲ **Loblolly Pine**

*Ecological modeling studies show how many important forest species, such as the Loblolly Pine (*Pinus taeda*), are being affected by climate change.*

ECOLOGICAL MODELING

Ecological modeling shows how Loblolly Pine (*Pinus taeda*)
species distribution in the eastern United States might
change in different future climate scenarios with low
and high atmospheric carbon dioxide concentrations.
(Source: Climate Change Atlas, USDA Forest Service.)

Current conditions

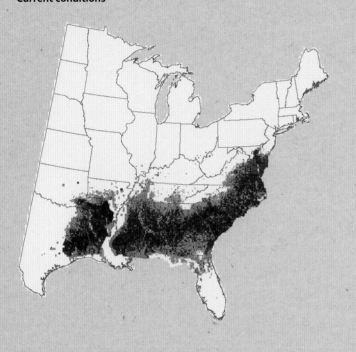

Importance value
(abundance of species)

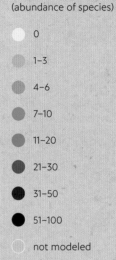

- 0
- 1–3
- 4–6
- 7–10
- 11–20
- 21–30
- 31–50
- 51–100
- not modeled

Future 1—moderate emissions

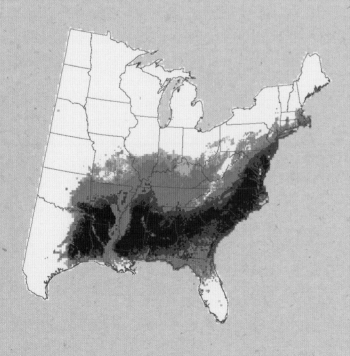

Future 2—high emissions

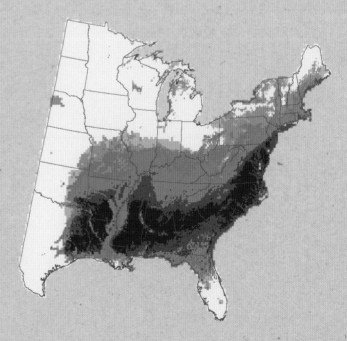

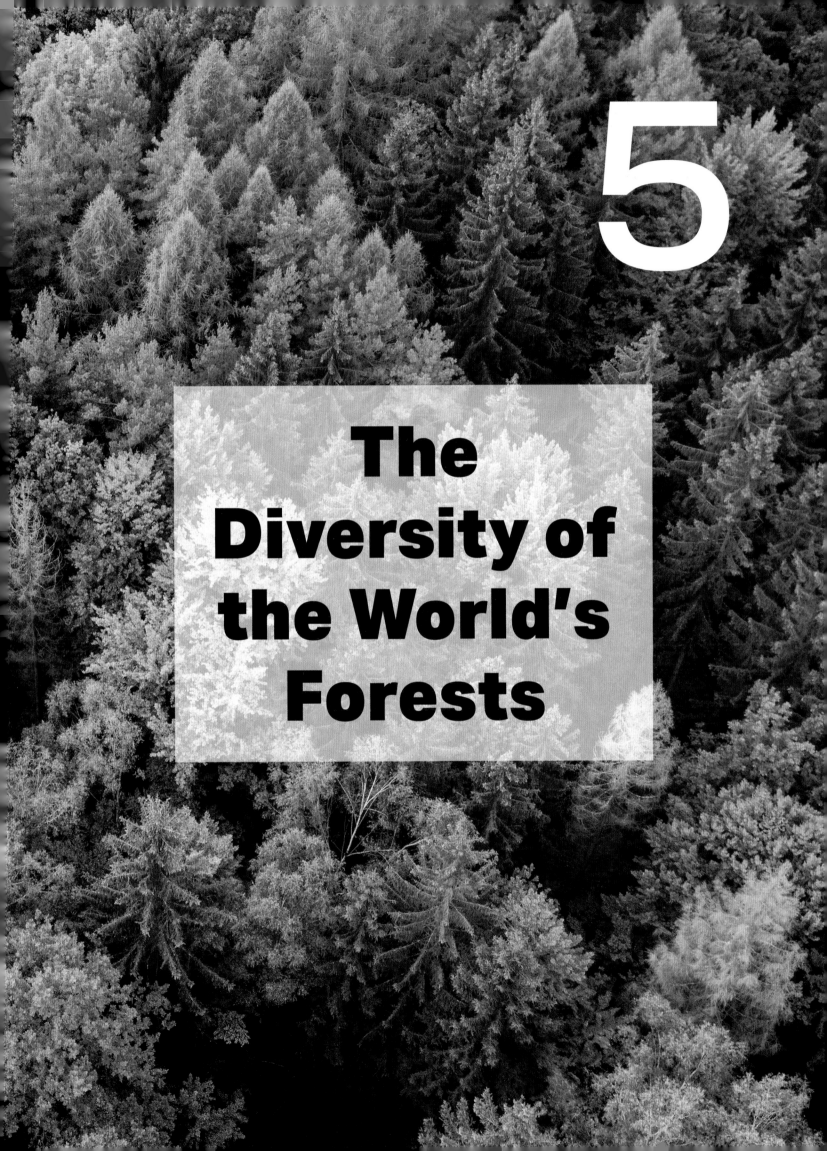

5

The Diversity of the World's Forests

Some unexpected forests

On September 26, 1836, Charles Darwin, then a 27-year-old naturalist on HMS *Beagle* and decades from the work that would secure his place in history, wrote in his diary: "I am strongly induced to believe that as in Music, the person who understands every note will, if he also has true taste, more thoroughly enjoy the whole; so he who examines each part of [a] fine view may also thoroughly comprehend the full and combined effect. Hence a traveller should be a botanist, for in all views plants form the chief embellishment."

PRINCIPAL FOREST BIOMES

The Earth's biomes are defined by environment, ecosystem structure, and the array of living organisms present. The distribution of the biomes is controlled by climates, ranging from warm to cold and from wet to dry. (Source: MA, 2005.)

- Tropical and subtropical moist broad-leaf forest
- Tropical and subtropical dry broad-leaf forest
- Tropical and subtropical coniferous forest
- Temperate broad-leaf and mixed forest
- Temperate coniferous forest
- Boreal forest / taiga
- Tundra
- Mediterranean forest, woodland, and scrub
- Tropical and subtropical grassland, savanna, and shrubland
- Temperate grassland, savanna, and shrubland
- Montane grassland and shrubland
- Flooded grassland and savanna
- Mangrove
- Desert and xeric shrubland
- Rock and ice

Each part of a fine view

In examining each part of the fine view of a forested landscape, nineteenth-century naturalists began to document and map the geographic patterns they saw on their travels (see Chapter 4, pages 116-119). Many of these explorers, like Darwin himself, came from the temperate latitudes of Europe. The low-hanging fruit, of course, was the latitudinal gradient that spans the boreal forest (Chapter 7), temperate deciduous forest and conifer forest (Chapter 9), to tropical rain forest (Chapter 6). The patterns in the southern hemisphere, while also driven by climatic gradients, had interesting differences in that land surface did not extend as far from the equator as in the northern hemisphere, limiting the expression of a boreal zone, and the greater ratio of sea surface area to land meant that winter temperatures were generally more moderate at any given mean temperature. Mountains were especially interesting everywhere for their sharp environmental gradients, high diversity, and the fact that their elevation zones were both similar to, and different from, the zones that were controlled by latitude.

Leaf size, shape, and the evergreen–deciduous divide

Zooming in farther on "each part" of Darwin's "fine view" reveals patterns in the morphology and seasonality of tree leaves that can be used to describe patterns in vegetation structure within and between the continents. Average leaf size in humid forests and the percentage of leaves with entire margins (those without jagged teeth along the edges) both increase from colder to warmer climates. About 80 percent of the trees in tropical forests have entire leaf margins, compared to 20 percent in high-latitude forests. Paleobotanists realized that they could measure these characteristics on fossilized leaves and then use the results to infer the temperature and moisture regimes that occurred thousands to millions of years ago.

A third geographical pattern in understanding the world's vegetation is the divide between evergreen and deciduous leaves. "Deciduous" trees have leaves that live for one growing season only and all leaves are shed with the onset of unfavorable conditions. In temperate climates, this occurs at the beginning of winter, but there are deciduous tropical forests in which leaf shedding occurs at the beginning of a dry season. By contrast, evergreen trees have leaves that persist through the unfavorable season, with life spans of 1-10 years. When new leaves are produced, older sets of leaves are still present, hence the plant is always green—not because the leaves live forever, but rather because the yearly sets overlap.

Evergreen leaves are more energetically costly to produce. They are thicker relative to surface area, with thicker protective cuticles on their surfaces to allow them to survive a wider range of humidity and temperature than deciduous leaves. They

▼ **Entire leaf shape**

Some species have leaves with smooth edges, as shown here with Avocado (Persea americana), native to the New World tropical forests.

retain nutrients through multiple growing seasons and therefore can occur where nutrients are less immediately available in the soil. By contrast, deciduous leaves are thinner and energetically cheaper to make. Deciduous trees must generate their entire leaf areas at the beginning of the growing season, and they generally support more rapid recycling of nutrients. The deciduous strategy is not only about avoiding a long unfavorable season, but equally about rapidly taking advantage of a long favorable season.

Leaf type also generates positive feedbacks that can amplify each strategy. Evergreen leaves are generally slow to decay, increasing soil acidity and decreasing nutrient supply—the very conditions that evergreens tolerate. In addition, evergreens produce year-round shade, thus influencing the type of seedlings that can grow beneath them. Deciduous leaves generally decay more quickly, promoting higher rates of nutrient cycling.

▲ **Jagged leaf shape**

*Some species have leaf margins that are jagged, as shown here with Silver Maple (*Acer saccharinum*). The individual points are called "teeth," as in a saw blade, and the leaf is said to be "toothed."*

▲ **Laurophyll forest**

A mossy laurophyll forest in Garajonay National Park, La Gomera, Spain.

Deciduousness and evergreenness as plant strategies

Deciduousness is a strategy that allows leaves to avoid the unfavorable season (dry or cold) and be rapidly deployed at the onset of long favorable seasons (see pages 280–285). The distribution of the evergreen strategy has more complexity. In humid climates, broad-leaved evergreen species increase along the gradient from temperate to tropical climates (see pages 154–155). Temperate and even cool temperate forests in regions with extremely high rainfall and mild winters are usually dominated by evergreens (see pages 162–165 and 166–169). Evergreen species are found across a wide range of latitudes when the favorable season is short and their leaves have been designed to withstand drought. These include sclerophyll forest (see pages 148–153) and some temperate conifer forests (see pages 292–295), needle-leaved forests at the treeline (see pages 156–161), and the boreal forest (see Chapter 7)—although deciduous needle-leaved larch trees appear in the boreal forests with the most extreme winter cold. Finally, temperate ecosystems with acid and nutrient-poor soils are often dominated by needle-leaved evergreens, including those on well-drained sandy soils (for example, the pine barrens of southeastern North America) and in bogs and swamps. Note that because evergreen and deciduous strategies both have costs and benefits, the evergreen-deciduous divide is a continuous transition and not an abrupt tipping point. Indeed, the two strategies coexist in many forests.

Consistent patterns on separate continents among unrelated evolutionary lineages suggest that convergent evolution has been at work—the independent evolution of similar adaptations. This presents us with the opportunity to phrase and test generalizations about the rules that govern forest distributions. Further, these traits can be observed and recorded by ecologists even when the underlying taxonomy has not been finalized. This also likely appealed to the first biogeographers venturing into unfamiliar lands.

Forests at the extreme

The chapters that come next describe the planet's major forest zones, each with its own sets of environmental conditions and each located along the gradients of evergreenness to deciduousness and other leaf characteristics described above. However, there are a number of forest types that necessarily get left out of that approach or are hard to place within the framework based on major climate zones. In this chapter the focus is on those "left out" forests. These are forests that occupy generally small areas, although they can be very ecologically important. For instance, temperate rain forest, cloud forest, and laurophyll forest are all critical to the generation of water supplies when they occur on upper mountain slopes, and mangroves are important for biotic diversity and as nurseries for marine food chains, while protecting shorelines from sea-level rise and tropical storms.

In one way or another, these forests also occur at environmental extremes, including very dry (sclerophyll forest), very wet (cloud forest, temperate rain forest), very cold (forests at the treeline), wet environments at the border of warm temperate and subtropical regions (laurophyll forest), and on harsh substrates (mangrove forest). All these examples, it turns out, are dominated by evergreen trees, albeit with leaves designed to function in these disparate and challenging environments.

▼ **Mangrove forest**
A mangrove forest in Krabi province, Thailand.

Sclerophyll forest

Sclerenchyma cells are the rigid, thick-walled cells that provide mechanical support in all plant tissues—roots, stems, and leaves. In wood, they have very thick secondary walls that contain compounds collectively known as lignin, which comprises 17–35 percent of the dry mass of wood. In Mediterranean climates, sclerenchyma cells also underlie distinctive leaf traits: sclerophyllous leaves are characterized as hard, tough, leathery, and remarkable for their ability to resist wilting. They are also usually evergreen. It is this distinctive leaf form that gives sclerophyll vegetation its name.

The vegetation of Mediterranean climates

Sclerophyll vegetation is associated with Mediterranean climates and adjacent climate zones. It occurs over a relatively small portion of the terrestrial surface (see opposite). Most of the precipitation falls during cool winters and the summers are hot and quite dry. Two "Goldilocks" growing seasons (more moist but not too cold, and not too hot) provide conditions favorable for plant growth. The first of these is at the end of winter. This "spring" period of plant growth lasts into the dry summer, until the plant root systems can no longer reach the deeper soil water. The other, shorter growing season occurs after the summer, when rainfall increases but it is not yet too cold to halt growth.

Six vegetation formations are found where these climatic conditions dominate. One, in the basin surrounding the Mediterranean Sea and called *maquis* in French, has hotter summers than the others. The other five are influenced by cold ocean currents. They lie between latitudes 30° and 40° in both the northern and southern hemispheres, and are typically found on the western edges of continents. The vegetation of these five "cool-summer" Mediterranean climates are the fynbos of southern Africa, the Chilean matorral, the Californian chaparral, and in southwestern Australia, the kwongan (south of Perth, Western Australia) and the Australian pyric heathlands (around Adelaide, South Australia).

Species from different plant families dominate in these various Mediterranean ecosystems. The similarities among the plants arise from adaptations to their environments much more often than from taxonomic relatedness. Despite these different floristic origins, there is great convergence of form across all six vegetation types. The dominant vascular plants are primarily woody, sclerophyllous, evergreen, deeply rooted shrubs. The vegetation can be extremely flammable in the dry summer. The reproductive strategies of the component species are tuned to wildfires of different intensities and frequencies—different species prosper under different fire regimes. Sprouting after wildfires is a common trait. With the combination of frequent wildfires and dry summers, one might expect a relatively lower diversity of species to prosper under such hostile conditions. However, these ecosystems are remarkably diverse.

COOL SUMMER ZONES

Mediterranean climate zones. Trees occur in the wetter, cooler regions in and adjacent to these zones. Generally, trees in these zones are low stature (usually less than a few meters tall).

Chaparral

Maquis

Matorral

Fynbos

Kwongan

Australian pyric heathlands

Australian sclerophyll

The vegetation of Mediterranean climates is primarily low-statured shrubland, with only a few monopodial trees or multi-stemmed shrubs that are taller than 30 ft (10 m). At the montane and coastal edges of these shrublands, where there is more precipitation, trees occur in sufficient density to be recognized as forest. Remarkably, some of these trees are also among the tallest on Earth. While forests are found in all six of the Mediterranean climate areas, Australian vegetation provides by far the most extreme expression of the ecological success of sclerophyllous trees. Here, there are large tracts of sclerophyll woodlands, mallee (multi-stemmed trees and shrubs sprouting from lignotubers), and forests. The range of variation in the appearance of these ecosystems is made more exceptional by the fact that many of these forests are dominated by trees of a single genus, *Eucalyptus*. There are more than 700 species of *Eucalyptus*, almost all of which are endemic to Australia—only 15 are found as native species elsewhere and among these are just nine non-Australian species.

A general term often used for Australian sclerophyll forest is eucalypt forest. In this usage eucalypt refers to a collective of *Eucalyptus* and two closely related genera. The first of these is the genus *Corymbia*, including bloodwoods (named for their carmine blood-like sap, which is produced when a tree is wounded), ghost gums, and spotted gums. There are about 100 *Corymbia* species, which were taxonomically separated from genus *Eucalyptus* in 1995). The second is the genus *Angophora*, consisting of nine species of tree or shrub called by the common name "apples," because to European settlers they looked like apple trees.

Patterns and abundances of species or genera in forest communities are often used to classify forests. For example, White Oak (*Quercus alba*)/ Chestnut Oak (*Q. montana*) forest is the name used for the vegetation of upper mid-elevation slopes in the Appalachian Mountains of the United States. In Australia the case is more complex, and sclerophyll forests are often classified by the patterns in dominance among broad groupings of eucalypts. For all the regional diversity of eucalypts, locally one often finds categories based on bark (stringy barks, ironbarks, and halfbarks, with bark releasing from the trunk about halfway up the tree), leaves, or other features. A forest in one location might have one gum (smooth-barked, with heavy sap production when wounded), one stringybark, and one ironbark. If there is one species of each in a eucalypt forest, then it is less likely there will be another. A second location might also have the same combination of eucalypt types, but while the overall appearance would be similar, one, some, or all the species could be different. "What's the ironbark growing around here on the middle hillslopes?" is the question a visiting forester asks a local colleague to become oriented to a new region. Stands dominated by a single species of *Eucalyptus* occur frequently.

◄ **Snow Gum**
A hardy Snow Gum (Eucalyptus pauciflora) *growing around granite in Australia's Snowy Mountains. Its dramatic bark is smooth, textured, and colorful.*

▼ **Eucalyptus forest**
Sclerophyll forests are dominated by Eucalyptus *trees.*

▼ **Bloodwoods**
Red blood-like sap produced by a burned Red Gum or Marri Tree (Corymbia calophylla), *Ambergate Reserve, Western Australia.*

▶ **Firestorms**

*Devastating wildfires
burning over eastern
Australia on December
7, 2019 (1: Brisbane, 2:
Sydney, 3: Canberra, 4:
Mallacoota). The NASA
satellite AQUA captured
the smoke plumes and
fire outlines (red).*

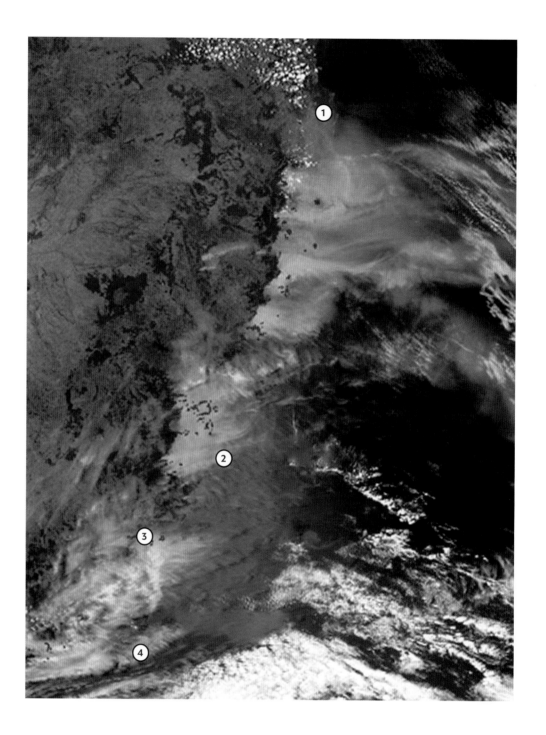

Firestorms in sclerophyll forest

We perceive, perhaps as never before, a world on fire. The media presents visions of
terrible wildfires in Australia, as well as other fire-prone forested regions—notably
in Africa, Siberia, and western North America. The combined effects of planetary
warming, more people living in what were formerly remote locations, and improved
worldwide satellite reconnaissance of fires on sub-daily intervals have converted
wildfires from being local news to the physical representation of planetary change
and violent danger.

For Australia, the bushfire season of 2019/2020 was collectively known as the Black
Summer. Throughout this austral summer, wildfires burned 71,800 square miles
(186,000 sq km)—about three-quarters the area of Britain—and 34 people were
killed and 5,900 buildings destroyed. The height of burning was from December

2019 to January 2020. On January 7, 2020, the smoke plume from Australia reached across the South Pacific to Chile and Argentina, some 6,800 miles (11,000 km) away. The costs are still being tabulated, notably the longer-term effects of smoke on human health and how many formerly endangered species are now extinct.

An earlier nightmarish Australian wildfire was the Black Friday Fire of 1939, which killed 71 people and generated firestorm effects—great tornadic vortices of fire, lifting 300 ft-tall (90 m) Mountain Ash (*Eucalyptus regnans*) trees from the ground and throwing them about as if they were jackstraws. On the day of the fire, Friday the 13th of January 1939, Melbourne recorded a temperature of 114 °F (45.6 °C). It was dry and had been so for six months. After the fire, a Royal Commission headed by Judge L. H. B. Streeton gave an account of the disaster, saying, "the speed of the fires was appalling. They leaped from mountain peak to mountain peak, or far out into the lower country, lighting the forests 6 or 7 miles in advance of the main fires ... such was the force of the wind that, in many places, hundreds of trees of great size were blown clear of the earth."

Such events may be increasing in frequency and duration as a result of climate change, especially in many already fire-prone regions. It is a challenge to know what should be done under threat of such fires. In Australia, the national policy for wildfires is to "prepare, stay and defend, or leave early." With super-fire events such as Black Friday or Black Summer, "leave early" may be the only real option, which in turn requires that notification systems are in place and evacuation routes planned. The interfacing of our capabilities to collect satellite images of fires over vast areas, to fuse weather models with wildfire models, to understand risk to human life as a fire changes dynamically and sometimes very quickly in space, is an absolute necessity. The remarkable flammability of sclerophyll forest is the harbinger of a more global problem involving climate change. This situation is likely to worsen under climate warming—as long as there are forests left to burn.

Fire adaptations

Fire is often the apex disturbance in *Eucalyptus* species, both in their native Australia and in the many countries where they are now naturalized. One adaptation to wildfire is the formation of lignotubers, resulting in the mallee growth form. Another striking adaptation is the abundance of epicormic buds beneath the bark in many eucalypts. When a wildfire burns away leaves, twigs, and branches, these epicormic bubs are activated, creating "fuzzy trees" (pictured) whose limbs and trunks are covered with new sprouts.

Laurophyll forests

Laurophyll forests take their name from Lauraceae, the laurel family. The leaves of laurel trees are evergreen, ovate, dark green, shiny, and moderate in size (4-7 in²/25-45 cm²), with margins that are entire (have no jagged teeth). While laurophyll forests often contain members of the laurel family, similar leaves occur in a number of other plant families found here, as an adaptation to the humid growing seasons with mild and short winters.

Global distribution of laurophyll forests

Laurophyll forests are medium to tall evergreen forests found predominantly in subtropical and warm temperate climates, but they can also occur in tropical montane forests, including cloud forests (see pages 162-165). They extend into temperate and even cool temperate areas in the southern hemisphere because the strong maritime influence lessens the severity of winter cold. Laurophyll forests have dense canopies, making forest interiors dark and shady year-round. Consequently, like tropical rain forests, laurophyll forests have few forest-floor herbaceous plants.

Unlike tropical forests, many laurophyll forests experience a cold season with a risk of frost, but are ultimately eliminated if winter temperatures are severe. These forests are also limited to areas with high moisture availability during the growing season. In subtropical to warm temperate areas with winter rain and dry summers, sclerophyll vegetation dominates instead (see pages 148-149).

▲ **Laurophyll leaves**

Laurophyll forest is named for the typical leaf form of the dominant trees, characterized by entire leaf margins, evergreenness, and moderate size.

Laurophyll forests have their greatest spatial extent in Southeast Asia, where they form part of a continuous latitudinal gradient from tropical forests to temperate deciduous forest. Asian laurophyll forests once covered 800 square miles (2,000 sq km) between 24°N and 32°N latitude, but now only fragments remain, many of them on temple grounds and in sacred groves. They also occur in Japan and on other east Asian islands.

In pre-Pleistocene Europe and northern Africa, laurophyll forests formed a wide latitudinal zone similar to that observed in Asia, but, with subsequent cooling and drying, these forests became restricted to small fragments in sheltered locations, including the coasts of Portugal and Spain, and parts of Italy. Laurophyll forests in the Macaronesian islands, including the Canaries and Azores, are also descendants of the once more widely distributed forest. Although not forming a continuous zone as they do in Southeast Asia, laurophyll forests are also found in Africa, Mexico, the Himalayas, western Asia, New Zealand, Australia, and South America.

As climates warm, winter cold is becoming less severe. One prediction is that frost-limited broad-leaved evergreen trees will move poleward and to higher elevations. In Europe, this process has been given the name "laurophyllization" and, indeed, a number of studies have shown that laurophyll trees have been spreading from their former climatic refuges in southern Switzerland and northern Italy to surrounding areas.

▲ **Sacred laurel**

The giant camphor tree legendarily planted by the high priest Shinran Shonin by the gate of Shoren-in Monzeki temple, Kyoto, Japan.

◀ **New Zealand**

A laurophyll forest in the southern hemisphere— Green Bay Beach and Karaka Park, Titirangi, Auckland, New Zealand.

Forests at the treeline

All climates and continents have mountains, so montane forest patterns have been described in many chapters of this book. Here, we turn to an extreme in the nature of forests: forests at the treeline. The treeline has been a major bioclimatic indicator in studies of past climates, and climate warming is challenging ecologists to predict future changes in its position.

As one moves upward in elevation or poleward in latitude, falling temperatures, shorter growing seasons, and increasingly severe winter temperatures ultimately limit tree growth. The tree growth form requires that photosynthesis is not only sufficient to produce reproductive structures and seeds, but also to create and maintain an above- and below-ground woody frame.

Types of treeline

Treelines take several forms and have been defined in several ways. The absolute climatic limit of trees, the physiological limit, has been called the "tree species line." In some areas, especially on windy mountain slopes, trees become gradually stunted until they form a low scrub called krummholz. In this case, the treeline and the tree species line are often treated as one. In other areas, closed forests yield gradually to small groups and isolated individuals. Here, the treeline is often treated as occurring where trees have reached an arbitrary maximum height (often 6½–10 ft /2-3 m) and density, even when individuals at lower heights and densities occur beyond this, finally reaching the physiological limit of the tree species line. Other treeline-related designations have been used: the "forest line" as the limit of closed forests, and the "timberline" as the limit of trees of merchantable sizes.

Taking a global and large-scale view, the most important environmental factor predicting treeline is temperature. A general rule is that the treeline is reached when the growing season falls to approximately 95 days, the growing season daily minimum temperatures average 33.6 °F (0.9 °C), and the growing season air temperature averages 43.5 °F (6.4 °C). Many other factors can influence treeline occurrence, including human disturbance (pastoralism, tree removal, fire), wildlife grazing, winter conditions that increase mortality (snow depth and exposure to winter desiccation when soils are frozen), and summer conditions that limit growth (low rainfall, windiness, maritime influences such as cool and cloudy summers). Species differ in their reactions to the thermal regime and these other factors, so the treeline can include a variety of taxa depending on environment and location, including the evergreen conifers spruce, fir, and pine, the deciduous conifer larch, and broad-leaved deciduous trees such as birches, alders, and willows.

▶ **The upper limit**
Ascending the Canadian Rockies in Loughheed Provincial Park, closed forests of spruce and fir give way to rock, snow, and open alpine grasslands.

Krummholz

Small trees, sometimes of great age and resembling Japanese bonsai, are found at the treeline in evergreen conifer forests. This vegetation is called krummholz, from the German words *krumm* (meaning "crooked" or "twisted") and *Holz* (meaning "wood"). Krummholz trees live in cold, difficult conditions and are pruned of their buds by ice blasts driven by high winds and from the drying effects of these winds. The locations in which they grow are sheltered by rocks, boulders, or snow cover, allowing the lower branches to develop dense foliage. When the harsh, icy winter winds come mostly from one direction, the damage is concentrated on one side of the tree trunk, forming "flag trees" or "banner trees." Krummholz is also maintained in avalanche zones, where there is a higher mortality among taller trees. Often the trees are selected over many generations for a small, prostrate stature, and remain so when they or their seedings are transplanted to favorable situations. In other cases, they grow larger and taller after they are transplanted.

▼ **Flag trees**

"Flag trees" (also called "banner trees") have branches missing from the windward side of the trunk.

Sideways

A Utah Juniper (Juniperus ostersperma) that has been shaped by the extreme environmental conditions, including wind, low humidity, and cold.

Stunted

In windswept areas at treeline, species that normally produce singled stemmed, upright trees can become low, horizontally growing mats of stunted individuals.

▲ **Gradients**

On elevational and latitudinal gradients, cold temperatures and short growing seasons ultimately limit tree growth and closed forests give way to alpine and arctic tundra vegetation.

▶ **Rockies**

The Canadian Rockies show a clear line, above which the cold temperature limits tree growth.

Mountain treelines

In 2015, Severin Irl and colleagues published a global overview of mountain treelines, contrasting continental treelines with those of continental islands (islands forming along the shorelines of continents and part of the continental shelf) and oceanic islands (volcanic islands that are isolated from continents). The continental treelines showed decreasing elevations toward both poles, but a dip in elevations in the tropics. Recall that a characteristic feature of the tropics is that the day-night cycle of temperature is more extreme than the summer-winter cycle of temperature. This treeline dip occurs because outside the tropics seasonality produces warmer periods without frost, whereas within the tropics, mountains that are sufficiently tall experience frost nightly, with no frost-free season. The analysis also showed that continental and oceanic islands did not show this dip in the tropics, presumably because maritime conditions reduce nighttime cooling here. Across latitudes, treelines were lower on isolated islands than on continental ones.

Treeline is a major marker for ecosystems and climates. A warming world leads to the question: are treelines moving up in elevation or poleward in latitude? Once again, we find ourselves on the frontier of scientific discovery. In their 2021 paper, Amanda Hansson, Paul Dargusch, and Jamie Shulmeister summarize the results for 447 study sites: 66 percent of these sites are confirming the expectation, with treelines moving both higher in elevation and poleward, and with latitudinal treelines moving faster than elevational ones.

Cloud forests

The broadest definition of cloud forest is forest in which clouds are frequent and fog drip is a significant input of moisture, although no lower limit has been universally established for cloud frequency or quantity of fog drip. Cloud forests occur at all latitudes in both coastal and mountain situations.

▼ Appalachians
Morning mist in the mountains on the Blue Ridge Parkway

Effects on forests

Where humid air masses meet cooling temperatures, clouds, fog, and mists form when the condensation point is reached and water moves from a gaseous form to a liquid. This is most frequent in two situations: first, on mountain slopes, if the mountains are tall enough for the condensation point to be reached; and second, on coastlines where humid air moves inland and cools.

Clouds, mists, and fogs dramatically affect local environmental conditions in that they reduce direct solar radiation and temperature, and thereby also reduce evapotranspiration (the water evaporated from surfaces, soils, and leaves), while also directly adding to water supply through condensation. Of course, the extreme is rain itself, but one of the interesting early discoveries was that as clouds sweep through forest canopies—over the complex surface area of leaves, twigs, and branches—the forest acts like a comb for the airborne cloud droplets. Even when it is not raining, water can be seen dripping from the tree canopy and running down along branches and tree trunks to keep soils moist. Measurements have shown that this cloud or fog drip can double or even triple the total precipitation to the recipient forest compared to the rain received in a rain gauge exposed to the open sky.

Let's take the case of mountains. As air masses are forced up mountain slopes, air pressure drops, causing temperature to drop—anyone who has climbed a mountain has experienced this and learned to pack extra clothes for the summit. The rate of the drop in temperature with elevation is called the adiabatic lapse rate. In the Appalachian Mountains of eastern North America, clouds are correlated with the lower elevational limit of montane spruce and fir forests. The condensation of moisture and formation of clouds happens abruptly with elevation. Because this change stores thermal energy, and water itself buffers the rate of temperature change and clouds reduce insolation, clouds affect both the moisture and temperature regime. Thus, the cloud ceiling is a manifestation of a critical interaction between temperature and moisture supply. If it remains at its historic position, the cloud ceiling may buffer higher-elevation systems from climate change but, if it moves to higher elevations, ecosystem change is likely to happen quickly. Some research in the Appalachians, led by Andrew Richardson, has indeed shown that cloud ceilings are moving to higher elevations.

There are frequent clouds, fog, and mists along some coastlines, too (see pages 166-169). Again, this requires humid air masses that cool as they cross from the sea to land. Land temperatures fluctuate more than those of the sea, setting up the circumstances when relatively cool land produces fog from sea breezes. The redwood forests of northern California and southwest Oregon, renowned for extreme tree heights and tree ages, are a dramatic example of the importance of coastal fogs. These forests depend on fog drip as a source of moisture in a landscape that is otherwise characterized by low precipitation and summer droughts.

▲ **Fog drip**

As fogs, mists, and clouds penetrate forests, condensation occurs on plant surfaces. Needle-leaved species, like Coast Redwood (Sequoia sempervirens), have been shown to be the most efficient in capturing this fog drip, greatly augmenting other sources of precipitation for forest growth.

Cloud forest features

The term "cloud forest" is often used in a narrow sense for tropical montane forests in which air masses are almost always humid and the adiabatic lapse rate guarantees that the condensation point will be reached. Clouds, fog, and mists can be a daily occurrence in these forests throughout the year. Because tropical montane cloud forests experience no deep winter cold and, in the extreme, lack dry periods, they have no seasonal pause in the rate of photosynthesis or in other life processes. As a result, they are dominated by broad-leaved evergreen trees in dense, shady forests. As with lowland tropical rain forests, cloud forests are crowded with life-forms, including epiphytes (plants that live on the branches of trees high in the canopy) and epiphylls (mosses and liverworts that can grow across leaf surfaces). Mosses often cover tree trunks and branches. Because decomposition is slower in cool mountain temperatures, the forest soils have a greater content of organic matter and tend to be acidic. On ridgelines and steep upper slopes where soils are thin and wind is prominent, trees can be low in stature with the branched canopy closer to the ground, leading to the colorful name "elfin forest" for this variant.

The role of clouds in water supplies

Mountain slopes that generate cloud cover and frequent rain and fog are also potent "machines" for the production of human water supplies. The Food and Agriculture Organization of the United Nations has estimated that more than half of the world human population depends on water supplies that originate in mountains. The world's major rivers originate on mountain slopes, and downstream reservoirs store the water that derives from the adiabatic cooling

CLOUD FOREST LOCATIONS

Where humid clouds meet cooling temperatures, as on mountain slopes or along some coastlines, persistent clouds provide abundant moisture.

that results in precipitation and fog drip and from the melting of mountain glaciers. One should never observe the rushing waters of low-elevation canyons, gorges, and waterfalls, or the even the languid and meandering rivers of flatter lands, without also thinking of mountain slopes. Water supply connects our most developed cities and our most remote mountains.

This dependence also suggests another critical concern about climate change. On the one hand, cloud formation can buffer local climate warming by reducing solar radiation and increasing moisture so that evaporation slows temperature rise. But on the other hand, warming temperatures may raise the elevation of the cloud ceiling and therefore lower the cloud inputs to total precipitation. The impacts of climate change on water supply are more difficult to predict than impacts on temperature, but they will prove critical to both natural systems and human populations that depend on supplies deriving from mountain slopes.

▼ **Elfin forest**
A mossy montane "elfin" rain forest above Rio Nangaritza Valley Cordillera del Condor, Ecuador.

Cloud forests, coffee, and biodiversity

Tropical montane forests are also economically important as the setting for coffee production. Coffee is produced from the fruits of tropical shrubs in the genus *Coffea*. Originating in Ethiopia, coffee production was soon expanded by colonial powers, which introduced the plants throughout the tropical world. While the wholesale conversion of tropical montane forests to coffee plantations is a significant threat to the biodiversity of these forests, wild *Coffea* shrubs (right) are understory species that are tolerant of some shade. In recent decades, alternative "shade-grown" coffee has been promoted to reduce the impacts of coffee production on these forests.

Maritime temperate rain forests

Trees in maritime temperate forests grow in what amounts to "tree heaven," with year-around rainfall, a relatively narrow annual temperature range, and few temperature extremes. Summers are mild and winters are cool but not cold. They are the photogenic landscapes that illustrate hundreds of cruise ship brochures.

Maritime temperate rain forests are the wet coastal forests that prosper in the cooler climate conditions of the west coasts in higher middle latitudes (35-60°) of continents with cold offshore ocean currents. A prominent example is the Pacific Northwest coast of North America. There is relatively little land in the southern hemisphere south of 35°S, but such forests are found on what land there is—Tasmania, southeastern Australia, New Zealand, southern Chile, and southern Argentina.

The maritime rain forests of the northern hemisphere share many ecosystem details. They feature evergreen needle-leaved conifers as the dominant trees, and they manifest similarities in their regional distribution patterns, which are driven by the global circulation of the atmosphere. Inland from the coasts, very similar forests can occur at higher elevations with rain, mists, and fog occurring through the day. Equatorward from most temperate rain forests, the summers become drier, resulting in tall forests and eventually Mediterranean forests and shrublands. A relatively similar climate, but not as wet as that associated with temperate maritime rain forest, covers western Europe. The winters here become colder and the summers hotter eastward from the European Atlantic coast.

Seasonal events

Temperate rain forest is characterized by striking seasonal events. Salmon migrate upriver in Russia, British Columbia, and Norway at densities that can turn rivers red—a seemingly venerable ecological feature. The adult salmon migrate from the sea to the very stream where they were born. When there, they stir the bottom sediments to build nests, they spawn, and in almost all cases, they die. The new generation hatches and develops into free-swimming salmon fry. The fry move from their stream to a series of ever larger streams, to rivers, and into the sea to grow into mature adults.

This multiscale convergence of fish and forest is made more extraordinary in that these ecosystems formed in their current locations within the past 10,000 years— not many generations for long-lived trees. How does the intricate clockwork of ecological interactions in these forests—growing on formerly glaciated terrain— assemble itself? If we are altering the planetary climate, we probably need to know.

Tongass forest
The Tongass National Forest is the largest National Forest in the United States. Its principal vegetation cover is Pacific maritime forest.

Wildlife haven
Tongass National Forest is home to a diverse range of wildlife, including agile black bears.

Coastal forest
The narrow climate conditions of global coastal forests mean unexpected similarities are found worldwide.

Southern hemisphere maritime temperate rain forests

In the southern hemisphere, the maritime temperate rain forests of Tasmania, southeastern Australia, New Zealand, and the southern tip of South America have dominant vegetation that derives from Gondwana. These landmasses once formed part of the ancient supercontinent, breaking apart over millions of years. Africa and South America separated from Antarctica about 180 million years ago, and Antarctica, New Zealand, and New Caledonia began to separate from Australia about 85 million years ago. The descendants of the plant species that grew in Gondwana are now shared across the southern maritime temperate rain forest. A typical example is the genus *Nothofagus*, the southern beeches of Australasia and southern South America, which can be deciduous or evergreen. As you hike through a New Zealand *Nothofagus* forest, it takes little imagination to be transported to a forested Antarctica at a time when dinosaurs ruled the Earth.

The Marbled Murrelet

The alcids, birds in the family Alcidae, are black-and-white saltwater divers of northern rocky coasts—flighted analogues to the flightless penguins of the southern hemisphere. Mental images of alcids evoke the sound of crashing surf, the smell of saltwater, and flights of auklets, murres, guillemots, and puffins. Marbled Murrelets (*Brachyramphus marmoratus*) are stocky little North Pacific alcids, slightly smaller than the pigeons that flock the plazas of modern cities—about 10 in (25 cm) from beak to tail. They swim by "flying" in the water with their flipper-like wings and can dive to a depth of 260 ft (80 m). In flight, they look a bit like large bumblebees, with short wings propelling pudgy bodies. Initially, no one really knew where these creatures nested. We now know that, unlike any related alcids, Marbled Murrelets nest in trees. A single egg is laid in a nest on the mossy limbs of large conifer trees of the old-growth maritime rain forests of the Pacific fjordlands. A fledgling's first flight is directly to the sea. Marbled Murrelet populations are declining due to a loss of the nesting habitat of the birds. This habitat loss springs from forest harvest and from insect epidemics killing trees already weakened by changes in climate.

Mangrove forests

Mangrove forests line the intertidal zones of tropical and subtropical coastlands. Northward and southward from the tropics, the tidal fringe lacks trees and is dominated by saltmarshes and other herbaceous vegetation.

▶ **Underwater**

In tropical and subtropical climates, salt-tolerant mangroves line the ocean's edge. Some species are able to grow in submerged areas, creating an underwater structure and organic production vital to a variety of species.

Vital role

Although mangroves are not high on the list of forests by areal extent, they play a critical role as buffers for adjacent lands and human populations against the damaging waves generated by hurricanes, typhoons, and tsunamis. Further, climate change puts mangroves at the frontline of defense against rising sea levels. The forests also create critical habitat for a large number of invertebrates and vertebrates, and as a result they have been called "keystone" species. They have also been tagged "ecosystem foundation" species, because they create forest habitat through trapping sediments and tolerating high salt levels, thereby producing forests where there would otherwise be none.

From the point of view of plants, the intertidal zone has harsh and fluctuating environmental conditions. It is a wonder that any plants—let alone trees—have evolved to dominate this environment. Salinity can vary from that of the open sea to lower concentrations in places where fresh water periodically flushes through the substrate, and to higher concentrations in places exposed to evaporation at low tide. Thus, mangrove tree species must cope not only with the general toxicity of salt, but also fluctuating levels.

Salt is toxic to most plants. Easily dissolved in water, the positively charged sodium ions replace essential nutrients that plants are doing their best to accumulate. Further, the negatively charged chlorine ions can accumulate in plants and interfere with cellular processes, including photosynthesis. High concentrations of salt can literally dry out a plant, causing water to leave it via osmosis across cell membranes. Even the application of road salt to improve winter driving conditions can be toxic to roadside trees.

Not all mangrove species are adapted to the full range of salinities that occur. Some mangrove trees prefer lower-salinity wetlands that have an influence of fresh water from terrestrial habitats, whereas others thrive in the outer zone, with the salinity of sea water at high tide and concentration of salt at low tide.

Salt is not the only problem. Due to the constant flux of seawater, mangrove roots also face low oxygen levels in the substrates on which they grow. In addition, they must be securely rooted to these substrates and have architectures that allow them to resist storm waves.

SALINITY ZONES

Within mangrove forests there are gradients defined by salinity conditions. In addition, areas that are more inland can support taller trees than those at the interface with the sea, where lower, more wave-resistant forests are found.

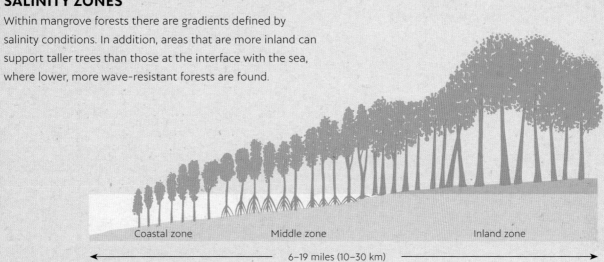

Coastal zone   Middle zone   Inland zone

6–19 miles (10–30 km)

MANGROVE FOREST LOCATIONS

Mangrove forests line the intertidal zones of tropical and subtropical coastlands.

Mangrove adaptations

How do mangrove forests deal with these conditions—conditions no other forests
on Earth face? The amazing adaptations include a trait most uncommon in plants,
vivipary, or live birth. In mangroves, vivipary means that seeds germinate while still
attached to the parent tree and then disperse. Mangrove species also have stilt roots,
allowing oxygen to be absorbed above the fluctuating sea, and they produce breathing
tubes called pneumatophores that extend from the submerged roots to reach above
sea level. Finally, the thick stem and cell surfaces of the plants, along with their
metabolic salt pumps, exclude and secrete excess salt.

Adapting to these harsh conditions is difficult and has been accomplished by
relatively few species. Individual tropical rain forests can be home to hundreds to
thousands of tree species, yet the coastal mangrove forests nearby have just a few at
most. An interesting evolutionary fact is that the adaptations of mangroves, although
rare among trees, have occurred independently in several plant lineages, with 50-
plus species distributed among 16 plant families—another example of convergent
evolution (see page 146). But not all mangroves have the exact same adaptations—
there has been room for innovation as well.

Independent evolution also means that the word "mangrove" does not refer to a single
closely related group of trees, at least if we look at the genus and family. By contrast,
trees we call "maples" are all related to one another at the genus level (in this case,
the genus is Acer). What trees called "mangroves" have in common is that they live
in coastal forests, rather than that they are members of a single genus of plants.

Global patterns of diversity

A final evolutionary lesson from mangrove forests concerns global patterns
of diversity, in that some regions have much higher diversity than others. One
expectation from ecology is that two areas with the same environmental conditions
ought to have similar diversities. But, interestingly, sometimes places with similar
environments have different diversities. This is called a diversity anomaly, and the
mangrove forests represent one such anomaly. A diversity anomaly also occurs in

the temperate deciduous forest (see pages 288-289), but part of that is explained by differences in habitat heterogeneity from one continent to another, namely that Asia has a greater latitudinal and longitudinal distribution of mountains than eastern North America.

In mangroves, the anomaly is made even more dramatic in that the salt gradient is similar in all areas and there are no elevation or soil differences to consider. Although mangrove environments could hardly be more similar, the global diversity of mangroves is highest in Southeast Asia—in fact, three to four times higher than in the Caribbean. The most likely explanations are that mangroves have evolved over a longer period in Southeast Asia, thus producing more speciation; that climates in Asia have not fluctuated as greatly as those in the New World, thus producing lower extinction rates; and that Southeast Asia has more islands and a greater length of coastline to support diversification.

◀ **Mangrove seedlings**

Red mangrove seedlings grow suspended from this tree branch in the Florida Keys. Seeds germinate while still attached to the parent tree.

6

Tropical Rain Forests

Rain forests as cradles

Tropical rain forests are natural wonders, with lofty trees growing over 100 ft (30 m) tall. These form a dense, complex thicket of leaves—the canopy—with tangles of lianas winding their way through, all pollinated and fed on by myriad insects, birds, bats, and other animals.

Tropical forests are not only an unparalleled cradle of biological diversity, but they have also nurtured many of the ideas of evolutionary biology and ecology. Through the nineteenth century, major thinkers of the discipline—including Alfred Russel Wallace (1823-1913), Charles Darwin, Eugen Warming (1841-1924), and Henry Bates (1825-1892)—developed their ideas after being exposed to the tropical experience. At the same time, anthropologists were also attempting to understand and document the sophisticated and sustainable interactions of forest peoples with their environment all over the world. It is unlikely this was a chance event: for nineteenth-century scientists, tropical forests had a magnetic attraction.

▼ Rain forest canopy

Looking down into the tropical forest in Borneo shows the several layers of leaves, the diversity of plant types, and the ground layer cover with leaf litter.

The missing pollinator

The tropical nature of evolutionary biology is nowhere expressed as vividly as in the example of the missing pollinator problem. In 1862, Darwin was sent a specimen of the rain forest orchid *Angraecum sesquipedale* from Madagascar, with its astonishingly long (12 in/30 cm), thin spur-shaped nectary. Darwin surmised that there should be an animal capable of pollinating this odd-shaped flower, and predicted that it would likely be a moth. A few years later, in 1867, Wallace published

a study on an African moth species that had a proboscis long enough to collect the nectar of this orchid, and predicted that this moth should be present in Madagascar, which was confirmed in 1903, more than 40 years after the initial hypothesis. The pollination of this orchid—now known as Darwin's Orchid—by a moth is a typical case of a coevolution, where two species have evolved as closely interdependent.

At about the same time, Bates was studying the butterflies of South America and noticed how they protected themselves against birds and dragonflies, their natural predators. He showed that some butterfly species were toxic, such that their predators learned the hard way not to bother them. Other palatable heliconid butterflies, however, mimicked the color and shape of toxic species to deceive their predators. Mimicry provided strong evidence in favor of natural selection. The recent genomic revolution has shed new light upon this process, revealing one region of the heliconid butterfly genome that is closely involved in the coloration patterns of wings, which could be exchanged through hybridization across species.

Concern for biological diversity and its erosion due to human disturbance and pollution is a more recent theme, but one that has been promoted most convincingly by tropical biologists. American biologist Edward O. Wilson, who is credited with coining the word "biodiversity," has spent the majority of his academic career studying tropical forest ants. Botany in particular is a largely tropical discipline: by some accounts, 47,000 of the world's 48,500 forest tree species—more than 96 percent—are found in the tropics. This figure alone illustrates the importance of tropical rain forests for biological diversity.

▼ **Batesian mimicry**
Some tropical butterflies mimic the showy colors of other species to keep their predators at bay.

▲ **Darwin's Orchid**
The long spur of this orchid has challenged nineteenth-century botanists. Charles Darwin surmised that it had to be pollinated by an unknown moth.

A museum of species

Much of the biological diversity seen in the world today arose in the climatically hospitable and extensive tropical rain forests. Most of the tropics have remained under conditions favorable for life for millions of years. In contrast, plants living in the temperate and boreal zones require a sophisticated biological equipment to survive, such as an adaptation to frost. To some extent, the large species diversity of the tropical forest biome may be attributable to its age and its stability, as Wallace originally surmised, comparing tropical forests to a "museum" of species. However, the extraordinary number of biological interactions in tropical forests also suggests that species are constantly adapting to their hosts, parasites, or predators, in an endless arms race. These selective forces lead to the divergence of populations and eventually to the more frequent appearance of new species, a process known as speciation. That speciation should be higher in the tropics because of the more complex network of ecological interactions has been speculated, but this proposal remains contentious.

How old are tropical rain forests?

Fossilized wood is rare in the tropics, but the oldest example of tree-like fossils with tropical attributes dates back some 50 million years. Detailed analysis of leaf shape helps define diagnostic criteria: rain forest leaves tend to be medium to large in size, with an entire margin, and with the characteristic "drip-tip" pattern at the end of the leaf blade. Another characteristic feature of tropical rain forest leaves is that they tend to be eaten by a wide diversity of insects. Leaf traces may be present as external bites, paths of leaf-mining insects, galls, or the marks of piercing-sucking insects, and these are preserved in the fossil record. Combining these characters, evidence points to the presence of tropical rain forests between 66 million and 60 million years ago. However, by reconstructing the evolutionary history of typical tropical rain forest families, biologists have suggested that tropical forests are quite a bit older (around 100 million years old).

▶ **Tropical fossils**

Palms are strongly associated with tropical forest formations, and this fossil palm frond discovered in the Green River Basin, Wyoming, is evidence that this area was subtropical around 50 million years ago.

CHONDRODENDRON TOMENTOSUM, *Ruiz & Pav.*

◀ **Dating the
rain forest**

*Botanists suggested
that tropical forests
are quite a bit older,
by reconstructing the
evolutionary history
of tropical rain forest
families such as
Menispermaceae, a
typical tropical plant
family including the
liana* Chondrodendron
tomentosum, *which is
the plant Amerindians
use to extract the
arrow poison curare.
DNA dating of the
Menispermaceae
suggests an age around
100 million years old,
much older than the
fossil record.*

Over this long time span, the Earth's climate has varied enormously. Some 50 million years ago, during the Eocene, the temperature was several degrees higher than it is today—so hot that the polar ice caps did not exist. What is today temperate region was then occupied by tropical forests. The city of London in England is built on a thick clay layer that dates back to this period. Clay is waterproof and easy to tunnel through, so it was the ideal setting for the construction of the world's first underground railway system, in 1863. But the London clay has also long been known to conceal botanical treasures from the Eocene flora, and much to the surprise of early botanists, the plant fossils uncovered were of tropical forest groups, including palms. Southeast England was covered with tropical forests 50 million years ago!

New World tropical rain forests

According to one estimate, tropical rain forests cover about 5 million sq miles (13 million sq km), or around 8 percent of the Earth's land surface. Of this area, it is estimated that less than 4 million sq miles (10 million sq km) is undisturbed. Tropical rain forests are found in the Americas, Africa, Southeast Asia, and Oceania, but there are profound differences between these and even within each continent. By far the largest extension of tropical rain forest is in the Americas, the New World.

NEW WORLD RAIN FOREST LOCATIONS

Tropical rain forests in the New World are located in South America, Central America, and the Caribbean islands. Around half of the world's tropical rain forests are in Brazil and Peru.

- Tropical rain forest
- Tropical moist forest
- Tropical dry forest
- Tropical mountain system
- Other ecological zones

▶ **Tropical nature**

Tropical rain forest in Costa Rica, La Fortuna waterfall.

Central America

New World tropical rain forests expand from Cuba to the northern tip of Argentina. Central American rain forests have seen the rise and fall of the Olmecs, Toltecs, Maya, and Zapotecs, and over the last 500 years the incredible architecture of these major civilizations has been fully covered by a dense thicket of vegetation, to the extent that only the recent development of airborne lidar scanning has unraveled the sheer extent and complexity of the Central American cities. The majority of the Central American Arc is a volcanic ridge, and for this reason soils are fertile even in the lowlands, whose nutrients have been weathered from the uplands. This has been both a blessing and a curse. Soil fertility is the reason why Central

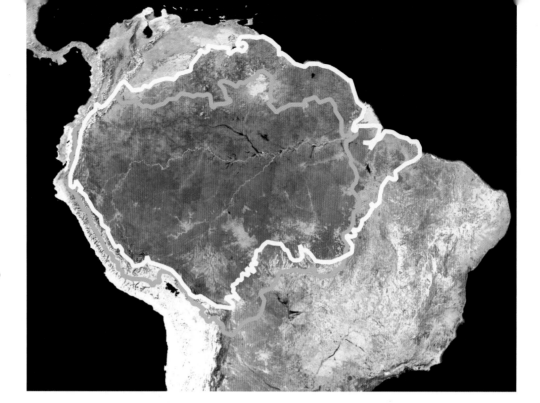

► **Amazonia**
The large majority of the Amazonian forest is restricted to the watershed of the Amazon River, which flows over more than 370 miles (6,000 km) across the continent. However, part of the same forest grows in the Orinoco River, and several other rivers of the Guianas.

America has been a major hotspot for human cultures, and a key center of plant domestication, including maize, squash, cacao, avocado, and cotton. More recently, however, Central American forested landscapes have been heavily transformed to give way to cattle ranching. The number of cattle heads rose threefold from 1960 to the mid-1980s, and over the same period of time forest cover was almost divided by a factor of two. This was a strong impetus to initiate some of the earliest tropical forest conservation programs: in Costa Rica, more than a quarter of the country is now under some form of protection status.

Floristically, Central America is quite different from South America. This is because the two subcontinents were separate until recently, at least in geological terms. Until 3 million years ago, North and South America were separated by a stretch of sea, drastically limiting the migration of species. Thus, South America was in splendid isolation from the rest of the world for most of the past 80 million years. The creation of the Isthmus of Panama generated a massive interchange of species: the Puma (*Puma concolor*) invaded South America from the north, while armadillos took the same route but in the reverse direction.

The Caribbean and South America

Caribbean islands have a hospitable, mild climate, and for this reason they were prized by early European settlers, who deforested much of the land—originally covered with tropical rain forest—for sugarcane plantations. Hispaniola was the first landing spot of Christopher Columbus in 1492, and at the time was probably mostly forested. Today, the island's lowland forest cover is barely more than a few percent in area.

In South America, the Amazon rain forest covers more than 2 million sq miles (5 million sq km), harbors an incredible biological diversity, and plays a key role in major processes of the Earth, including its water and carbon cycles. From west to east, it stretches more than 1,800 miles (3,000 km), the distance between Washington, DC, and Mexico City. In maps, the forest appears as homogeneous and endless, but a closer look reveals a different picture. The Amazon River carries by far the most water of any river on the planet, and is more than 6 miles (10 km) wide at the city of Macapá in northeast Brazil. As much as one-third of Amazonia is seasonally inundated, with the trees living here adapted to survive in waterlogged soil for part of the year. North of the Amazon, a huge hilly area of sandstone mountains covers much of Venezuelan Amazonia, including the tepuis, spectacular tabletop mountains rising vertically from the forest below (see pages 184-185).

South America has a great variety of tropical forest types. On the Pacific side of the Andes, the Chocó province of Colombia has some of the highest levels of biodiversity and most pristine rain forests in the world. The central part of tropical South America is slightly too dry to support rain forest, and is instead occupied by a woodland savanna called the Cerrado. Growing here is a mixture of vegetation types, with emblematic trees such as the beautiful Ipê-do-cerrado (*Handroanthus ochraceus*). Further southeast, rainfall coming in from the Atlantic Ocean increases and a long strip of rain forest extends along the coast for some 1,200 miles (2,000 km). This Atlantic rain forest is the birthplace of Brazil, with the cities of Rio de Janeiro, São Paulo, and Salvador all located in the biome.

▼ **Venezuela**
Black water river flowing through a stretch of Amazonian forest, Venezuela.

Tepui forest

North of Amazonia, the Guiana Highlands include the tepuis, spectacular tabletop mountains towering over dense tropical forest—pictured here in Canaima National Park, Venezuela. These sandstone formations are the result of ancient erosion, and they shelter a unique biodiversity.

Exploring the Amazon rain forest

The first written account of travel along the entire Amazon River was by missionary Gaspar de Carvajal (c. 1500-1584), who chronicled the epic journey of 57 men led by Francisco de Orellana (1511-1586) from their departure from Quito, Ecuador, in February 1541 to their arrival at Cubagua Island, Venezuela, in August 1542.

The most striking part of Carvajal's account is his description of the bustling communities they found while traveling down the Amazon River. The next major expedition was in 1637, led by Portuguese explorer Pedro de Teixeira (d. 1641). The journey was recorded by the missionary Cristóbal de Acuña (1597-c. 1676), who described thriving life along the waterway, but the area was already under intensive exploitation, with large stores of manioc in villages defended by palisades, farming of turtles, and fisheries.

Smallpox spread in the mid-seventeenth century, followed by many other diseases, including imported strains of malaria. Jesuit missions, and then secular Portuguese settlements in the first half of the eighteenth century, contributed significantly to the collapse of the Indigenous population, which in turn had a complex impact on the environment. On the one hand, the Portuguese actively depleted forest resources in favor of cacao plantations, and they also hunted manatees and turtles. But on the other hand, the collapse of the Indigenous population in Amazonia, from about 10 million people in 1500 to just a million in 1700, probably led to a massive forest recovery. Some authors believe that this forest recovery created such a potent carbon sink that it may explain the reduction in atmospheric carbon dioxide observed between the sixteenth and eighteenth centuries.

Amazon rain forests have thus long been occupied by humans, who domesticated manioc, sweet potato, chili peppers, the Brazil nut, and a great variety of palm species. While the image that Amazonia represents the ultimate primary forest, virgin of human occupation, is a myth, the inference that Amazonia was planted by the Amerindians is also an exaggeration. With a population density of 2.5 people per square mile (one per square kilometer), and a higher concentration near the rivers, Amazonia was much less densely populated than Central America and the Andes even prior to European contact.

◀ **Flood survivors**
Blackwater flooded forest in the Amazon, locally called "igapó." Trees of the igapó forest survive with their roots underwater for up to six months a year. Some of the trees have their seeds dispersed by fishes.

◀ **Amazonian societies**
Amazonia is home to a large cultural diversity and much evidence confirms that these societies have profoundly shaped their environment. This rock art was painted 12,000 years ago in Serranía de la Lindosa, in Amazonian Colombia, and illustrates an astounding and now extinct megafauna.

Old World tropical rain forests

On the other side of the Atlantic Ocean, Africa also has large expanses of tropical rain forests. Some 90 million years ago, Africa and South America were part of the single supercontinent of Gondwana, and they share some geological features. However, much has happened since then, and the tree flora of Africa is almost totally different from that of South America.

OLD WORLD RAIN FOREST LOCATIONS

Old World forests are found in Africa, South Asia, and Oceania.
They span a range of forest types and climate regimes.

- Tropical rain forest
- Tropical moist forest
- Tropical dry forest
- Tropical mountain system
- Other ecological zones

Cotton Tree

*A small girl shows the scale of one of the largest Cotton Trees of Senegal (*Ceiba pentandra*).*

Seed dispersal

A chimpanzee sitting in a tree reaching for food, Kibale Forest National Park, Uganda.

There are rare commonalities between the rain forest flora of Africa and South America. These include trees such as *Carapa procera*, famous for the oil extracted from its nuts, Boarwood (*Symphonia globulifera*), and the Cotton Tree (*Ceiba pentandra*). The latter is sacred in Central and South America, and it is difficult to find someone who will agree to cut one down. When freed slaves returned to Africa and founded the city of Freetown in Sierra Leone in 1792, they built it around a Cotton Tree at its center, symbolizing the sanctity of their new lives.

Africa

For the most part, African rain forests are found within or around the Congo River watershed, in south Cameroon, Gabon, the Republic of the Congo, and the Democratic Republic of the Congo (DRC). This vast forested area is home to an

exceptionally high ethnic diversity, with more than 200 different languages spoken in DRC alone. Tropical forest research has been conducted at sites such as the Lopé National Park in Gabon and the Okapi Wildlife Reserve in DRC. At Lopé, with its complex mosaic of dense forests interspersed with savannas, research has been carried out on seed dispersal by animals, including the African Forest Elephant (*Loxodonta cyclotis*), Western Lowland Gorilla (*Gorilla gorilla*), and Chimpanzee (*Pan troglodytes*). At the Okapi Wildlife Reserve, foremost botanists such as Corneille Ewango have helped increase our understanding of why some tropical forests may be dominated by only a few tree species, such as *Gilbertiodendron dewevrei*.

Several other regions of Africa also support rain forest, including three biodiversity hotspots. The first of these covers the region from Guinea-Bissau to Nigeria in West Africa and the large forest remnants in Liberia. On the other side of the continent, Afromontane tropical forests of the Eastern Arc Mountains and Albertine Rift (DRC, Uganda, Rwanda, Burundi, and Tanzania) shelter many endemic species, including the Eastern Chimpanzee (*Pan troglodytes schweinfurthii*). Finally, Madagascar has remnant tropical rain forests on its east coast, although these are currently being deforested at a rapid pace.

Forest fortress

Sigiriya, near Dambulla in the Central Province of Sri Lanka is a rock fortress built during the 5th century CE. Although the forest around Sigiriya appears pristine from the image, some of the oldest landscaped gardens are found in the area.

Southeast Asia and Oceania

Some 100 million years ago, Madagascar was connected to India as part of Gondwana. However, the Indian tectonic plate then broke away and started an amazing journey toward the northeast, eventually colliding with Asia to create the Himalayan Mountains and Tibetan Plateau. At that time, a small plant family, close to the Madagascar endemic family Sarcolaenaceae, hitchhiked on the Indian Plate as it made its way toward Asia. This family, the Dipterocarpaceae, was to become one of the most successful radiations of tropical forest trees, being dominant today in Southeast Asian forests and a key timber species. India therefore plays a special role in the history of Asian tropical forests.

Asian tropical rain forests are home to iconic animals such as orangutans (genus *Pongo*), whose common name means "people of the forest" in Bahasa Indonesia, the funny-looking Proboscis Monkey (*Nasalis larvatus*), and the Borneo Pygmy Elephant (*Elephas maximus borneensis*). As observed early on by Wallace, there are major differences in biodiversity between Papua New Guinea and Australia, which have always been separated by a sea channel. The magnificent birds of paradise of Papua New Guinea are found only on the Asian side of this divide, known as the Wallace Line, while the Platypus (*Ornithorhynchus anatinus*), echidnas, and other monotremes are all found only to the east of it.

Southeast Asian tropical forests are threatened by massive land-use change, especially oil-palm plantations in Malaysia and Borneo. This threat is compounded by occasional droughts that are triggered by warm El Niño phases. During the El Niño drought in 2015, for example, fires in the tropical forests of Indonesia burned so intensely that they created a smoke plume that stretched halfway around the world. El Niño events can be of global significance. An extreme event occurred in 1788-93 with devastating consequences: the monsoon failed in India, leading to catastrophic famines that killed up to 11 million people. This climatic anomaly may also have been the proximal cause of the French Revolution (1789-1799), with severe crop failures in Europe in 1788 leading to widespread unrest.

Island tropical forests

A last mention is reserved for tropical forests on islands. These have been disproportionately hit by environmental change, as seen in the Caribbean islands and other parts of the planet. St. Helena, a key stopping point for European ships on their way to India following its discovery in the sixteenth century, was so thoroughly deforested that several endemic tree species are now believed to be extinct, such as the Dwarf Ebony (*Trochetiopsis melanoxylon*), or nearly extinct, such as the Bastard Gumwood Tree (*Commidendrum rotundifolium*). Other tropical islands have been victims of biological invasions, including Hawaii and Tahiti, where the Neotropical Velvet Tree (*Miconia calvescens*) is known as the "purple plague" for the massive disruption it has caused in the local forest ecosystems.

▼ **Threatened forests**
Conversion of Southeast Asian tropical forests to oil palm plantations is a major threat to these ecosystems and their wildlife. The oil of African oil palm (Elaeis guineensis) is the most traded vegetable oil. In Borneo, almost 80 percent of the oil palm plantation area (c. 22 million acres/9 million ha) was old-growth forest in the early 1970s.

Complex life at the canopy top

The topmost canopies of tropical rain forest trees are a world unto themselves, supporting clumps of ferns, orchids, cacti, and succulents found nowhere else. Many of these plants are epiphytes—plants that grow on other plants for support. The diversity of life that forms at the tops of the world's rain forest is both great and unexpected.

▶ **High canopy**

The canopy tops of New World rain forest trees display an extreme diversity of plants. Tank bromeliads, the vase-shaped plants with green-and-white-barred leaves in the illustration, hold stored rainwater that nurtures a vast array of animals— including a small crab in Jamaica.

Plant diversity

Unique to the New World tropical forest canopies are the bromeliads (family Bromeliaceae). These are represented by about 3,320 species in 52 genera, and are all found in the Americas—mostly in the tropics. The single exception is *Pitcairnia feliciana*, which is found in rocky outcrops in tropical West Africa. Bromeliads demonstrate wide variation. The most familiar may be the pineapple gracing the shelves of the local grocery store, while Spanish Moss (*Tillandsia usneoides*), seen hanging from oak trees in the American Deep South, is an iconic species of that region. In the wild, tank bromeliads provide a habitat for a variety of life, including several predators of mosquito larvae that help regulate mosquito outbreaks.

Other wonderful examples of plants predominantly found in the topmost canopies of rain forest trees are orchids (family Orchidaceae), the largest plant family of the world with about 27,801 species in 899 genera, well over half of them epiphytes. Aroids (3,368 species and 117 genera), members of the Arum family (Araceae), form another distinctive group. Their large flowers warm up to 95–113 °F (35–45 °C) when mature, to attract pollinating beetles. Many of these canopy-top plant species find an alternative life as office plants, because they need relatively little care other than watering.

In 1987, in a 10,700 sq ft (1,000 sq m) patch of Ecuadorian tropical rain forest, the botanists Alwyn Gentry and Calaway Dodson recorded the total number of plant species. They found no fewer than 365 species, a third of which were epiphytes. This proportion tends to drop rapidly in more seasonal tropical forests, because epiphytes are heavily reliant on nighttime water condensation in ever-wet forests. Beyond plant epiphytes, the top canopies are teeming with a variety of life-forms.

Insect diversity

The hyperdiversity characteristic of top canopies goes beyond plants. In the late 1970s, the American entomologist Terry Erwin fogged the top of a tropical tree with pesticide and collected the knocked-down insects. He found that a single tree harbored up to 1,200 species of beetle, some 160 of which were found only on that particular species. Erwin used these results of host specificity to infer that the worldwide number of beetle species must exceed 30 million—far more than the 1.5 million estimated by biologists to this day. Arthropods are the main group of animal species found in tropical forests, be they sap-suckers, leaf eaters, mushroom eaters, or scavengers. When asked by theologians what one could conclude as to the nature of God from a study of his creation, the British biologist "Jack" Haldane is said to have answered that the Creator must have had "an inordinate fondness for beetles."

MINI RESERVOIR

The cross section of a Tank Bromeliad reveals some of the animals found in the stored water. Spiders, snails, tree frogs, and insect larvae are all typical inhabitants of this miniature ecosystem. Other animals found in Tank Bromeliads include salamanders, ostracods (small crustaceans commonly known as "seed shrimp"), and a wide array of insects and their larvae.

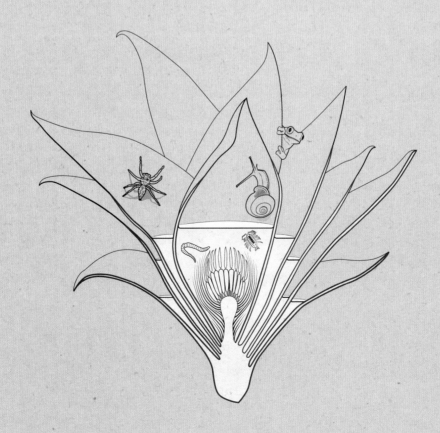

Pollination and regeneration in rain forests

Tropical forest animals are essential for the pollination of flowers and the dispersal of seeds. The only sensible explanation for why so many flower shapes, colors, and sizes have evolved is that they have adapted to their pollinators, an even more diverse cohort of creatures.

Animal pollinators

The Central and South American Cannonball Tree (*Couroupita guianensis*) produces large pink-red flowers with a pale hood. Carpenter bees are known to visit the flowers, and while searching for the nectar within they are dusted with pollen, which they occasionally transport to other trees, thus ensuring pollination. More than 98 percent of tropical rain forest plants are animal-pollinated. Insects are the main pollinators, especially bees, moths, butterflies, and insects. Occasionally, bats have been documented pollinating trees, and nectar-eating birds, especially hummingbirds, are also active pollinators. It is no exaggeration to say that without the animals of the forest there would be no pollination at all.

Animals are also major seed dispersers: they eat the pulp of the fleshy fruit and defecate the seeds some distance away. They may also carry seeds unintentionally, attached to their fur. Neotropical agoutis, common rain forest rodents, are another type of gardener. They hoard seeds by burying them in small stores. Often these caches are forgotten and the seeds germinate, already planted in the soil. Many tropical forest plants produce brightly colored berries, and these are apparent adaptations to attract dispersers. When ripe, the seeds of South American Virola trees, in the nutmeg family (Myristiceae), split open by two valves, displaying their single seed. This is covered by a brightly colored and nutritive fleshy part, eaten by the birds and monkeys that are primary dispersers of these seeds.

▼ **Eye-catching seeds**
Seed of Virola surinamensis, *in the nutmeg family (Myristicaceae), Amazonia. These fruits split open when ripe, revealing conspicuous seeds that are highly sought after by canopy wildlife.*

Survival strategies

Once dispersed, seeds are exposed to many risks. Large seeds are rich in starch, allowing them to germinate even in the shade, but as a result they may be eaten by predators, or parasitized by insects or fungi. The germination of these seeds does require at least some light—even brief sun flecks are sufficient. So, there is no incentive for a large seed to delay the germination process. Because animal predation may be a crucial factor for a tree's survival at the seed stage, some species produce massive amounts of large seeds, all of which germinate at once, carpeting the ground with small seedlings. This so-called "mast fruiting" strategy is most famous in the Southeast Asian Dipterocarpaceae. Dipterocarps reproduce only once every 4-6 years, but when they do, they are so prolific that they over-satiate their potential predators.

In contrast to large seeds, small seeds lack the resources to germinate in the shade and are not attractive resources for predators. For these seeds, it pays off to adopt a "sit-and-wait" strategy. In one study in Panama, minute seeds of the *Croton billbergianus* tree collected from the soil were found to be 38 years old and still viable even after this long dormancy. When large trees fall, they open a gap in the canopy that lets through a great deal of light. Seeds—some of which had been waiting for decades for this event to happen—suddenly escape their dormant stage, and the newly emerged seedlings set off on a race for light with their neighboring trees and lianas.

▼ **Efficient dispersers**

Seeds can stay about 30 minutes in the digestive tract of toucans before being dispersed. During this time, toucans travel more than 330 ft (100 m), making them efficient seed dispersers.

▶ **Striking flowers**

*Abundant flowers and fruits of the Cannonball Tree (*Couroupita guianensis*) in the Brazil nut family (Lecythidaceae).*

Partnerships and parasites

Pollination is an example of a service rendered by an animal to a plant in exchange for a reward. Other types of beneficial two-way partnerships—termed mutualisms—are frequent in tropical rain forest, as are parasitic relationships, which benefit one party at the expense of the other.

Ant patrols

South American *Allomerus decemarticulatus* ants live exclusively in the plant *Hirtella physophora*. The plant feeds the ants with nectar and also provides them with shelter. In return, the ants protect the plant against potential herbivores. They create a sophisticated insect trap by cutting and weaving the plant's hairs in a gallery along the branches, and mortar this construction using a fungus they grow. When an insect lands on the plant, the ants rush out of their leaf pocket shelter and tie the legs of the unfortunate visitor, eventually dismembering it in a medieval torment. The Novice Tree of Amazonian forests, *Triplaris americana*, is another example of a beneficial relationship with an ant species. Only the uninitiated would be bold enough to touch it, soon to discover that it is defended by fierce *Pseudomyrmex triplarinus* ants, whose bite is a painful and unforgettable experience.

▼ Symbiosis
Some tropical ants nest within natural holes in plant stems, and in return they patrol the plant to deter plant predators. In this example from Cameroon, the ant Petalomyrmex phylax *inhabits the plant* Leonardoxa africana.

Root power

Plants gain the water and nutrients they require from the soil. Tropical forest soils are generally infertile, and most of the nutrient uptake happens at the soil surface—the poorer the soil, the shallower the mat of roots. Experiments using radiolabeled nutrients sprinkled on root mats have shown that 99 percent of the nutrients are absorbed by the plants. Thus, most of the nutrient resources come from the in situ decomposition of litter, rather than from the soil's own resources.

Plant parasites

Biological complexity is mind-boggling. In the tropics of the Caribbean and Central and South America, the forest floor is occasionally colored by the flowers of a plant emerging from the ground but with no apparent leaves— *Voyria* flowers. These plants have lost the ability to produce sugars by photosynthesis, and instead act as parasites on the mycorrhizal fungi of other plants. They belong to a group of plants called mycorrhizal cheaters. These include tropical orchids, which also parasitize fungi, although orchid fungi themselves feed upon dead organic matter.

NETWORKING

How can roots be so efficient at absorbing nutrients? The answer is that they get a little help from tiny friends in the form of fungi. Soil fungi grow a web of microscopic conduits called hyphae. On encountering a fine root, some fungi enter the cells and grow a microscopic tree-shaped structure within them, called an arbuscule. In return for supplying nutrients to the tree via the arbuscules, the fungus feeds on the plant's sugars. Fungi associated with plant roots are called mycorrhizae, from the Greek words meaning "root fungi." The type of association described here is called an arbuscular mycorrhizal association, and neither the plant nor the fungus can survive without the help of the other; this is called a symbiosis. Arbuscular mycorrhizal associations are not restricted to tropical rain forests, but they are especially important in soils depleted in one major nutrient, phosphorus, as is the case in the tropics.

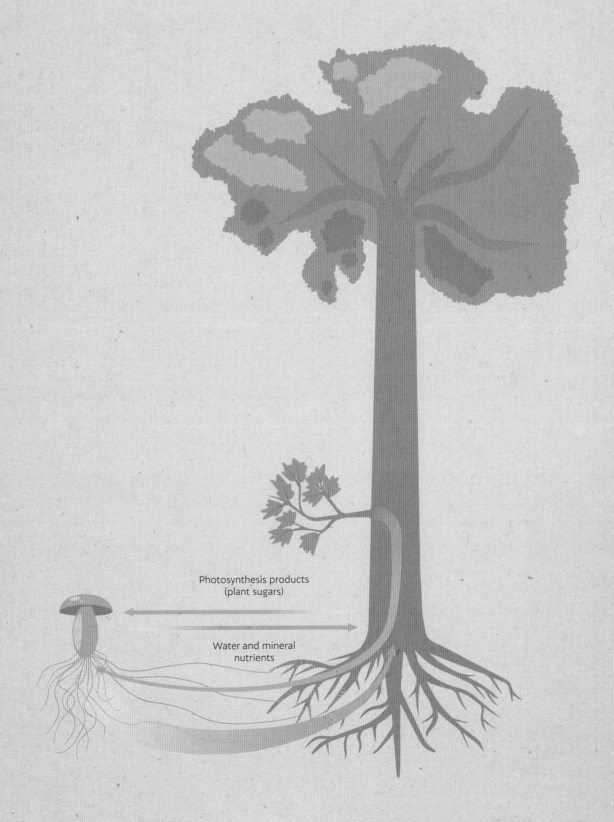

Photosynthesis products
(plant sugars)

Water and mineral
nutrients

Functional tree types of the rain forest

Faced with the extreme complexity of tree diversity in the tropical rain forest, and with a diverse array of morphologies and plant associations, botanists have sought to categorize them into smaller groups of plant types, each characterized by a unique set of ecological functions. This conceptualization is important in understanding why species common in open habitats become rare in old forests, and to model forest regeneration pathways.

▼ Light-demanding
Cecropia *trees*
viewed from below,
Florianopolis, Brazil.

Germination and seed size

Germination defines a first main axis of variation. Small-seeded species can sometimes enter a dormant phase and persist for years in the seedbank, waiting for the ideal conditions for them to emerge as a seedling. Other species have large seeds and must germinate within weeks or months—assuming, of course, that they are

not eaten in the meantime. Seed size thus controls a major difference in plant regeneration strategies, separating those species that require light for their germination from those that tolerate shade.

Light and shade

Light-demanding species are commonly found growing along tropical roadsides. In addition to having small seeds, they grow quickly, have large leaves that are shed often, and have short life spans. Examples of light-demanding trees are *Cecropia* and *Vismia* in the Neotropics, and *Macaranga* and *Musanga* in the Paleotropics. These species are said to have a "James Dean" strategy—they live fast and die young. They are unable to survive in the shade of a forest and persist only by growing in the treefall gaps, quickly producing massive amounts of seeds before they are outcompeted by shade-tolerant species. These seeds then lie dormant, waiting for the next treefall gap to occur. Shade-tolerant trees constitute the contrasting strategy, with larger seeds, an ability to persist as saplings for a long time in the understory, a slow growth rate, and a long life span.

▼ **Fast reproduction**
Early-successional tropical trees produce massive amounts of tiny seeds that are dispersed into forest gaps by animals. A fruiting Macaranga peltata *tree, India.*

Stature

Another dimension of functional variation in tropical trees is stature. Some species never grow large and complete their full life cycle in the understory. This does not necessarily mean that understory tree species have a fast turnover rate; in the low-light environment of the tropical forest understory, plants have to live more slowly. Some plants less than ¾ in (2 cm) in trunk diameter have been radiocarbon dated as more than 100 years old, whereas other species could grow as canopy emergents in less time than this. Both light-demanding and shade-tolerant species can be tall or short (see Chapter 2, pages 76-77 for examples and a discussion).

Exceptions to the rule

A more careful look at plant functional types shows that some species do not comply with these ideal types. Some trees need full sunlight to germinate and grow in their first life stages, but then they are perfectly able to persist for decades, if not centuries, in the canopy of mature forests. The ericoid tree *Agarista salicifolia*, endemic to the Mascarene Islands and called Rampart Wood there, grows as a shrub on lava fields but can persist in mature rain forest as a large tree reaching well over 65 ft (20 m) in height. In addition to its remarkable morphological plasticity, Rampart Wood is known for its toxic leaves; a Creole proverb has it that two leaves of this plant can kill a cow. Trees like Rampart Wood are economically important species, because they grow as large trees, they produce relatively light woods, and they grow quickly. Other examples are the South American Mahogany (*Swietenia macrophylla*) and *Aucoumea klaineana*, a species endemic to Gabon, where it is used for the production of plywood.

◀ **Shade-tolerant seedlings**

Seeds germinate amid fallen leaves and they are exposed to all sorts of herbivores who feast upon them.

◀ **Shade-tolerant trees**

One giant tree of the tropical forest in Ecuador—the oldest tropical forest trees wait decades to centuries before reaching the light of the canopy.

Rain forest exploitation and land conversion

The conversion of temperate forests to agricultural land has been a long process, extending over much of the past 2,000 years. Contrasting with this, tropical forests remained largely untouched until the nineteenth century.

▶ **Tea plantation**

Workers in a tea plantation newly established after forest clearing, Sri Lanka (former Ceylon), c. 1900.

Impacts of crop cultivation

Historians have calculated that both tropical and temperate pre-industrial cultures needed about 1 acre (0.4 ha) of cultivated land per person for subsistence. In 1700, roughly equal areas of land were cultivated in the tropical and temperate worlds—some 640 million acres (130 million ha) in total—suggesting a global human population of around 625 million. At that time, almost no tropical rain forests were converted for the culture of global commodities. An exception was in Aceh province on the Indonesian island of Sumatra, where the production of pepper for exportation to Europe began as early as the seventeenth century.

It was not until the nineteenth century that the cultivation of global crops began to have a significant impact on tropical forests. In Sri Lanka (then known as Ceylon), the British colonists had deforested more than 500,000 acres (200,000 ha) by 1880 to make space for tea plantations. In the first half of the nineteenth century, about 1.8 million acres (750,000 ha) of the Atlantic rain forest of Brazil were converted to sugarcane plantations, then the most profitable staple crop. These were then replaced by coffee, known as "green gold," by the end of the century.

Colonialism and deforestation

In many tropical countries, colonialism was a potent cause of deforestation, and colonial countries claimed that their plundering of the forest was justified by the inability of local populations to manage their own forest resources sustainably. Madagascar exemplifies the problem. According to some estimates, about 40 percent of the island was covered in moist rain forest before humans arrived around 2,350 years ago. Part of the island was too dry to support a rain forest biome, and the abundance of typical savanna species endemic to the island suggests that a large fraction was always covered by natural fire-prone savannas. At the time of the French colonization of Madagascar in 1898, two-thirds of the moist forest was still in place, a proportion that had dropped to 33 percent by 1960, when Madagascar won back its independence. Yet, the French colonial administration developed the narrative that 90 percent of Madagascar was originally forested, and that the Indigenous Malagasy people were to blame for the destruction of much of its original cover. In 1927, the French established natural forest reserves on the island, allowing no provision for the Malagasy who relied on access to forests for their resources. The control of the land based on conservation has been a powerful device of power for colonialism.

TROPICAL RAIN FOREST LOSS

Tropical forests have been cut down to give space for plantations since the nineteenth century, but the rate of tropical deforestation has massively accelerated since the 1950s. (Source: IGBP, 2004.)

% loss (area)

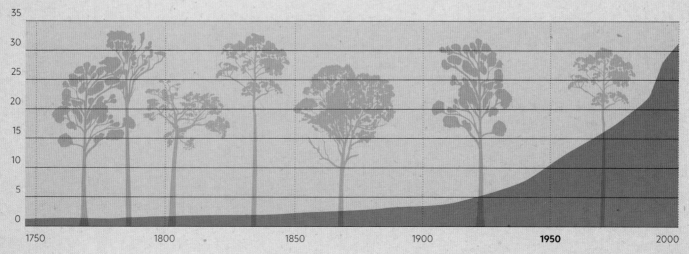

Escalating deforestation

Although deforestation has taken place in the tropics since ancient times, it was only after the First World War and the establishment of an international system of trade that tropical deforestation became a massive phenomenon. In the tropics, it is estimated that 20 million acres (8 million ha) were deforested per year during the period 1920-1949, increasing to 25 million acres (10 million ha) per year for 1950-1979 and to 35 million acres (14 million ha) per year for 1980-1995. Causal factors were a combination of a demographic explosion, leading to an increased demand for agricultural and urban land, and improved technology in the forestry sector, such as chainsaws, forest trailers, and log loaders.

Exploitation of the forest as a resource for wood is a major factor in forest conversion, and it has been so for a long time. In the process of converting forested land, timber trees are usually logged first and either used for local construction or sold to the international market. Before the fossil fuel era, the non-timber wood would be used as firewood, which remains an important resource in many regions of the world today. However, forest logging alone cannot explain the rapid deforestation in the tropics. After several cycles of heavy logging, there is a strong incentive for conversion to crop plantations. Thus, deforestation is usually caused by a combination of actors, including logging companies, urban developers and policy makers, international agro-industries, and local landowners.

DEFORESTATION DRIVERS

In tropical America and Asia, agro-industrial projects are the main cause of deforestation, often associated with the forest industry. In Africa, local shifting agriculture is the main impact on forests. (Source: Curtis et al., 2018. *Science.*)

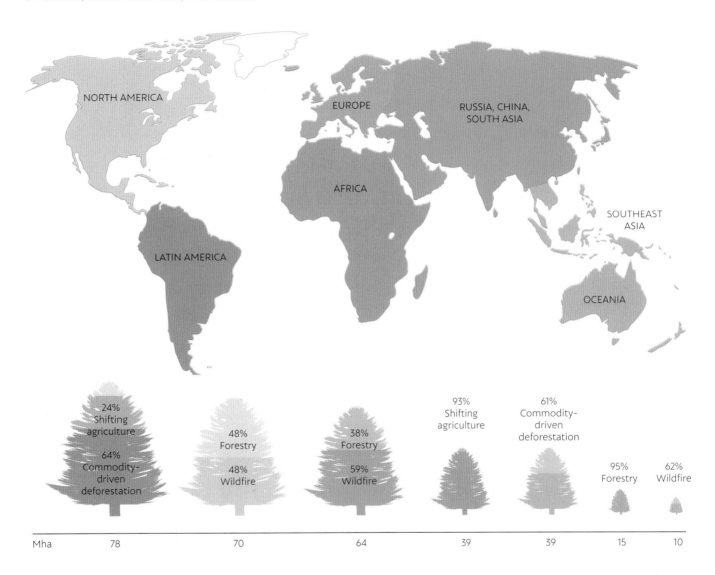

24% Shifting agriculture	48% Forestry	38% Forestry	93% Shifting agriculture	61% Commodity-driven deforestation	95% Forestry	62% Wildfire
64% Commodity-driven deforestation	48% Wildfire	59% Wildfire				
Mha 78	70	64	39	39	15	10

Global drivers

Analyses of the drivers of tropical deforestation reveal contrasting patterns. In Latin America and Southeast Asia, two-thirds of the deforestation is driven by global commodities, mainly cattle ranching in Latin America and oil-palm plantations in Southeast Asia. In Africa, however, deforestation is of a different nature, being caused mainly by the local demand for agricultural products. This leads to small-scale disturbances that recover their forest cover more quickly after abandonment than large-scale land conversion.

Unless the soil has been compacted, polluted, or eroded, forests naturally encroach on abandoned tropical land. Deforestation is not irreversible, and many reforestation projects have been successful. One important motivation is that tropical forests offer a great potential for the capture of atmospheric carbon dioxide, and the reforestation of large areas could help mitigate global warming. Whether this nature-based solution can be implemented at a large scale remains to be seen.

The fragmented forest

Tropical forests once formed large areas of unbroken canopy across Central and South America, Africa, and Southeast Asia. Today, however, they are highly fragmented. In the Atlantic rain forest of Brazil, it is estimated that less than 20 percent of the remaining forest fragments are more than 125 acres (50 ha) in size. In 2018, ecological modeler Franziska Taubert and colleagues found that the median size of tropical forest fragments was the same in the three continents—around 32 acres (13 ha).

Edge effects

As a result of forest fragmentation, plants and animals live in a matrix dominated by edge effects. Near forest edges, the air is drier and the temperature is higher. This favors light-demanding plant species, at the expense of shade-tolerant ones. Another important consideration is that these remnant forests are often on private land, and owners may further degrade the forest patches or hunt the wildlife they support. The fragmentation of large tracts of old-growth forests has implications for the ability of these forests to store carbon, and perhaps also to withstand drought episodes.

▼ **Sugarcane plantations**

An aerial view showing remnants of the Atlantic Forest in Goiana city, near Recife, Pernambuco, Brazil—fragmentation driven by sugarcane cultivation.

Dry tropical forests

Dry tropical forests rank among the most fragmented forest types of the world. The prime targets of agricultural systems are reasonably fertile soils where the annual water balance is neither too dry nor too wet. In climatic zones with seasonal rainfall but marked dry seasons, natural pests are less of a problem, and any seasonal water shortage can be managed by drainage

systems. Dry tropical forests areas have therefore been the prime target for sugarcane plantations and cattle ranching. The dry forests of Central America were the first to be degraded in the early twentieth century, and many efforts in tropical forest conservation can be traced back to the protection of the dry forest in 1971 in what is now the Guanacaste Conservation Area in northwest Costa Rica. However, the protection status of dry tropical forests remains unevenly distributed across countries. In Colombia, only 8 percent of the 22 million acres (9 million ha) of dry tropical forests remain today, little of which is under any protection status. Because of the size of the country, which stretches from the Caribbean coast to its border with Ecuador, these dry forests include a widely varied biodiversity. In an effort to protect the dry forest fragments that remain, Colombia's Alexander von Humboldt Institute has conducted research to document these and establish a viable conservation plan.

The prevailing narrative that tropical forest fragments are lower-grade forests may have adverse consequences on forest conservation. Why invest effort and resources in preserving fragments if these are not the tall-canopy, ideal-type forests that Western cultures have recognized as "real" forests, at least since Romanticism has been in vogue? This perception bias has certainly played a role in the sprawl of human activity in the Amazon. The 1965 Brazilian Forest Code required that Amazonian landowners maintained the majority of their land under native vegetation. However, enforcing the law in such large areas is an extremely difficult task. Even though the Brazilian Institute of Environment and Renewable Resources has played a crucial role in this, the 2012 update of the Brazilian Forest Code has pardoned any illegal deforestation on private land prior to 2008, effectively removing accountability for past misdeeds.

▼ **Study plot**

Experimental long-term research has been conducted in the central Amazon initiated by biologist Thomas Lovejoy in 1979. This project, the Biological Dynamics of Forest Fragments Project, explores how forest functioning and biodiversity persists in artificial forest fragments of various sizes.

7

The Boreal Forest or Taiga

Patterns of the boreal forests

The boreal zone, or taiga, is the largest terrestrial biome, stretching across the top of North America, Europe, and Asia above about 50 degrees north. It comprises the vast conifer-dominated forests of Canada and Alaska, Russia, and Fennoscandia. Some ecologists use the term taiga to describe the more sparsely forested, northern part of the biome, found mostly in Russia, and boreal forest for the more southern part, but here we use the two words synonymously.

BOREAL FOREST REGIONS

The northern hemisphere boreal forest covers 11.5 percent of the Earth's land area (6.6 million sq miles/17 million sq km). While its area is extensive, its diversity of tree species is low and drawn from a relatively small number of primarily conifer genera.

Boreal forest

▼ **Summer and winter**

The Siberian taiga is the largest forest in the world. Top: Dark coniferous fir forests in the summer on the slopes of the Altai Mountains. Bottom: Siberian taiga in the winter with snow-covered spruce trees.

Diversity and seasonal variation

The taiga has relatively low tree diversity compared to other forested systems. Fifteen species of tree are locally dominant across all the North American taiga, and 14 species across Fennoscandia and Russia. Locally across the biome, six or often fewer tree species encompass the tree diversity. This is less than a tenth of the equivalent number found in many temperate forests, and much less than a hundredth for most tropical rain forests. There is no southern hemisphere equivalent to the taiga; the world's southernmost forests—the Magellanic subpolar

forests in southern Chile and Argentina—are cool temperate forests with southern beeches (genus *Nothofagus*) as the dominant trees.

The taiga is a cold forest with strong seasonal variation. Summers across the zone are short, moderately warm, and moist, and winters are long, extremely cold, and dry. The fluctuations of average monthly temperatures are particularly pronounced in inland continental regions—for example, there is an 80 °F (44 °C) range between the highest and lowest monthly average temperatures in interior Alaska, and a 100 °F (56 °C) range in eastern Siberia. Both of these regions can also have episodic high temperatures exceeding 100 °F (38 °C). These heatwaves promote catastrophic wildfires—one of the main drivers of change in the taiga, along with regional insect outbreaks. In addition to the pronounced temperature variation within years, there is also strong interannual variation.

Day length also varies with both date and latitude, with the seasonal change in day length being greatest at high latitudes. Daylength change has strong control over the timing of events such as budbreak, leaf-out, flowering, and so on. When southern varieties of trees are transplanted north of their natural range by foresters hoping to take advantage of warming temperatures, they can fail when their new light regime induces them to break their buds too early, resulting in frostbite.

◀ **Mountain taiga**
Siberian Pine or in Russian, "Cedar," (Pinus sibirica) growing in the East Sayan Mountains, Buryatia, Russia.

Alpine equivalents

Vegetation types in different latitudes frequently have altitudinal equivalents—in the case of boreal forests, these mirror the alpine forests of North America and Eurasia. These forests are similar in structure and share the same tree genera and sometimes even the same tree species. However, when detailed comparisons are made there are significant environmental differences. For example, alpine forests do not have the extreme seasonal changes in day length seen in high-latitude boreal forests. In terms of light transmission through the atmosphere, the shorter distance that light travels, the less it is filtered by the air—meaning that higher altitudes have less atmospheric filtering and so alpine forests have more exposure to harmful ultraviolet light. Low partial pressure of oxygen at altitude makes it hard for us to breathe. The increase in breathing rate in such conditions required to obtain oxygen also increases water loss—one needs to drink more water than usual to stay hydrated at high elevations. For plants, the partial pressure of carbon dioxide in the air in high mountains is lower. To cope with this, plants growing at altitude have a greater number of stomata (the pores that open to allow carbon dioxide to diffuse into the leaves) per unit area. Elevated stomatal indices can allow greater inward diffusion of carbon dioxide, but they also cause leaves to lose more water. The photosynthesis payoff per quantity of water lost (the water-use efficiency) therefore drops at altitude.

Boreal forest species

The taiga and alpine equivalents are often composed of the same genera operating in comparable ecological roles worldwide. Deciduous angiosperms, which in the taiga include species of *Betula* (birches) and *Populus* (poplars), are often the first trees to colonize a site after a disturbance. The dominant trees in mature taiga are drawn from the same small number of genera: *Picea* (spruces), *Abies* (firs), *Larix* (larches or tamaracks), and *Pinus* (pines). The general replacement patterns among these genera are consistent across the boreal zone, such that a Russian ecologist arriving in Canada can "read" the broad history of a Canadian landscape, identifying where there has been a recent fire or a windstorm a decade previously. The reciprocal, a Canadian ecologist taking a first look at a Siberian landscape and then interpreting it, also holds true. However, there are some surprising exceptions, in particular the extensive and very cold larch forests of Russia. These are deciduous and extend over an area only slightly smaller than that of the United States' contiguous 48 states, and do not have an equivalent in the North American taiga.

The canopies of boreal conifers are columnar or conical in shape, with branches that often reach down to the ground. The extended conical shape also helps the trees shed snow and reduces the risk of branch breakage from snow loading. The incoming direct sunlight, which is low to the horizon at high latitudes, is better captured by the sides of

▼ **Birches**

In the boreal forest worldwide and specifically in Siberia, broad-leaved, deciduous birches (genus Betula*) are often one of the first trees to colonize after a wildfire.*

tall, columnar tree canopies. The conifers are needle-leaved and usually evergreen; they have very high absorption of incoming light and so are called "dark conifers." Their needles are geometrically arranged to better trap incoming light, and they also have a thick, waxy coating to reduce desiccation. When the needles are shed, they decompose and in doing so mineralize nutrients that can be taken up by competing trees, as well as shrubs, herbs, and mosses.

There are, however, costs to evergreenness. The leaves of evergreens are typically more efficient at using sunlight to drive photosynthesis when young, becoming less so with age, and the trees often suffer from exposure to the dry air typical of boreal zones. Unlike spruces, firs, and pines, larches drop their needles annually. Prior to leaf-fall, they move nitrogen compounds from their leaves into their branches for winter storage—an adaptation to the low-nitrogen, carbon-rich conditions.

▲ **Conical canopies**

In the high latitudes of the taiga, the sun is never overhead and the direct sunlight is more horizontal. The trees have conical shapes and canopies with leaves to the ground to capture this light.

Changes in permafrost

Boreal forests can be divided into three zones with respect to the presence of permafrost, or permanently frozen soil, from less cold to progressively colder conditions: no permafrost, discontinuous permafrost, and continuous permafrost. The zone of discontinuous permafrost has permafrost in some locations but not others. The actions of thawing and refreezing of permafrost, particularly in the discontinuous permafrost zone, produces dramatic landforms and also makes the environment unviable for many tree species. The freezing and refreezing of soils has several consequences, including cryoturbation, or churning of the soil, and thermokarst, or the formation of small pits, mounds, sinkholes, and the like. With global warming, many of these soil dynamics are becoming more apparent in locations in the continuous permafrost zone as it begins to thaw.

▼ **Drunken forest**

Drunken forest at a small lake, Denali Highway, Alaska. The reeling "drunk trees" are striking physical consequences of soil freeze/thaw processes.

The Dahurian Larch

The Dahurian Larch (*Larix gmelinii*) of eastern Siberia is the world's northernmost tree. By shedding its leaves annually, it avoids potential damage from freezing internal water in the leaves, breakage from high winds, and winter abrasion ("ice-blasting") from windblown ice crystals. Dahurian Larches are adapted to withstand temperatures below −40 °F (−40 °C), requiring special adaptations to protect their cells from damage through freezing. Adaptations for survival in these super-cold conditions include thick-walled cells that resist cell rupture when frozen, tissue dehydration to reduce the amount of free water in tissues, and, as already mentioned, deciduousness. Dahurian Larch can survive temperatures as low as −94 °F (−70 °C).

◀ **Thermokarst crater**

A thermokarst crater, Batagay, Russia. Permafrost freeze/thaw can produce powerful internal pressures in the soil and create large features such as this crater. The thawing of permafrost can release large amounts of the greenhouse gas, carbon dioxide, along with volumes of the much more potent greenhouse gas, methane.

A shared history

Worldwide, boreal forests share a common history. During the Last Glacial Maximum 26,500-19,000 years ago, the world's glaciers were at their fullest extent and much of the area under the current boreal forests was covered by glacial ice, polar desert, or a steppe-tundra biome. It was inhabited by a striking and mostly now extinct collection of large animals, including the Woolly Mammoth (*Mammuthus primigenius*), Woolly Rhinoceros (*Coelodonta antiquitatis*), horses, bison, and muskox.

Migrating species

The dominant boreal trees are wind-pollinated. Some of this windblown pollen is deposited in lakes and sediments, providing a historical record of the trees present. In the past, trees of the boreal forests were sparser, as indicated by the lower volume of pollen falling into lakes worldwide. The evidence from fossil pollen clearly indicates that, as the ice receded following the end of the last glaciation about 12,000 years ago, different boreal trees extended their range in different directions from sources to the south to form the current boreal forests in the far north. This is true for the entire circumpolar zone. It appears that the boreal forests did not initially migrate south in lockstep as the ice age temperatures fell and then move back north with the glacial retreat. It is more the case that the boreal forest ecosystem coalesced in the far north from individual tree species migrating northward with considerable independence.

For all these similarities, there are also some important broad differences when comparing the Russian, Fennoscandian, and North American boreal forests. The northern treeline in Russia is formed by needle-leaved deciduous larches; in North America, the northernmost trees are needle-leaved evergreen spruces; and in Fennoscandia, broad-leaved deciduous birches are the treeline species. Over longer time intervals, the retreats and advances in treelines have not usually been synchronized over the different parts of the boreal forest. The situation we see today is unusual, with the forests advancing into the tundra across all the world's boreal regions. The last time this occurred was between 6,000 and 4,000 years ago.

Paludification

Owing to its relatively recent frozen past, the boreal zone has young soils, often with high ratios of carbon to nitrogen. This condition has attendant slow decomposition rates and an associated slow release of nitrogen for tree nutrition. Boreal forests tend to accumulate organic peaty matter, which ties up nutrients. Through the process of paludification they may convert over time to bogs, mires, fens, and swamps. Paludification is a major challenge for boreal foresters.

NORTHERNMOST TREELINE SPECIES

The northern treelines of the three boreal forests feature different genera with different types of trees. At the northern treeline of the North American boreal forest the terminal tree species is Black Spruce (*Picea mariana*), an evergreen conifer that can tolerate permafrost. It can reproduce vegetatively by layering, the sprouting of roots when branches touch the ground. In contrast, at the boundary of the Fennoscandian forest the northernmost species are Downy Birches (*Betula pubescens)*, which are broad-leaved and deciduous. While this is the opposite of the needle-leaved spruce treeline in North America, Downy Birches do have chlorophyll for photosynthesis in their twigs, which provides a kind of "faux-evergreenness." Iceland was about 25 to 40 percent forested when colonized by the Vikings, with forest and woodlands of Downy Birch but the current forestation is between 1 and 2 percent. Greenland also has a presence of Downy Birch on the western site of its southern tip. Finally, at the cold treelines of the Russian boreal forest are needle-leaved deciduous conifers: larches (genus *Larix*). At the coldest, most northern treeline, Dahurian Larch (*Larix gmelinii*) is the only tree species to be found.

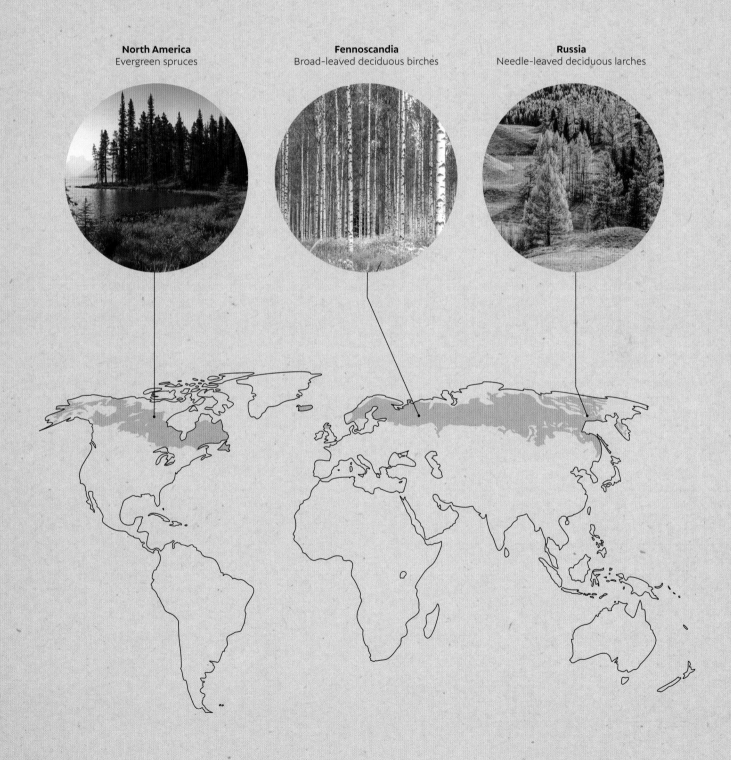

North America
Evergreen spruces

Fennoscandia
Broad-leaved deciduous birches

Russia
Needle-leaved deciduous larches

Forest dynamics

Boreal forests produce contrasting landscape elements as a response to local and regional ecosystem dynamics. Consider an idealized forest succession on north- and south-facing slopes after a wildfire in the boreal forests near Fairbanks, Alaska. The fire recoveries on the two slopes are quite different and demonstrate the actions of physical and biological processes that can drive forest dynamics in the boreal zone. On warmer south-facing slopes, a tree-killing wildfire creates opportunities for herbaceous plants and tree seedlings to regenerate. Over time, shrubs begin to dominate the area and tree saplings gain in size. Resin Birch (*Betula glandulosa*) and Balsam Poplar (*Populus balsamifera*) establish early on but are smaller trees and are eventually overtaken by White Spruce (*Picea glauca*). The mixed spruce-hardwood forest eventually transforms to a forest dominated by White Spruce trees in its canopy. The organic soil layers deepen over this time and White Spruce remains the dominant species until the next wildfire triggers another recovery.

Meanwhile, cooler, less sunlit, north-facing fire-damaged slopes have a very different fate. The soils here have a frozen permafrost layer and some of the peaty organic layer insulating the permafrost is burned away in a fire. This initiates several feedbacks that are quite different relative to those experienced on south-facing slopes. In total, these feedbacks slow tree growth, increase the growth of moss and hence peat development, and amplify one another to produce a forest with a frozen, carbon-storing soil.

The moss accumulation on north-facing slopes (see the diagram opposite) results in colder, wetter soil and less decomposition of organic matter, which in turn causes the soil to become more acidic and wetter still, and slows decomposition even further. At the end of this carbon-storing feedback system, more moss accumulates and the cycle closes and repeats. With the reduction in soil insulation, the permafrost thaws to a greater depth, and the active layer—the part of the soil that is not frozen in the summer—deepens. As the permafrost recovers and a deep peat layer grows, a progression of herbaceous plants and then shrubs colonize the area, and over time an increasingly dense cover of Black Spruce (*Picea mariana*) develops. With the increased insulation from the nighttime flux of heat to the sky provided by the greater tree cover, the permafrost moves closer to the surface and a mature Black Spruce forest develops. The thawing, heaving, and refreezing of the permafrost in this forest can produce "drunken forests," with tree trunks tilted off vertical and pointing in different directions.

WILDFIRE RECOVERY ON SOUTH- AND NORTH-FACING SLOPES

Secondary succession following a wildfire on south-facing slopes near Fairbanks, Alaska displays very different patterns of recovery on the permafrost-free south-facing slopes versus the cold north-facing slopes with underlying permafrost.

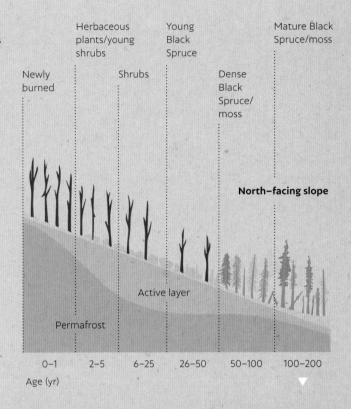

South–facing slope

Newly burned	Herbaceous plants/ seedlings	Shrubs/ saplings	Dense hardwood (Birch and Aspen)	Mature hardwood	Mixed White Spruce– hardwood	Mixed White Spruce/moss

Active layer

Bedrock

0–1	2–5	6–25	26–50	51–100	100–200	200–250+

Age (yr)

North–facing slope

Newly burned	Herbaceous plants/young shrubs	Shrubs	Young Black Spruce	Dense Black Spruce/ moss	Mature Black Spruce/moss

Active layer

Permafrost

0–1	2–5	6–25	26–50	50–100	100–200

Age (yr)

South-facing recovery
On the Dalton Highway from Fairbanks to Prudhoe Bay, Alaska, an autumn day reveals the footprint of a wildfire 50 to 100 years before in the golden and yellow leaves of the deciduous hardwood trees in the regenerating forest.

North-facing permafrost
A drunken forest in Fairbanks, Alaska where trees collapse into the ground due to permafrost melt, corresponding to the 100–200 year forest stage on the diagram above.

Disturbances in the taiga

Flying over the taiga reinforces the feeling of vastness of the boreal forest, and it also reveals the large-scale effects of the principal disturbances that drive boreal ecosystems. Vistas of burned and blackened landscapes, mile upon mile of insect-killed trees standing dead with brown leaf canopies, drowned landscapes produced by the complex actions of freezing and thawing ice … these are all signs of major disturbances producing change and death over extensive areas.

▼ **Wildfire**

Komsomolsk, Russia, June 2007. A forest fire in a remote region of the Siberian taiga.

Disturbance regimes are the sum of the characteristics of natural disturbances in a given region (see page 83). Boreal forests occupy the latitudinal belt where most climate models have predicted the greatest changes in temperature through anthropogenic global warming. It is also the zone where the most substantial warming has been observed in recent years. The disturbance-regime change compels ecosystem change. If the intensity or frequency of disturbances in boreal forests change, then this will alter the features of their ecosystems. There are three current significant disturbances in taiga systems: wildfires, insect attacks, and forest harvesting. These disturbances are all intensified by climate change. Forest harvesting, particularly in Russia, is expected to increase under warming with the greater maritime transportation afforded from the melting of the Arctic Sea. In addition, the thawing of the permafrost from climate warming also can cause high levels of tree mortality and landscape-level change.

WILDFIRES IN CENTRAL SIBERIA

Graphic from a scientific research paper detailing 20 years
of wildfires in Central Siberia. The top image shows the
study area divided into five transects for detailed analysis.
The graphs below show the numbers and area burned each
year since 1996 to 2015. The trends for total number of fires
and the total area burned have significantly increased.
In addition, the most extreme years above the trends are
among the most recent. (Source: Ponomarev et al., 2016.)

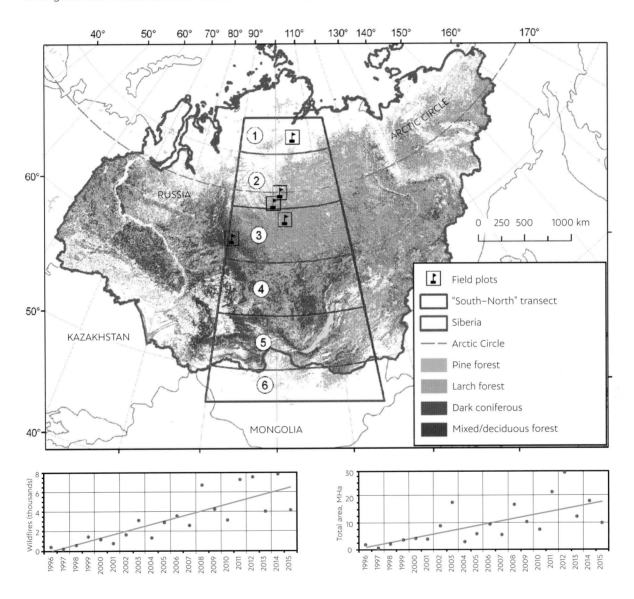

Wildfire

Relative to other forests, boreal forests experience wildfires that are episodically
very large. The Black Dragon fire, which occurred in the Greater Khingan
Mountains of northeastern China, started on May 6, 1987 during a hot, dry period
under ideal conditions for a wildfire propagation. It eventually spilled across the
Sino-Russian border and lasted for a month, burning 2,500 sq miles (6,500 sq km) of
forests and 1,359 sq miles (3,500 sq km) of other landcover types—Russia lost about
five times more forest than did China. The Russian firefighting strategy was to let
the fire burn, whereas the Chinese authorities deployed 60,000 soldiers and workers
to fight it. When it was finally extinguished on June 2, one-sixth of China's timber
reserve had been destroyed, 191 people had been killed, and 33,000 were homeless.

This sad parable exemplifies the current wildfire fighting strategies in the northern forests of Alaska, Canada, and Siberia, where protecting people takes precedence over protecting trees. In 2020, for example, the policy of Russia's Federal Agency for Forestry was to ignore 91 percent of the fires that occurred, in a year with a much greater incidence of wildfires than usual. Many of these fires were in "control zones," with no effect on local populations. In such cases, the economic cost of extinguishing the fire is considered greater than the residual damage the burning will cause.

Fires in the taiga are episodic over large regions. The area of forest burned by wildfires in Alaska and Canada has been estimated by ground and airplane survey since 1950. In some years the fires burn relatively little of the forest, but in other years as much as 17 million acres (7 million ha) have been burned in a single year. Research indicates that both the size and intensity of the fires are increasing and the frequency interval between events is reducing. In 2016, Evgenii Ponomarev and colleagues computed the number of wildfires in larch forests across an area in central Siberia covering about one-third of the total area of Russia over the 20 years between 1996 and 2015. During this period, the number of fires increased from a few hundred in 1996 to about 6,000 per year by the end of the interval, and in 2014 alone there were 8,000 wildfires that together burned about 42 million acres (17 million ha) of forest. This significant upward trend in the numbers and intensities of fires in the taiga is a well-anticipated signal of the biome's responses to global warming.

Insect outbreaks

As with wildfires, insect outbreaks in the taiga of both Eurasia and North America are episodic events and can destroy millions of acres of forest. A general conceptual model of the relationships between boreal trees and insects typically indicates some shared, interacting components. The dominant boreal trees use quantitative chemical defenses such as resins and tars to fend off attacks by insects. These sticky defenses are produced in large amounts and "gum-up" the insects. The other alternative, qualitative defenses plants use are toxic compounds such as alkaloids, cyanogens, and terpenes to poison herbivores, but these are more common in short-lived herbaceous plants than boreal trees. In the great game of chemical warfare, trees are like castles with defensive materials to use against the invading insect horde. The insect invaders win by mustering large numbers to attack the trees and drain them of their defenses.

Siberian Fir die-off

The Siberian Silk Moth (*Dendrolimus superans*) is a pest of boreal forests across much of the Russian taiga, from the Ural Mountains to the Russian Far East. Its caterpillars feed on the needles of conifers in general, notably the Siberian Fir (*Abies sibirica*) and larches. The species overwinters

▼ **Forest pest**
Caterpillars of the Siberian Silk Moth (Dendrolimus superans) attack conifers in the Russian taiga.

▲ **Double disturbance**

Dead trees that have been killed by a beetle infestation in Jasper National Park, Alberta Canada with an erosion slide on the rocky ground.

as a pupa, and the adult moths emerge after winter and actively lay eggs on branch tips and leaves from later June to early August. The caterpillars hatch and repeat the cycle when they pupate. If the trees are hardy, they can withstand attack from the caterpillars using their chemical defenses. Should the moths gain an advantage, however, such as if the trees are compromised by a drought, the insects can increase dramatically in number over just a few years. This build up of numbers is followed by an insect outbreak that destroys large areas of forest. With the massive numbers of tree deaths, the moth's food supply catastrophically collapses and insect numbers plummet. At the same time, the landscape is covered by dead trees with dry leaves and wood, providing a ready source of fuel for wildfires.

The weak link in the chain occurs early in a potential insect outbreak, when young, regenerating trees are vigorous and insect numbers are low. At this critical time, the moths survive by locating weaker trees that have been damaged by a lightning strike or toppled by a windstorm. Using these sites, they can maintain a low presence, waiting for the opportunity to prosper. For foresters hoping to control tree damage caused by insects, this is the time to focus on eliminating the pests. This is true for the Siberian Silk Moth, and also more generally for other insects associated with forest-damaging outbreaks.

Up until the collapse of the Soviet Union in 1991, the State Forest Service flew about 600 flights a day to detect Siberian wildfires and deployed "smoke jumpers" (firefighters who parachute into an area to fight wildfires) in an attempt to control the fires. In the off-season they flew a similar number of flights to find damaged trees or small areas being attacked by insects. The smoke jumpers then worked as "forest sanitation" crews to clear and burn these insect patches, with the overall goal of preventing insect outbreaks across the landscape. The cycle of regeneration, tree regeneration and tree growth, slowing of growth, a stress trigger, and insect outbreaks is a common pattern in boreal tree species and the insects that feed on them. While the actors may change across the different boreal forests around the world, the play stays the same.

Forest harvesting

The global taiga constitutes about 45 percent of the world stock of growing timber (wood of merchantable dimensions). The total increment of timber production is greater than the annual harvest, but this harvestable proportion varies nationally. Most Alaskan boreal forestry is excluded from timber production. In Russia and Canada, it is not economically feasible to harvest 32 percent and 19 percent of the closed-canopy forest, respectively, using current technology and transportation. The equivalent figure for Norway is 14 percent, for Sweden 9 percent, and for Finland only 2 percent. There are also considerable national differences in land ownership, with primarily public ownership across much of Alaska, Canada, and Russia, and mainly private ownership in the Nordic nations.

▲ **Managed forest**
Thinning in a pine forest with a harvester.

In managed forests, which dominate the boreal forest of Sweden and Finland and the southern part of the boreal forest in Canada, the focus is on controlling or limiting the effects of fire and insects. In the northern half of the taiga, the forest is less intensely managed and disturbances are active and obvious in shaping the landscapes.

▼ **Timber production**
The boreal forest harvesting provides about 17 percent of the annual global forest roundwood production.

Forestry—particularly boreal forestry—as an economic endeavor is currently facing a time of change and uncertainty caused by complex changes in global demand. Pulp and paper production is increasing outside the taiga region, as is plantation forestry. There was a one-third drop in employment in the forestry sector between 2000 and 2010 in Finland and Canada and a 50 percent drop in Russia over the same

period, and China has now surpassed the United States as the largest producer of paper and paperboard. Even though there are predictions of a possible 6 percent increase in taiga productivity by 2050 through the effects of global warming, corresponding increases in insect attacks, wildfires, droughts, and so on will increase the economic uncertainty of the boreal wood supply. There is a possibility that the increased melting of the Arctic Sea ice could open up currently inaccessible northern regions, particularly in Russia, which could reduce the costs of exploiting this part of the taiga. At the same time, however, these forests represent pristine nature, and their future value may instead lie in their recreation potential, carbon storage, and conservation, not the extraction of traditional timber resources.

MANAGEMENT STATUS OF BOREAL FORESTS

Forests are delineated as: unmanaged, managed (harvested and regenerated commercially); managed certified (certified as being under sustainable management); intact forest (unbroken expanses of natural ecosystems with no signs of significant human activity and large enough to maintain all native diversity); intact certified (intact forests certified sustainable). (Source: Kraxner et al., 2017; IIASA; IBFRA.)

- Unmanaged
- Managed forest
- Managed certified
- Intact forest
- Intact certified

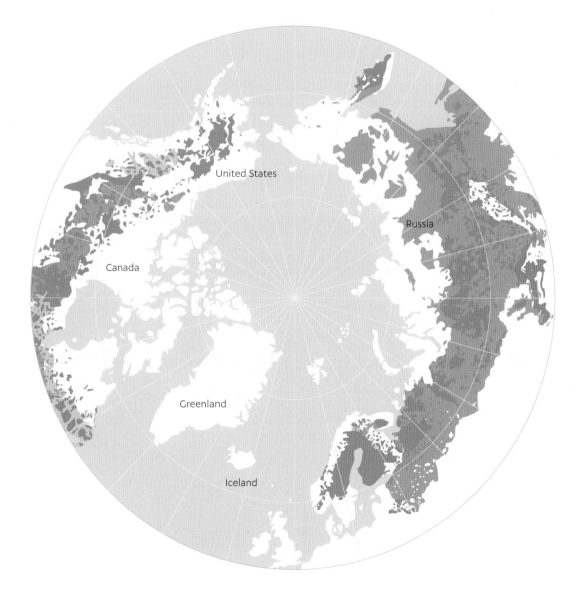

Climate change in the boreal forest

Today's boreal forests are in a dynamic state and the associated uncertainty will only increase with the changing world climate. Global warming is expected to alter the patterns of disturbance in the taiga, which in turn will affect the biome's boundaries and adjacent ecosystems.

BOREAL FOREST BOUNDARIES

Shifts in the boreal forest zone under a climatic warming of around 3.6 °F (2 °C) could produce vegetation and soil change over about 40 percent of its current total area. These changes release carbon dioxide into the atmosphere, which sets up an initial positive feedback with warming producing more greenhouse gas emission, in turn producing more warming. Further, a northward migration of boreal forest into the tundra also has the potential to enhance global warming.

Boreal forest

Temperate broad-leaf and mixed forest

Temperate coniferous forest

Tundra

Temperate grassland, savanna, and shrubland

Shifting the boundaries

The polymath Alexander von Humboldt defined and used isotherms to map vegetation distribution and relate vegetation responses to change in latitude and altitude (see page 118). He established the isotherm of a given location by computing the average of two temperatures taken in that location at dawn and 2:00 p.m. every day over the course of a year. In modern use, isotherms are the average temperatures for a given location over a designated time interval. The boreal zone is bounded by the July 64 °F (18 °C) isotherm on its southern border and the July 55 °F (13 °C) isotherm to the north. The difference in the July isotherms for the northern and southern boundaries is 9 °F (5 °C). If this isothermal relationship persists, then at first approximation a climate warming of 3.6 °F (2 °C) will displace the boundaries of the world's boreal forest zone poleward enough to change 40 percent of the current boreal forest to some other biome.

Such changes would involve shifts in the transitions between boreal forest and other biomes, including tundra to the north, deciduous forest at warmer, wetter boundaries, and grasslands at warmer, drier boundaries. The boreal forest is also bounded by oceans or by maritime forests associated with ocean margins. Transitions along these boundaries have a spectrum of controlling conditions, each with different responses to change. Many of the boundaries seem to be controlled by the disturbance regime. For example, grassland (steppe) and taiga boundaries are often mediated by wildfires, particularly the frequency of these events. The study of these transitions occurs over large areas and over long periods of time. For these reasons, our understanding of them is based on hypotheses about forest change and long-term paleontological data.

Fire danger indices

Fire disturbances are expected to increase in intensity under modeled global warming predictions. The fire danger indices that are often displayed on signs at entrances to forest parks and other recreational sites are based on how easy it is to ignite a fire in the conditions, how rapidly a fire would spread, how dangerous an ignited fire would be to fight, the expected height of the flames, and so on, depending on the particular model used. The higher the fire danger index, the more dangerous a fire will be should it start in the area. If the fire danger index is high enough, then entrance to the forest is prohibited. The indices are computed using mathematical models that rely on weather and forest data—the dryness of the potential fuel, the conditions controlling the rate of heat transferred by the fire, and the weather conditions (dry, hot, windy, and so on). Many of the components of fire danger indices are predicted to greatly increase with a warming world, with current evidence suggesting this is already happening.

The Russian border between tundra and taiga can be abrupt and expansive. In this photograph, larch forests are advancing into tundra. Indeed, on all the northern continents, boreal forests are similarly advancing northward. This unusual simultaneous global event has not occurred in the past several thousand years.

Fire at the boundaries

For regions as extensive as the taiga, the factors that ultimately control the edges between the forest and other biomes can vary with location. Influencing factors involve the lay of the land, including the orientation of the slope (north- and south-facing slopes show great differences in incoming light, with resulting consequences), drainage conditions, soil variation, elevation, and aspect. That said, the transition between the northern boundary of the taiga and tundra vegetation, and between part of the southern boundary that transitions into grassland, both often involve wildfires.

At the taiga-tundra boundary in northern Canada, investigated for decades by biologists Serge Payette, Luc Sirois, and colleagues at Quebec's Laval University, the timing of fires is the critical issue. If a fire occurs when the forest has developed a high reproductive capacity, then there is ample seed production following the event and the population density of the fire-adapted trees increases. The closed forest therefore maintains itself and may also colonize open patches in the adjacent tundra. However, if a fire occurs under climate and forest conditions that trigger only limited seed production, then there is limited tree-regeneration potential following the disturbance and the vegetation move toward more open woodland or bare land. Because soil surface response to wildfire is heterogeneous, the advances and retreats of forest against tundra vary along the boundaries between the two.

The boundaries between the taiga and drier grasslands have a conceptually similar control process relating to wildfire. While tundra burns rarely in comparison to taiga, grasslands have a higher frequency of burning event than the forests. Frequent fires along the grassland edges of the taiga promote an increase in the frequency of fires in the forest itself, as it provides ample fuel for ignition. Following ignition, fire behavior is controlled by the factors used to establish fire danger indices (see box on page 229). When conditions are hot, dry, and windy, and when the fuels of forest litter, leaves, dead trees, and branches are dry, then a single ignition can a promote forest-destroying fire. Repetition of fires along the grassland boundary at short intervals eliminates seed sources and seedlings, and thus the transition of forest to grassland.

Along wetter boundaries of the taiga, the transitions between boreal forest and deciduous forest (or boreal forest and mixed evergreen-deciduous forest) are less clear because boreal trees grow more poorly on their southern edge, even though their growth rates are often highest here. The same pattern is also seen in the alpine equivalents to boreal forests, at their downslope transition to deciduous forests. In this case, it is not environmental conditions that are controlling the location of the southern boundary of the boreal forest, but rather the change in competitive interactions among trees, which themselves may be mediated by environmental conditions. Computer models that simulate the interactions among individual trees in a forest and with each tree's immediate environment have supported this conjecture.

▼ **Wet boundaries**
The landscape scale actions of permafrost as an agent simultaneously drain and produce wetlands to create complex landscapes— Black Spruce (Picea mariana) trees on the higher ground; lakes, bogs and mires, shrubs, and dead trees from paludification (swamp creation). Yukon Territory, Canada.

Tree competition

Competition in trees as a scientific concept is complicated by some fundamental issues in tree biology. Most ecological theory and associated models concerning tree competition are based on two simple assumptions: that the unique features of individuals, including individual trees, their sizes, and their relative locations, are sufficiently unimportant that individuals are assumed to be identical; and that the population is "perfectly mixed," so that there are no local spatial interactions of any important magnitude. However, contradicting the first of these is the fact that trees vary greatly in size, from small seedlings to gigantic canopy trees that sometimes exceed 330 ft (100 m) in height. And trees do interact with nearby trees in quite important ways. For forest ecologists, competition is seen as a tree-versus-tree interaction, in which size and location do matter.

Since neither assumption describes the apparent workings of tree competition particularly well, computer models have been developed to avoid these problems. One important type of computer-intensive models are gap models, named in deference to Alex S. Watt's concept of the importance of gaps in the mosaic forest (see pages 68-69 and 72-73). Each year they compute the growth, death, and regeneration of each tree on a small ¼-acre (0.1 ha) patch of land, which is the typical size of forest sample plots and gaps in the forest canopy. The death of a particular tree, the regeneration of seedlings, and the year-to-year variation in environmental conditions are all expected to have chance variation. The average of hundreds or thousands of individual patches of land are then simulated to determine overall forest change over time, mimicking the pattern and process dynamics of a mosaic forest.

In 1986, John Pastor at the University of Minnesota Duluth and W. M. "Mac" Post of the Oak Ridge National Laboratory developed an individual-based forest simulator capable of tracking the expected changes in soils as well as the performance and regeneration of each simulated tree. They then used the model to investigate the transition from boreal forests to deciduous forests at 11 sites near the southern boundary of the boreal zone in eastern Canada (Quebec and Ontario) and the United States (Maine and Minnesota). As one might expect, the model predicted that forest productivity increases in warmer sites with adequate moisture, and the reverse at locations of increased dryness. A significant finding was that the change in the species composition and the decomposability of the leaf litter has strong reinforcing feedbacks within the forest nitrogen cycle. They found a "the rich get rich and the poor get poorer" situation, in which increased productivity increased nitrogen availability, which increased productivity, and so on, and also the reverse, with less productivity leading to less available nitrogen and so on. They opined that when subjected to climate change, forests are as sensitive to indirect changes from such feedbacks on the soils as they are to the direct effects of changes in temperature on tree growth.

▶ **Mixed-wood forest**
The mixed-wood forest of the Canadian Maritimes occurs between boreal forest to the north and temperate deciduous forest to the south. In this diverse forest, species that are diminished in the face of losing competition rally to persist when conditions in time and space become fleetingly favorable. Jacques Cartier National Park, Quebec, Canada.

The taiga's unique global role

One of the wonders of forests is that there are many things about them that seem to follow a set of similar rules. The rise of tall monopodial trees repeatedly and independently in the evolution of plants, the effect of trees and forests on soil development … these and many other factors make forests seem familiar regardless of their origin. A New Zealand forest, separated from other landmasses for 85 million years, seems familiar to a forest ecologist no matter where they come from.

SEA ICE CONCENTRATION

Ice reflects radiation and darker, unfrozen seawater absorbs radiation making the changes in sea ice a power factor in the planet's climate. A similar situation is seen in the Siberian forest, where seasonal surface changes lead large annual changes in net radiation fluxes. For the global boreal forest, forest clearing may produce seasonal surface changes that increase the net radiation flux and promote cooling. However, forest changes produced by climate warming may have the opposite effect—warming interacting with forest begats more warming.

September 2020

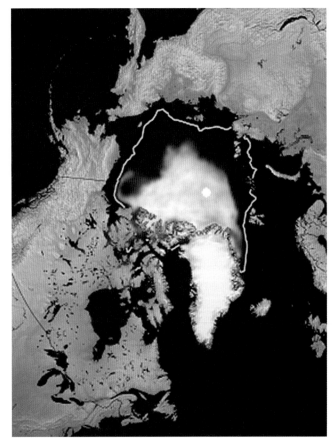

March 2021

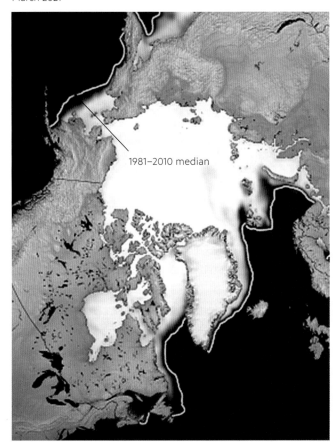

1981–2010 median

Sea ice concentration (%)

0   25   50   75   100

Similar yet different

For all the similarities between forests, there are also many differences, and a comfortable familiarity is only illuminated by uniqueness. One unique aspect of the taiga is its potential to leverage change in climate at the global scale through regional shifts in the abundance of its relatively few species. In 2000, British meteorologist Richard Betts posed an interesting question for the application of a global climate model: "Growing trees store carbon and reduce the atmospheric CO_2 [carbon dioxide] that is involved in global warming. More trees also increase the capture of incoming radiation and thus increase heating. Since one of these effects produces cooling and the other warming, then where is it best to plant trees to reduce global warming?" He found that forestation with evergreen conifers at high latitudes would increase warming from sunlight (through radiative forcing and a warming effect) and outweigh the cooling effect of reducing atmospheric carbon dioxide. Reducing global warming is more complex than simply saying, "Let's grow more trees." Where the trees are grown is important.

▲ **Dark conifers**

A forest of dark conifers in Teberda Nature Reserve, located on the slopes of the Caucasus Mountains, Karachay-Cherkessia, Russia.

The larch forest of eastern Siberia

A unique aspect of the taiga is the extensive larch forest of eastern Siberia. The effects of global warming in the region should favor the natural replacement of the current, more sunlight-reflective, bitterly cold larch forests with the more southern "dark forest" of Russia. Dark conifers capture more incoming radiation than do the "light conifer" larches and hence produce a shift toward warming. In addition, the larch forest is deciduous and when it loses its leaves, the surface condition is dominated by winter snow, which reflects even more light. The conversion of larch to dark conifers therefore leads to the absorption of more radiation, in turn leading to the growth of more evergreens and further warming. This is called positive feedback—a small initial change promotes more change in the same direction. Positive feedback behaves like a reverse-wired thermostat: when it is hot, it turns on the heat; when it is cool, it turns off the heat.

"Evergreenification"

There are other parts of the world where seasonal variations in the surface affect the radiation budget. A significant example is the freezing of sea ice. Ice with a covering of snow reflects radiation from the sun, whereas darker, unfrozen seawater absorbs radiation. This major effect has to be taken into account in global climate models. A similar situation is seen in the Siberian forest, where seasonal surface changes lead to changes in radiation fluxes—including in the larch forests. The overall changes in the forest radiation budget could add a multiplier to the equation and increase the effect of global warming. Much more analysis is needed here, but rough calculations indicate that the leverage from replacing the Russian larch forests over the long term could add about 1.8–2.7 °F (1–1.5 °C) of warming on top of a 5.4 °F (3 °C) warming.

A worrisome aspect of this is that the "evergreenification" of the Siberian larch forests may already have begun. Viacheslav Kharuk and colleagues from the Sukachev Institute of Forests in Krasnoyarsk, Siberia, have found evidence of larch replacement by evergreen conifers (spruces, firs, and pines) in the far north of Siberia and also at high elevations. In 1992, American environmental scientist Gordon Bonan and colleagues experimented with climate models and found that global-scale climate consequences could arise from boreal deforestation. A northward migration of boreal forest into the tundra could increase the percentage of incoming radiation absorbed by the planet and produce further warming. A considerable amount of similar work in Amazonia has indicated that the destruction of tropical forest may lead to warmer and drier conditions. The parallel that the potential of boreal forests to influence the northern hemisphere climate points to a great need to improve our understanding of these forests as interactive components of the global system.

LARCH REPLACEMENT

Under warming conditions, the cold-tolerating Siberian larches are losing their competitive advantage over other conifers. Over time this implies a conversion of deciduous larch forest to evergreen conifer forests. This phenomenon appears to be occurring over large areas both in level terrain and in alpine conditions. These changes are expected to affect the forest radiation balance toward warming—warming produces forest change, which produces warming, which produces forest change—and hence promote a positive feedback loop with existential implications.

● Larch

● Siberian Pine

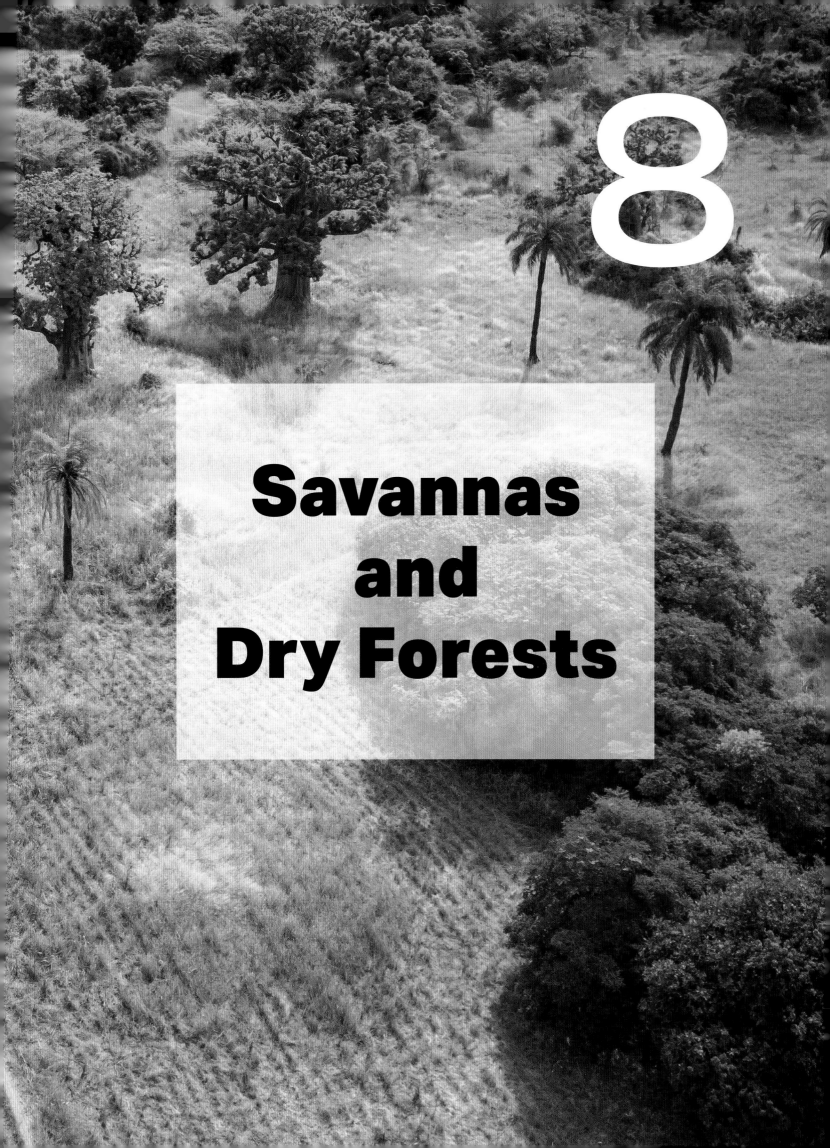

8

Savannas and Dry Forests

Savannas and associated woodlands

Savanna is characterized by a mixture of woody plants and grasses, and is found in tropical and subtropical climate zones with a pronounced dry season in winter and a hot, wet season in summer. The so-called Mediterranean climates and their associated vegetation have the reverse seasonality of rainfall, being wet in winter and dry in summer.

SAVANNA LOCATIONS

A complex mixture of trees, grasses, and shrubs form the world's savanna ecosystems. They are extensive, heterogeneous, and home for one-fifth of the human population.

Tropical and subtropical grasslands, savannas, and shrublands

Temperate grassland, savanna, and shrub

A relative newcomer

Savannas are complex mixtures of grasses and woody plants, often covering vast areas. Here, the term "grasses" refers to both the true grasses (family Poaceae) and sedges (family Cyperaceae). Most of the woody plants in savannas are "rain-green," meaning that they lose their leaves during the extended winter dry season and then grow new ones with the arrival of the rains and the onset of the wet growing season. Leaf-out occurs slightly before the wet season for many of the species. Worldwide, savannas cover a total of between 10 million and 12.5 million square miles (25 million and 33 million sq km), depending on one's exact definition of the biome. A fifth of the human population lives in savannas. If the words of Shakespeare's Antonio, in Act 2, Scene 1 of *The Tempest* apply—"Whereof what's past is prologue; what to come, in yours and my discharge"—then the prologue for savannas is short, for they are newcomers relative to other major terrestrial biomes. What is to come and in our discharge is that we are changing our planet and, with it, savannas.

The savanna ecosystem

The explanation of how savanna ecosystems function and how they might respond to change resembles a Gordian knot of causes and responses whose untangling is progressing, particularly through ongoing ecosystem-based synthesis. The task of explaining savannas has been a forum for biogeographers, ecologists, and naturalists. Savannas have considerable natural ecosystem complexity, which fuels scientific argument. Even the meaning of savanna as a word has changed through history. Etymologically, "savanna" derives from an ancient word in the Arawakan language spoken by the Taíno people of the Caribbean. Arawakan was a major source of new words borrowed into the languages of the European explorers and colonizers—in this case Spanish. The Spaniards used Sabana as the place-name for a treeless plain near the court of the Taíno king, Carlos, likely located in the current Madungandí indigenous province in Panama. Its current use has drifted from the original "treeless plain" meaning, which makes it tricky to interpret the notes of Spanish explorers on the nature of the vegetation at certain locations.

The prevailing ecological use of the term savanna denotes communities or landscapes with a continuous grass layer and scattered trees. The balance in abundance and patterns of the trees and grasses are products of dynamic interactions among climate, topography, soils, geomorphology, herbivory, and fire.

▷ **Australian savanna**
A Golden Wattle (Acacia dealbata)—the floral symbol of Australia— blooms in the country's extensive red heartland called "the bush" or "the outback."

▲ **African savanna**
The African savanna contains the greatest diversity of large mammals on Earth. Much of this diversity is housed in game reserves, such as Maasai Mara, Kenya—the site of this Acacia tree.

Why the mix?

Questions as to what allows grasses and woody plants to survive over vast areas as codominants have long invited theories—initially, what prevents one of these life-forms from performing better in a particular situation and dominating the other? This is certainly the case for the boundaries between other forests and grasslands. Why don't the winners really win, so that savannas become either tree-dominated forests or grass-dominated grasslands? Or if it is a matter of percentage, which

▶ **Savanna chemistry**
*Plants with different photosynthesis chemistries compose savannas. Trees, such as the African Baobab (*Adansonia digitata*), top, operate the C_3 photosynthesis pathway. About 3 percent of vascular plants, notably savanna or warm-season grasses (center) use a C_4 pathway. A third pathway, CAM, provides drought tolerance for cacti (bottom), agave, and many orchids, for example.*

factors are important in determining the percentages of tree and grass cover to change over time or location? Are the causes to be found in water availability? If so, exactly how does this work? Is it due to available nutrients? Is it due to a combination of water and nutrients? Is it due to fire? Is it due to grazing animals controlling the types of vegetation by their food preferences? These are all good questions, but the "correct" answer may vary with location or with small changes in the overall environment.

Different photosynthesis pathways

Plants can be categorized by their photosynthesis biochemistry as C_3 plants, C_4 plants, or CAM plants. Almost all woody plants use the ancient biochemical C_3 photosynthesis process, which evolved about 2,800 million years ago. It is the most common photosynthesis pathway and has the broadest geographical distribution—woody plants use the C_3 pathway, as do algae, mosses, and ferns. C_3 plants are most efficient in cool, wet climates.

The grasses in classical savannas have a modified biochemical process using a C_4 pathway, with a four-carbon-compound-based (hence C_4) biochemical pathway to concentrate carbon dioxide before feeding it into the ancient C_3 pathway. While only about 3 percent of the world's vascular plant species use the C_4 pathway, it is found in about half of grass species, which together produce about a quarter of the Earth's total photosynthesis. The C_4 grasses are often referred to as warm-season grasses, whereas grasses that use the C_3 pathway are called cool-season grasses. Warm-season grasses and other C_4 plants have advantages in hot, sunny climates and when there are lower levels of carbon dioxide in the air. C_4 grasses are very intolerant of shading, which makes them absent or rare under closed forest canopies.

The third pathway is used by CAM plants (named for their novel biochemistry, crassulacean acid metabolism), which have advantages in arid environments. As in the C_4 plants, CAM plants use an additional biochemical process to feed carbon dioxide into the ancient C_3 pathway. Typical CAM plants include cacti, agave, and many orchids. They are drought-tolerant and only rarely manifest as trees.

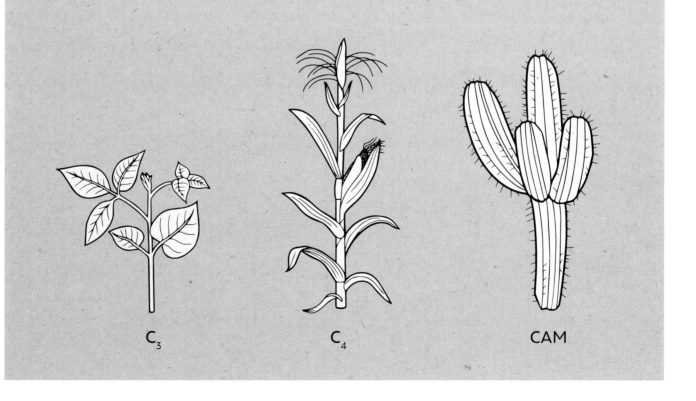

C_3 C_4 CAM

Evolution of the savanna

Savannas are mixtures of plants with two very different life-forms—woody plants and warm-season grasses—each with its own photosynthesis pathway (see box on page 243). C_4 plants evolved about 30 million years ago. Then about 8 million years ago the C_4 grasses dramatically expanded around the world in the space of about a million years—the blink of an eye in geological time. Savanna originated with this nearly synchronous expansion of C_4 grasses. What was the trigger? A lower concentration of carbon dioxide in the atmosphere would disfavor C_3 tree seedlings competing with C_4 grasses worldwide, but lower carbon dioxide levels had been in place for about 20 million years before the spread of savanna.

Some researchers have proposed that fire and feedbacks between fire, vegetation, smoke, and climate were the trigger. Grasses prosper over woody plants in more frequent wildfire-prone situations, and grasslands are more prone to fire than forests—a positive feedback. Most hypotheses about the processes in savannas discuss feedbacks involving fires, droughts, the reduction of grasses by grazing animals, the reduction of woody plants by browsing animals, and the reduction of successful grazers by predatory animals and thus the promotion of successful grazers, or vice versa. Perhaps combinations of some or all these causes are at work. However, one factor is likely more important above all others to the future of this young biome. At the end of the brief prologue, a new cast strode onto the stage—the setting is a new biome in a time of great change and the cast comprises the savanna hominids, with *Homo sapiens* in the central role.

▼ **Olduvai gorge**
Homo habilis, probably the first early human species, evolved from savanna species in East Africa.

Early humans

The first fossils of the earliest predecessors to share our genus, *Homo habilis*, date from 2.3 million to 1.8 million years ago and have been found in the East African Rift System. *Homo habilis* was followed with dramatic evolutionary changes manifested in the species *H. erectus*, which had 40 percent larger brains than their relatives, along with a larger body size, shoulders that allowed them to throw projectiles, and adaptations to long-distance running. Humans originated from a series of savanna species that evolved the ability to walk upright through their environment, and then continued to evolve in the direction of ecological flexibility and increased brain size. The first modern humans, *H. sapiens*, originated about 300,000 years ago in Africa.

We are now at a time when our species is a major force on savanna systems. We appear to have had a hand in the extinction of many of the very large mammals from Australian, New World, and Eurasian savannas. If the empowerment of C_4 grasses to outcompete C_3 woody plants arose from low levels of carbon dioxide in the atmosphere, then our burning of fossil fuels and clearing of land may have spiked that advantage by increasing atmospheric carbon dioxide. A complex, worldwide problem involves "woody weeds," trees, and shrubs that can outcompete grasses. A proliferation of woody weeds may be caused by a reversal in the very conditions that originally favored C_4 grasses (low concentrations of carbon dioxide in the atmosphere 8 million years ago) and may have triggered the creation of savanna, the eventual cradle of humankind.

▲ **Woody weeds**

Famine Weed (Parthenium hysterophorus) is a major invader of grassland savanna systems in Africa, Australia, and Asia. It produces greater levels of plant and animal toxins with increased atmospheric carbon dioxide.

Baobab trees

Giant Baobab (*Adansonia granddidieri*) trees growing in the "Avenue of the Baobabs" Morondava, Madagascar. There are eight species of baobabs (genus: *Adansonia*) with one native to mainland Africa, another species native to Australia, and the other six species native to Madagascar. They can live long and grow to remarkable size. An African Baobab (*A. digitata*) in Zimbabwe was carbon-dated to be 2,450 years old when it died in 2011; a baobab named "The Limpopo Baobab" had a circumference 154 ft (47m) and a diameter of 52 ft (15.9 m). This giant tree has now split in two parts.

Along with their striking appearance, the trees have considerable practical utility. The hard-shelled, spherical fruit has a pulpy center with a citrus flavor and is nutritious, so much so that it is exported as a safe food ingredient in the United States and UK. In Africa, it has found uses as a food additive in porridge and drinks in Zimbabwe; boiled and used as a base for the ice-cream-like *gelado de múcua* in Angola. Baobab leaves are edible by humans. In Australia, baobab leaves are used as "emergency fodder" to sustain cattle during droughts. The woody fiber of several species are used to make string and then woven into rope and baskets.

How the savanna works

Savanna vegetation as an object of study has shown a singular tendency to be the graveyard of simple explanations. Even the straightforward task of mapping where on Earth savannas occur is vexed by the many ways one could express the boundaries between the different vegetation types.

Savanna dynamics

Beyond the conceptual difficulties in mapping savannas is the problem of proper stewardship of these environments. Savannas can produce revenue for their owners through tourism or livestock production. However, they are the dominant vegetation type for some of the poorest nations based on economic metrics of per capita income. A conference on savannas held in Harare, Zimbabwe, in 1985, sponsored by the International Union of Biological Sciences, compared South American, African, and Australian savannas and spawned a generation of research. The working group of scientists proposed a complex synthesis of the dominant forces at work in savanna dynamics in the form of a general worldwide model of savanna function. They identified the principal forces operating to dynamically change savanna structure as shown in the diagram opposite.

The web of interactions is remarkably complex and many of these factors can be highly interactive. Different savannas on different continents are more influenced by any one of these factors, and these broad continental differences promote three case studies of change in savannas, explored on the following pages.

Today, the African savannas have the most intact large grazing-mammal fauna on Earth and so are a logical case location for inspecting grazing and herbivory processes. The arrival of humans in Australia some 65,000 or more years ago appears to have been accompanied by a substantial increase in the frequency of wildfires, and so the use of fire as a tool to manage the landscape promotes a case study from the continent. The third case study, of the Cerrado in South America, illustrates the interactions among nutrients and water to form large patterns in complex savannas.

A WEB OF INTERACTIONS

Many processes and their interactions drive savanna structure and pattern. Interactions among the soil and nutrient conditions with the climate set the stage for the possibilities of tree, grass, and shrub cover in a location as well as the dominant species. Herbivores, under the control of predators, selectively graze the vegetation and affect the composition and structure of the savanna. Wildfires and their frequency of occurrence favor grasses and fire-adapted woody plants. This complex concert of interactions allows experienced observers, scientists, and pastoralists to "read" the landscape history of a particular area of savanna.

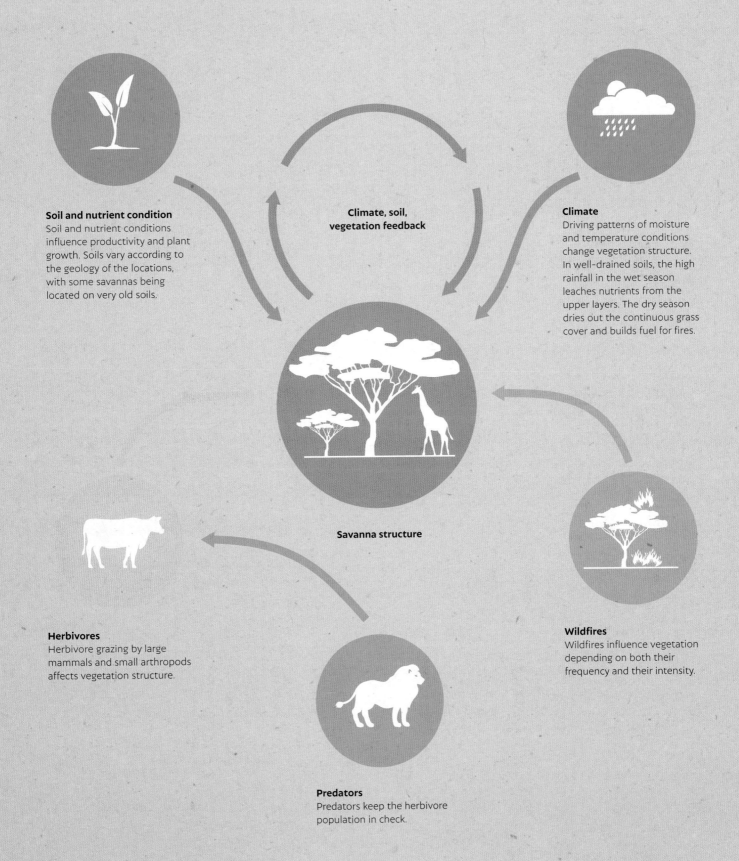

Soil and nutrient condition
Soil and nutrient conditions influence productivity and plant growth. Soils vary according to the geology of the locations, with some savannas being located on very old soils.

Climate, soil, vegetation feedback

Climate
Driving patterns of moisture and temperature conditions change vegetation structure. In well-drained soils, the high rainfall in the wet season leaches nutrients from the upper layers. The dry season dries out the continuous grass cover and builds fuel for fires.

Savanna structure

Herbivores
Herbivore grazing by large mammals and small arthropods affects vegetation structure.

Wildfires
Wildfires influence vegetation depending on both their frequency and their intensity.

Predators
Predators keep the herbivore population in check.

Grazing by large herbivores in African savannas

Predators at the top of a food chain could control the numbers of herbivores, such that the herbivores would not be abundant enough to overgraze the plants. Removal of these predators could therefore permit herbivore overgrazing, and thus one would expect a "healthy" ecosystem to feature predators that keep the herbivore density relatively low. This is referred to as a "trophic cascade" with "top-down" control—the predators control the structure of the ecosystem, and removing them would have a large, system-wide impact.

▶ **Elephants**

African Elephants can be destructive. Their action can push the plant mixture from trees toward grasses in savanna ecosystems.

▼ **Herbivores**

Large herbivores can potentially overgraze a savanna if predators do not keep them in check.

The alternative "bottom-up" control notes works on the premise that although the world may appear to be green with plants, it is not a gigantic tossed salad. The plants defend themselves against herbivory by being inedible, thorny, or poisonous to varying degrees—they therefore control the number of herbivores and hence the food chains. This implies that the pattern of the vegetation could be largely influenced by environmental conditions and that removing the predators would not make much difference.

In African savanna parks and nature reserves, the Lion (*Panthera leo*) is a significant top carnivore. Surveys of populations here demonstrate evidence for top-down control of herbivores by carnivores in some locations but not others. Closer observation reveals that the small- to medium-sized herbivores often appear to be limited by predation by Lions (the top-down case). However, the large herbivores—including the African Elephant (*Loxodonta africana*) and rhinoceroses—are not controlled by predation to any great degree, or only in exceptional circumstances. Elephants can be remarkably destructive animals, destroying forest and shrub cover in savanna ecosystems. They are a major agent responsible for knocking over trees, which potentially increases grasses and hence the frequency of wildfires. Other knock-on effects include increased forage for grass-eating herbivores.

In their 2003 paper, ecologists William Bond and Jon Keeley pointed out that fire can be considered as if it were a gigantic herbivore that selects for particular plant traits and consumes vegetation not eaten by other herbivores. Operating as surface fires in savannas, this "herbivore" often selectively consumes plants in the grass layer but not trees that are taller than 6½–13 ft (2–4 m). Alternatively, tree seedlings could be prevented from becoming established as saplings because surface fires block their emergence above the flame zone of grass fires. All of this implies a capability to manage fires as a method to manage savanna vegetation.

Fire as a management tool in Australia

Currently, savannas worldwide are burned using controlled fires to manage the vegetation toward desired goals. This occurs against a background of fires caused by natural events such as lightning strikes and accidental human-generated fires. The long record of wildfire use by Aboriginal people for at least 45,000 years makes Australia an interesting example for exploring the use of fire as a landscape management tool.

▼ **Wildfire knowledge**
Aboriginal peoples combine traditional knowledge of wildfires and modern bushfire science to manage wildfire.

It appears that traditional anthropogenic fires produced a mosaic of landscape types, with the "tiles" of the mosaic representing tracts of land burned at different times. Aboriginal people intentionally set small fires, and the resultant fire mosaics of burned and regenerating vegetation are more fine-grained. These fires increase local nutrient availability and enhance the short-term productivity of herbaceous plants typical of the early stages of recovering vegetation, a practice often referred to as "fire-stick farming." The fires are of lower intensity, and are often ignited in particular types of vegetation, but they are more frequent than Australia's natural, lightning-caused fires.

Fire hunting

An example involves traditional hunting by the Martu people in the Western Desert of Australia. The Martu sometimes use fires to "clean up" remote regions and to attract Australian Bustards (*Ardeotis australis*), turkey-sized birds that forage in burned areas, but most fires are set by women hunting large monitor lizards called Sand Goannas (*Varanus gouldii*). They set the fires to take advantage of the wind direction and use firebreaks to control the direction of spread. Winter is the fire-hunting season because fires at this time of year are easier to control and more effective for goanna hunting. The Martu women initiate fire hunts by igniting a suitable tract, then they walk behind the fire line and search for signs of fresh goanna burrows. If they find a burrow, they use a specialized digging stick to root the animal from its den.

In their use of fire to hunt goannas and other small game, the Martu women basically reconstruct the landscape ecosystem—their goanna hunting creates a landscape that is more favorable to their activities and that differs from the landscape that would occur without their efforts. Their fires rearrange the vegetation on the land into relatively small patches, creating more biological diversity at the same spatial scales as the foraging ranges of the hunters. The immediate effect of the Martu women's use of fire on their landscape is the creation of greater numbers of animals of the species they hunt. They effectively farm small game by traditional fire management.

The fire hunting or fire farming of the Martu people is echoed in traditional practices among Aboriginal peoples across Australia. Experts from different Aboriginal groups have merged their knowledge from traditional use of fires to become "rangers," a job that involves fusing modern and traditional practices to promote wildlife habitat. At the time of writing, this policy is in abeyance in several locations due to difficulty in obtaining fire insurance for the rangers.

▲ **Sand Goanna**

*Sand Goanna (*Varanus gouldii*) are the targets of fire-stick farming by the Martu people of Western Australia.*

Nutrients and moisture patterns in the Cerrado

The Cerrado is a large region in central Brazil and parts of Paraguay whose name is a Portuguese word translating as "savanna." The Cerrado is distinguished by having a significant proportion of trees with broad evergreen leaves, in contrast with the finer, deciduous leaves of trees growing in other savannas around the world.

Under conditions of frequent fire and lower soil fertility, the resultant vegetation in the Cerrado is called *campo limpo*, a grassland with few or no shrubs (the Portuguese word *campo* refers broadly to a grassland). With decreasing fires and a correlated increasing soil fertility, the vegetation transitions to a mixture of mostly grasses and small shrubs (*campo sujo*), to open shrubland with a few trees (*campo cerrado*), to a closed shrub layer with scattered trees in the overstory (*cerrado sensu stricto*, meaning "Cerrado in the strict sense"). Finally, under conditions with the best soil fertility and the lowest wildfire frequency, one expects to find *cerradão*, a dense, moderately tall forest. (Note here that Cerrado can also be used generally to refer to a mixture of all these different landscape elements over a large area; *cerrado sensu stricto* refers to one specific kind of vegetation in this collective.) As in the case of many savanna classifications, these Cerrado vegetation types are based on species proportions in tree-grass-shrub mixtures and the environmental conditions they indicate (fire frequency, nutrient availability, and so on).

VEGETATION TRANSITIONS IN THE CERRADO

The unique vegetation of the Cerrado—decreasing fire and increasing soil fertility results in a transition from grassland through savanna with scattered trees to dense forest.

GRASSLAND

Campo limpo (grasslands)
Grassland with few or no shrubs or taller woody plants.

SAVANNA FORMATION

Campo sujo
Grassland with scattered shrubs (7–10 ft/2–3 m tall).

 INCREASING FIRES

Influences on tree composition

In 2018, Brazilian Marcelo Leandro Bueno and colleagues conducted a massive survey of the distribution of 3,072 tree species based on 1,165 survey plots across the Cerrado. They analyzed a packet of 27 climate and soil variables at each of the survey plots to identify which were the most important for predicting the distribution of Cerrado tree species. They found that tree composition can be separated into three groups, with the makeup of each group being strongly controlled by the local conditions. The first group comprises forests with fire-adapted vegetation (*cerrado sensu stricto* and *cerradão*), the second group comprises dry forests found in conditions of high fertility soils but low water availability, and the third group comprises forests found in conditions of high soil water availability. This latter group includes both evergreen and semideciduous forests. Overall, the composition of tree species at a given location is controlled by local soil fertility, water availability, and flammability.

Rio de Janeiro

Cerrado

▲ **Cerrado area**
Map of the Cerrado vegetation, which is centered on Brazil.

WOODY SAVANNA

Campo cerrado
An open scrubland with few trees (10–20 ft/3–6 m tall).

Cerrado sensu stricto
A woodland with closed scrub and more scattered trees (16–26 ft/5–8 m tall) than *cerradão*.

Cerradão
A dense forest type (26–50 ft/8–15 m tall) that often has a completely-closed canopy.

INCREASING SOIL FERTILITY

Large-scale studies of savanna change

The demonstration of the importance of local factors as the dominant influences on the community composition across the Cerrado (see pages 254-255) implies a cohesion not always seen in other ecosystems. This then prompts questions around the stability of savanna systems in their response to change. The work of Bueno and his colleagues in examining controlling factors over vast areas of the Cerrado exemplifies the importance of expansive studies to our understanding of what produces pattern in savanna ecosystems.

We know that other ecosystems responding to climate changes since the end of the last ice age, such as temperate deciduous forests across the northern hemisphere, have demonstrated a lack of such community constancy. Different species of trees now found together were separated in the past, and vice versa. Perhaps ecosystems operating within a set of rules in the current climate could have "new" rules in a changed "new" climate, which could produce surprises. This applies across all biomes, including savanna.

Kalahari Transect pattern study

In Bueno et al.'s study of the Cerrado, the collection of well over a thousand survey plots and their associated climate and soil variables allowed complex statistical analysis to identify "rules," the likely controlling variables producing vegetation patterns. Studies on long transects can complement these studies by trying to isolate the "rule changes" in response to a single variable. The Kalahari Transect (KT) is one of a global set of "megatransects" designated by the International Geosphere-Biosphere Programme (IGBP) to explore the continental-scale links between climate, biogeochemistry, and ecosystem structure and function. For the KT, the focal variable is rain—the transect has a sharp precipitation gradient but otherwise is climatically and geographically uniform along its length. It has widely distributed, physically uniform soil (the Kalahari Sands) along a continuous gradient of increasing annual rainfall to the north.

Annual rainfall totals are highly variable, both seasonally and annually, ranging from 40 in (1,000 mm) in the north to less than 8 in (200 mm) in the extreme southwest, and decreasing from east to west and north to south. The rainy season starts in the southern hemisphere summer around October and lasts until April. The rest of the year (in the southern hemisphere winter) is very dry, with little or no rainfall—less than ½ in (10 mm) for the entire dry season. With its relatively constant soil, elevation, rainfall pattern and systematic change in rainfall, the KT resembles a very large natural "experiment."

KALAHARI TRANSECT VEGETATION PATTERNS

The Kalahari Transect in South Africa, Botswana, Namibia, and Zambia. This transect has a strong rainfall gradient (running from the wettest end in Zambia to the driest in South Africa), seasonal climate, but uniform sandy soils. It is a unique transect for the study of heterogeneous vegetation—areas of intensive study are indicated on the map below. Tree, shrub, and grass mixtures form woodlands, savanna, and shrubland. Its biomass patterns indicate complex vegetation responses to moisture.

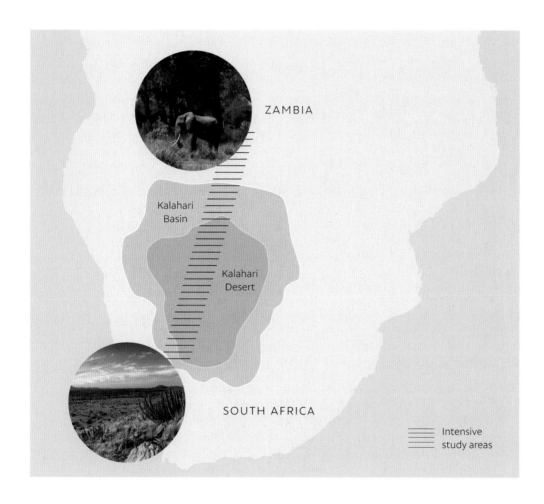

ZAMBIA

Kalahari Basin

Kalahari Desert

SOUTH AFRICA

Intensive study areas

▼ **Kalahari wildlife**
Sociable Weavers (Philetairus socius), below, build shared nests (below left). Note the open woodland with evenly spaced trees.

African savanna patterns

In a 2005 article in *Nature*, Mahesh Sankaran and 30 other savanna ecologists explored the factors that control the woody cover in African savannas. Note that this was a different focus from that of Bueno et al.'s study in the Cerrado (see page 255), which looked at species patterns, not woody cover. The scale of the Sankaran et al. study was also different, covering an area more than six times that of the Cerrado.

Collecting data from 854 locations across Africa, Sankaran and his colleagues found that the area covered by trees at a location seems to be constrained to about 80 percent for areas receiving $20^{1}/_{3}$ in (516 mm) or more of rainfall per year. Combining this information with similar data on average time between fires, herbivore biomass per unit area, percentage of clay in the soil, potential nitrogen available to plants, and the amount of soil phosphorus, they distinguished three savanna categories. Firstly, stable savannas, which receive less than $20^{1}/_{3}$ in (516 mm) of mean annual precipitation. These savannas have climatic rainfall-based limitations on trees that allow grasses to persist. Periodic differences in rainfall might cause the ratio of tree to grass cover to vary, but there would always be a mixture of grasses and trees. Secondly, unstable savannas, which receive more than 31 in (788 mm) of mean annual precipitation. In these areas the trees exclude grasses, so long as disturbances (fire, grazing, browsing, and so on) do not allow the grasses to persist. A relaxation of the intensities of disturbance would result in a transition to forest. Thirdly, a transition between stable and unstable savannas, characterized by $20^{1}/_{3}$-31 in (516–784 mm) of mean annual precipitation. In this transition zone, climate history and disturbance history could have a strong influence over the state of the ecosystem.

The researchers found that mean annual precipitation is a very strong determinant in each of these categories. For cattle grazers or wildlife-viewing eco-tourism operators, the management of unstable savannas under this theory could be difficult. Failures in management could lead to new tree-dominated systems, with an attendant drop in cattle production or a change in habitat for grazing and often charismatic wildlife.

The woody weed problem

Sankaran et al.'s precipitation-based stable, unstable, and transitional savanna categories are changing at the global scale in both tropical and subtropical regions. Woody plants (shrubs and trees) are increasingly encroaching on the former successes of grasses in savanna systems. Less intense, more regularly ignited fires often promote grasses, and they also reduce potential loss of life. These smaller, more frequent, "cooler" fires—such as those used in the traditional Martu practice (see page 253)—are safer for both human and animal inhabitants of the savanna. In addition, better management of the savanna for grazing animals often means management for grasses, be they cattle or wildlife grazers such as Cape Buffalo (*Syncerus caffer*), wildebeest, or White Rhinoceros (*Ceratotherium simum*).

Human effects

Globally, human activities strongly associated with the burning of fossil fuels have raised the concentration of carbon dioxide in the atmosphere, from around 285 parts per million at the start of the Industrial Revolution in the late eighteenth century to 416 parts per million today— and there is little sign of it stopping. One of the possible causes of the rapid increase in land under savannas about 8 million years ago is that a low level of atmospheric carbon dioxide at that time allowed tropical and subtropical C_4 grasses to exercise their advantage over less productive C_3 plants (see page 243). Will the human-generated increase in carbon dioxide that is occurring now lead to a similar effect, but this time in reverse? Certainly, the effects of elevated atmospheric carbon dioxide in increasing the efficiency of water use in woody C_3 plants (more photosynthesis per water evaporated) and in removing one of the advantages of C_4 grasses (higher photosynthesis under lower carbon dioxide levels) both conspire to change savanna patterns. In the future, the current rainfall limits delineating stable and unstable savanna categories can also be expected to change.

▼ **Tree-dominated savanna**
In general, the more rainfall and the less wildfire transition savanna toward greater tree dominance. The giraffe is a uniquely adapted animal for grazing tree canopies.

Patterned landscapes: tiger bush and tree clumps

In Chapter 2, the phenomenon of "fir waves" was introduced—a natural pattern generated by harsh winds in which trees are arranged into gap-replacement-based sequences, forming waves or stripes across the landscape (see pages 72-73). Similar striking patterns are generated by finer-scale processes in savannas.

Tiger stripes

"Tiger bush" is a naturally occurring pattern of alternating stripes of small trees and shrubs with bare ground between, and has been documented in savannas in Australia, Mexico, and elsewhere. The pattern is more difficult to see at ground level, but when viewed from an airplane or satellite it resembles a tiger-skin rug in a Victorian hunting lodge—except on the order of several square miles. The phenomenon occurs at the drier edges of the savanna-climate moisture spectrum (12-25 in/300-650 mm mean annual precipitation), on a long, flat, slightly tilted land surface, and on a soil with a relatively high clay content. The clay makes the soil less permeable, and rain from wet-season showers tends to run off the surface.

Each tiger stripe in the pattern is a naturally generated water-harvesting system. The pores in the bare soil are compacted by rainfall and are filled by clay when the soil dries. Rainwater falling onto the relatively impermeable bare soil flows downslope and into one of the tiger stripes. The presence of vegetation on the

▼ **Over-spaced vegetation**

Here, in the Kalahari, both the grasses and trees are over-dispersed. This means that on average the distances between plants are more even than one would expect at random.

upslope edge of a single stripe increases soil permeability here, allowing more water to be absorbed and the plants to grow. The trees and shrubs at the upslope edge get first chance at the runoff, with water diminishing downslope through the stripe. At the lower edge, the water is so reduced that the trees and other plants here are more likely to die. The area beyond this edge therefore transitions to bare soil, which reinitiates the process of routing runoff to the next downslope stripe.

Clumping in the KT

Tiger bush is perhaps an extreme case of an overall feature of savannas—namely a general tendency for non-random spatial patterns to be apparent in the distribution of trees and grasses.

For example, the savanna trees of the KT have an overall clumped pattern, from the northern, wet end of the transect at Mongu, Zambia, where tree canopies cover 65 percent of the surface, to the southern, dry end at Vastrap, South Africa, with 4 percent tree cover. The implication of this is that, over this distance of 927 miles (1,492 km), the chance of tree-seedling establishment increases with local tree density, and the probability of mortality increases with greater open space in the vicinity of a tree. This pattern could be caused by many processes depending on the location, but water availability seems the likely driver in the Kalahari.

▲ **Tiger bush**

On slightly sloped surfaces, torrential rain can run downslope and is collected by bands of small trees and shrubs to form self-organized stripes of vegetation.

Parkland

*Widely spaced trees
in parkland savanna
in Namibia. Trees in
parklands often show
regular geometries
involving ratios of the
area of ground, rainfall,
and area of tree crowns.*

Savanna parkland

Savanna parkland is characterized by clumps of trees that are relatively spaced on a uniform matrix of grassland. The sizes of the tree clumps can vary, right down to a single tree, but they are often regular at a particular location. The distance between clumps is also locally quite regular but can vary at different locations. The general appearance of the landscape pattern looks too "manicured" to be natural, hence the name parkland—the overall impression is that it has been created by management on some vast estate.

One interesting hypothesis derived from an ecological model of the physiological process of tree clumping asks the question: "Where on the landscape might seedlings grow best?" In dry conditions, the answer might be under a tree, where the shade reduces the high loss of water caused by heat from direct sunlight. This would encourage growth in clumps. If conditions are wet enough, however, it could be better for seedlings to grow in the open, where the high light levels drive more photosynthesis and the high water availability solves the heating problem. The result in this case would be a widely spaced savanna of single trees. This implies that after a reinitiating event such as a super-destructive fire, recovery in savannas with similar climates, soils, and so on could be different if there was a run of either dry years or wet years in the recovery phase.

Termite mounds

Another source of tree clumping in savanna ecosystems in the tropics and the subtopics arises from the presence of termites, which are a major faunal component of the biome. Astonishingly, termites represent about 13.6 percent of the mass of all terrestrial animals—to give this context, livestock animals globally represent about 21.7 percent of the terrestrial animal biomass and humans about 16.3 percent. Termites are found on every continent aside from Antarctica. They live colonially in termite mounds, with some living colonies dating back more than 1,000 years. Termites in savanna ecosystems aerate the soils and speed up decomposition, making plant nutrients more available for plant growth.

Some species of termite can build exceptionally large mounds, which concentrate nutrients, elevate the soils, and serve as islands of fertility across the savanna surface. Several mammalian herbivores selectively graze the resultant nutrient-rich forage, including the Sable Antelope (*Hippotragus niger*), which inhabits wooded savanna in East and southern Africa. The tall termite mounds are also used as viewing platforms for predators surveying the landscape for prey.

▼ **Islands of fertility**
Termite mounds, here from Litchfield, Queensland, Australia, have high concentrations of plant nutrients remaining from termite gut-symbiotic protozoa digesting the cellulose in plant tissue brought into the mounds.

Humans as agents of change

Humans have been a major agent in maintaining and altering savanna systems. We did not cause the explosion of savannas on Earth—that was 8 million years ago, well before our species walked onto the scene. However, we have been active in deploying wildfire in savannas for millennia.

Sometime in the prehistory of humans, we became adept at transforming and maintaining savannas through the use of fire—as seen among the Martu people in Western Australia (see page 253). However, savannas were burning long before we tamed fire, as seen in the presence of charcoal in marine sediments dating back millions of years. Indeed, there was a major increase of charcoal in marine sediments about 8 million years ago, when C_3 trees and C_4 savannas dramatically increased worldwide. This promotes the informed speculation for the role of wildfires in allowing C_4 grasses to gain ground against trees and "create" the savanna biome.

A problem in confirming the human role as agents of change in savannas lies in the fact that savannas are so dynamic it is hard to isolate any single cause. For this reason, the few experimental and long-transect studies that are undertaken in savannas are invaluable. Differences in fire frequencies and intensities, the soil, the weather record, the climate, and so on can all produce changes in the species composition and productivity of savannas—findings that likely would sound familiar to the Martu.

▶ **Grazing cattle**

Grazing Boran, a breed of African Zebu. Cattle and grazing husbandry is associated with the spread of Bantu speakers across Africa between 5,000 and 1,500 years ago.

In the simplest sense, savannas are grasslands or mixtures of trees and grasses occupying areas that might otherwise be forests in the absence of fires. Human actions on this tension between grasses and trees can have a surprisingly dramatic effect. This is consistent with a large body of theory and field observations, which indicate that the spectrum of possible mixtures of grasses and trees can have multiple stable states. For example, a location with grasses might have wildfires that block tree-seedling regeneration. The grass provides fuel for frequent wildfires, and the burn-and-repeat cycle—in which more fires produce more grasses, which in turn produce more fires—produces stable state 1. A change such as a run of years without fires can cause trees to break into the cycle, establish seedlings, and produce a forest with fewer fires. This different rhythm of fires might allow a cycle with more forest, leading to less grass, leading to fewer fires, leading to more trees to establish as stable state 2. If the landscape is managed to be in one stable state but an error is made, then it may transform to the other stable state. And it may be very difficult to reverse this process. One common comment from savanna land managers is that "northern hemisphere" management methods do not always work in the biome. In part, this may be because of the relative irreversibility of management errors in savannas, along with the fiscal restraints of repairing such mismanagement. Savannas are often bounded by dry woodlands under wet conditions, and shrubland and deserts under dry conditions. Multiple stable states across the entire gradient seem to be possible due to an array of factors.

▲ **Herding**

A Maasai girl herding goats in the Ngorongoro National Park, Tanzania. "Ngorongoro" in Maasai means "cowbells" and is a onomatopoetic to the sound of cowbells.

HUMAN EFFECTS ON SAVANNAS

Human actions affect the processes and their interactions that
drive savanna structure and pattern.

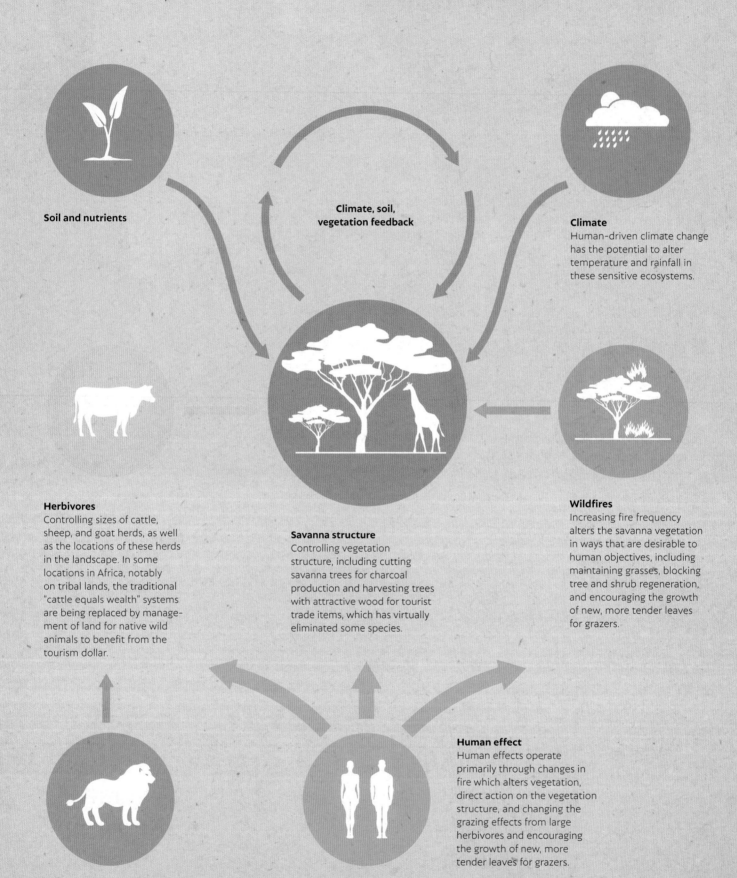

Soil and nutrients

**Climate, soil,
vegetation feedback**

Climate
Human-driven climate change
has the potential to alter
temperature and rainfall in
these sensitive ecosystems.

Herbivores
Controlling sizes of cattle,
sheep, and goat herds, as well
as the locations of these herds
in the landscape. In some
locations in Africa, notably
on tribal lands, the traditional
"cattle equals wealth" systems
are being replaced by management of land for native wild
animals to benefit from the
tourism dollar.

Savanna structure
Controlling vegetation
structure, including cutting
savanna trees for charcoal
production and harvesting trees
with attractive wood for tourist
trade items, which has virtually
eliminated some species.

Wildfires
Increasing fire frequency
alters the savanna vegetation
in ways that are desirable to
human objectives, including
maintaining grasses, blocking
tree and shrub regeneration,
and encouraging the growth
of new, more tender leaves
for grazers.

Predators

Human effect
Human effects operate
primarily through changes in
fire which alters vegetation,
direct action on the vegetation
structure, and changing the
grazing effects from large
herbivores and encouraging
the growth of new, more
tender leaves for grazers.

Current challenges

What are the current challenges in the management of savannas? This chapter began with a diagram of the major interacting components of a savanna ecosystem without humans (see page 243). The diagram left is this same but with the addition of human actions. Human effects are generally larger relative to other influencing factors. In fact, this "new" ecosystem is driven by human action to such an extent that it is effectively completely different.

Overlying all of these actions are anthropogenic changes at large scales, ranging from extractive mining operations, which can have very destructive effects on savanna systems, to global climate change, which has the potential to alter temperature and rainfall in these sensitive ecosystems.

▼ **Savanna sunset**
The will and knowledge to sustainably manage savannas in the face of increasing human use is an existential challenge, both for its inhabitants and the planet as a whole. We must not let the sun set on the savannas.

9

Temperate Forests

What and where are the Earth's temperate forests?

Temperate climates are distinguished from tropical ones by the occurrence of seasonal frost, but winters are not as long or as severe as in boreal climates. Temperate forests comprise a tremendous variety of ecosystems within this climate zone, from dense, tall forests in humid areas to the open woodlands and savannas in drier ones, and from broad-leaved deciduous forests to evergreen forests dominated by broad-leaved trees or needle-leaved trees, as well as mixed evergreen-deciduous forests.

TEMPERATE FORESTS WORLDWIDE

Temperate forests cover large areas in the northern hemisphere in areas of abundant growing season moisture. They are more restricted in the southern hemisphere because there is less land in temperate latitudes and climates are buffered by the great extent of southern hemisphere oceans.

● Temperate broad-leaf and mixed

● Temperate coniferous

This variation in structure and leaf type is correlated with environmental conditions. Starting with the temperate deciduous forest (with a growing season lasting about 4-9 months and abundant summer rainfall), the principal environmental gradients are: (1) in areas with ample summer rainfall, broad-leaved evergreen trees increase toward the equator as the length and severity of winter decreases; (2) as summer rainfall decreases, closed forests yield to open woodlands and savannas (fire and grazing animals are also important in the precise position of this transition); and (3) in warm areas with low rainfall and winter rather than summer rain, temperate forest transitions to sclerophyllous woodlands and shrublands (see pages 148-153).

Temperate coniferous forests

The description above focuses on temperate deciduous forest, the most spatially extensive of the temperate forest biomes. By contrast, the distribution of temperate conifer forests defies easy generalization. Within the deciduous forest, conifers are found across gradients from wet to dry sites and from warm to cold environments (see page 272). One common denominator of these sites is that they tend to have acidic and nutrient-poor soils and are often fire-prone; however, there are also conifers that are characteristic of soils with higher pH, such as some species of juniper and White Cedar (*Thuja occidentalis*). Temperate coniferous forests are also found outside the deciduous forest biome, including the complex and diverse array of conifer forests across the mountain ranges of western North America (see pages 292–295), along gradients from semiarid woodlands at low elevations to cold, wet subalpine forests at high elevations. Where rainfall is extreme in the Pacific Northwest of North America, temperate coniferous rain forests occur (see pages 292–295).

▲ **Deciduous temperate forest**

Temperate deciduous trees are leaf-bare in winter, produce a rapid flush of new leaves in the spring, and shed those leaves in the fall.

Topographic patterns

Topography creates environmental gradients and spatial heterogeneity that are ubiquitous in temperate forests. Rainfall and cloud cover increase and temperature decreases with elevation. Southern slopes (this and following references refer to the northern hemisphere—for the southern hemisphere, substitute "north" for "south") have the maximum solar radiation and northern slopes the minimum. Southwest slopes, which face the sun during the warmest parts of the day, are the warmest and northeast slopes are the coolest. In addition to the effect of elevation itself, moisture flows from convex upper slopes and ridges to concave valleys, creating strong moisture gradients. These topographic patterns also result in different kinds of natural disturbances, from dry, warm fire-prone areas, to valleys prone to flood scour, to flood-inundated low areas, and to steep, high-elevation slopes prone to debris avalanche (downslope sliding of materials that lie above bedrock in contrast to snow avalanches or avalanches that include the erosion of bedrock itself). The net result from all of these factors is that temperate forests are not one homogeneous entity, but vary in composition and structure at local to regional scales.

Great Smoky Mountains

The Great Smoky Mountains are renowned for their biological diversity. Its forest ecosystems change along complex topographic gradients that influence patterns of temperature, precipitation, and soil moisture supply.

The American plant ecologist Robert Whittaker (1920-1980) popularized a way of describing the distribution of the vegetation on the two strongest topographic gradients. These "Whittaker diagrams" show elevation on the y-axis and site moisture supply on the x-axis. Whittaker diagrams have been published for a variety of forests, including the Great Smoky Mountains of North Carolina and Tennessee, where Whittaker did his doctoral work, and the Rocky Mountains, following research by Whittaker's student Robert Peet (see page 292). The diagrams provide a useful way to conceptualize forest pattern, but they omit variation in geology, soils, and disturbance—although sometimes these can, themselves, be correlated with elevation and site moisture supply. In this chapter, we focus on two northern hemisphere landscapes: temperate deciduous forests and the diverse conifer forests of western North America.

Southern hemisphere temperate forests

In the southern hemisphere, the greater sea to land ratio means that winters are milder and summers cooler than in the northern hemisphere, with the result that the temperate forests here are largely broad-leaved evergreen forests, although there are also deciduous forests. Temperate rain forests are found on the western coastlines of the southern hemisphere landmasses (see pages 168–169). The evolutionary separation of the southern hemisphere continents (once united as the Gondwana continental complex) from the northern ones is evident in the unique genera here, principally the dominant trees in the genus *Nothofagus* (both evergreen and deciduous) and unique gymnosperm genera in the families Podocarpaceae and Araucariaceae.

▲ **Argentina**

A magical forest in Tierra del Fuego National Park, Beagle Channel, Patagonia, Argentina.

Nothofagus forest

The southern beeches (genus *Nothofagus*) comprise approximately 40 species with a tremendous diversity of leaf forms, including evergreen and deciduous species, a range of leaf sizes, and smooth-edged and toothed leaf margins. Once thought to be in the same family as the northern beeches (*Fagus*) so prominent in temperate North America and Eurasia, they are now placed in a separate, though related, group, the Nothofagaceae. They are now found exclusively in the southern hemisphere, including New Zealand, Australasia, and South America (*Nothofagus* in Los Glaciares National Park, Argentina, pictured here). Their current distribution mainly reflects their evolutionary history: this group evolved when the southern hemisphere continents were part of one landmass, Gondwana, and subsequently became widely separated because of continental drift. However, there is recent evidence in some lineages of long-distance dispersal within a few subregions of their overall range. The Botanic Gardens Conservation International has recently estimated that 30 percent of the *Nothofagus* species are threatened with extinction.

The temperate deciduous forest

Temperate deciduous forests are found in three great centers: east Asia, northern Europe, and eastern North America. These widely separated areas have climates with key similarities: warm summers, cold winters, and precipitation during the growing season. That summer rain is more important than winter rain can be seen in the contrast between otherwise similar deciduous forests in eastern North America and east Asia: both have rain in the growing season, but east Asia's is monsoonal and its winter precipitation is lower.

The demise of the American Chestnut

Chestnut blight, the fungus *Cryphonectria parasitica*, has eliminated the American Chestnut (*Castanea dentata*)—fruits pictured below—as a forest dominant over eastern North America. The story of the functional extinction of this tree is well known, caused by the accidental introduction of the fungus to North America from east Asia in the early twentieth century. At present, both breeding and molecular techniques are being used in an attempt to bring back this dominant and ecologically important species. The landscape that saw the demise of the American Chestnut is now witnessing further waves of mortality, caused by the balsam woolly adelgid (*Adelges piceae*), which attacks firs; the hemlock woolly adelgid (*Adelges tsugae*), which attacks hemlocks and spruces; the emerald ash borer (*Agrilus planipennis*), which feeds on ash trees; and other invasive insect pests.

Shared genera

The three centers of temperate deciduous forest harbor descendants of a once more widespread ecosystem that dates to the Tertiary period, some 66 million years ago. Because modern forests share this common descent, the current temperate deciduous centers share many genera of trees, including *Acer* (maples), *Quercus* (oaks), *Fagus* (beeches), *Castanea* (chestnuts), *Betula* (birches), *Fraxinus* (ashes), and *Ulmus* (elms). The centers have been isolated long enough that each continent has its own set of species in these genera, but many of the shared genera show an amazing niche conservatism considering the millions of years they existed in isolation. They occupy similar environments in each of the three centers and produce similar geographic gradients of composition, such as an increase in beech and maple in cooler environments, and an increase in oaks in warmer and drier ones.

Shared climates and genera among the three deciduous centers has had one important environmental consequence: the spread of forest pests and diseases through human activities, which can prove devastating in a new setting. Examples from temperate deciduous forests are many, including the well-known case of chestnut blight (see box), which originated in China and greatly affected chestnut trees in Europe and North America.

◀ **Japanese maple**

Temperate deciduous centers (east Asia, northern Europe, and eastern North America) share many tree genera—maples occur in all three.

Bald Cypress

Bald cypress (Taxodium distichum) are deciduous conifers that dominate the bottomland swamps of southeastern North America. The swollen trunk bases and the vertical root growth ("cypress knees") are distinctive. It has been speculated that the cypress knees function for mechanical support, root aeration, carbon storage, and nutrient cycling, but their function has not yet been definitively proven.

Transitions

Broad-leaved evergreen species increase as you move southward in all three deciduous forest centers, but this is especially marked in Southeast Asia, where broad-leaved evergreen forests (called laurophyllous forests; see pages 154–155) occupy a broad area and form a transition to subtropical forests. In North America and Europe, there are geographic circumstances that make the transition to the subtropics less obvious. In eastern North America, the deciduous forest confronts a wide coastal plain, with sandy, nutrient-poor soils originally dominated by fire-dependent longleaf pine savannas and mixed pine–hardwood forests, and to the south, the Gulf of Mexico. Mixed forests of deciduous trees and broad-leaved evergreens (for instance, beech–magnolia on more nutrient-rich soils and live oak maritime forests) occur but don't form a continuous vegetation zone. In Europe, the southern transition is marked by pine and oak woodlands, a climatic shift to winter rainfall and landscapes dominated by sclerophyllous forests and shrublands, and the Mediterranean Sea.

Westward in North America and Asia and eastward in Europe, increasing continentality and decreasing rainfall result in a shift to open woodlands, savannas, and, ultimately, mid-continent grasslands, with grazing animals and fire setting the precise position of the forest–grassland boundary. Continental aridity, familiar from the prairies and Great Plains of North America and steppes of Eurasia, sweeps almost to the coast of China at the latitude of Beijing and separates the moist deciduous forest there into northern and southern parts.

Conifers

Everywhere within the deciduous forest, needle-leaved coniferous trees can be found in a wide variety of environments and can sometimes dominate. These include cooler, more northern, and higher-elevation sites (transition to boreal and subalpine forest); warmer, drier, and more fire-prone sites (mid-elevation ridges with pine forests and the pine-oak forests of the European transition to Mediterranean climate); sandy, acid, and nutrient-poor sites (island-like glacial sands, called pine barrens in North America); wetlands (bogs and swamps throughout); and post-disturbance successional sites. Bald Cypress (*Taxodium distichum*), a deciduous conifer, dominates backwater swamps on the coastal plain of southeastern North America. It harbors the oldest trees in eastern North America, some more than 2,500 years in age. The coastal plain here is also home to unique and fire-dependent longleaf pine (*Pinus palustris*) forests, which are a biodiversity hotspot.

▼ **Longleaf pine**

The coastal plain of southeastern North America was once dominated by extensive forests of longleaf. Fires maintained an open park-like structure known as a savanna. This ecosystem is an important biodiversity hotspot.

Changing with the seasons

The deciduousness of leaves is not a passive response to unfavorable seasons, but rather an evolved strategy. Actively directed by the trees themselves, it requires the detecting and use of environmental cues to predict the seasonal rhythm of favorable and unfavorable conditions. There is partial reabsorption of nutrients from the leaves prior to leaf-fall and the formation of a corky layer (the abscission layer) that both seals the stem at the base of the leaf and weakens the leaf's physical connection to the stem, ultimately producing leaf-fall.

▶ **Fall forest**
A patchwork of autumn colors in the deciduous forests of Ontario, Canada.

Fall color

While senescing (aging) leaves can display color in any environments (for example, the swaths of yellow color in Quaking Aspen (*Populus tremuloides*) clones in the boreal forest), the temperate deciduous forest is renowned for the brightness and diversity of its color display. Where species diversity is high, the colors can span the spectrum, from pale yellow to orange to lighter and darker reds to purples. Like deciduousness itself, fall color is not a passive response to the onset of winter, but an active, self-directed process. We see leaves as green because the chlorophylls reflect much of the light in green wavelengths. But there are two other important classes of leaf pigment and these are the ones involved in the coloring of leaves in the fall.

The first class, comprising carotenoids and xanthophylls, are generally yellow. These pigments are present from the spring expansion of new leaves but are masked until fall by the green-reflecting chlorophylls. Chlorophyll is continually breaking down and being regenerated by the leaf. In the fall, the pace of chlorophyll regeneration lags behind its degradation and the already present yellows are revealed.

▶ **Fall leaves**
Tree species vary in the color spectrums they produce in the fall. Yellow pigments are present in most species from the first, though masked by the green pigments until the fall. Reds, which not all species produce, develop quickly in the fall when sugars become trapped in the aging leaf.

The second class of pigments are the anthocyanins, which produce many shades of red and purple. These pigments are produced in the fall as a byproduct of photosynthesis. As the nights grow colder, some of the photosynthetically produced sugars are transferred to cell vacuoles and transformed to anthocyanins. In individual leaves, this happens relatively quickly—over the course of even a few hours to a few days.

From this, we can see why the yellows in fall tend to be more constant from year to year: they are hard-wired into the cell photosynthetic machinery from the start. In contrast, the reds are dependent on photosynthetic generation of sugar, so there is more annual variation due to environmental variability. Anthocyanins can vary from year to year, vary over the fall season, vary from the sun-exposed to shaded leaves, and vary from wetter to drier habitats.

Genes set the stage for color

Not all tree species produce vivid colors and some don't produce much color at all, so there must also be a genetic basis to color variation. Some species, such as tuliptrees (*Liriodendron*), are always yellow in the fall. Others are known for their deep reds (including tupelos or blackgums, *Nyssa*), although in the shade where sugar production is lower, they can be predominantly yellow. Some species manage to create a blend of yellows and reds, and so produce orange—sugar maple (*Acer saccharum*) is one example. Others, such as sweetgum (*Liquidambar*), can produce shades from pale yellow to dark maroon on a single tree. Do fall colors have an evolutionary purpose? The jury is still out, but some scientists have proposed that these pigments act like a sunscreen, helping protect the metabolic cell processes from solar damage as the leaf goes through senescence to leaf-fall.

▲ **Colorful forest**
The contrast of dark green conifers and the yellow, oranges, and reds of deciduous trees illuminates this landscape.

▲ Early bloomers

Wood Anemones emerge in the spring and then die back in early summer.

▶ Ramps

Ramps leaf out in early spring and produce flowers in the early summer.

Spring ephemerals and backwards plants

Deciduousness is linked to a second, equally striking evolutionary story in temperate deciduous forests: in the canopy, it sets off a seasonal rhythm in the wildflowers of the forest floor below. When the trees are leafless, light reaches the ground. As temperatures warm in spring, this light presents an opportunity. While the risk of frost is still present, damage is more likely higher in the tree canopy than on the forest floor, which is warmed by the sun during the day and has its temperatures buffered by the mass of moist soil. Therefore, forest-floor plants can leaf-out in the understory before the canopy trees above do so. This early greening requires resources other than just light and is, therefore, most pronounced in soils that are moist and rich in nutrients.

The true "spring ephemerals" have the most extreme strategy. These wildflowers spend their entire above-ground life cycle in the 4-6 weeks of maximum sunlight in early spring and, thereafter, disappear—despite the fact that a long, warm, wet summer is ahead. In a few cases, such as North American ramps (a wild onion, *Allium tricoccum*), the leafing and flowering are separated in time. Ramps produce a flush of short-lived leaves (which are prized by foragers for soups and salads) in spring, but then flower a month or two later with no leaves at all.

The "backwards plants" take this a step further. The orchids *Tipularia* and *Aplectrum* of North American and Asian deciduous forests produce leaves in the fall and then lose them in the spring during canopy leaf-out, a seasonal pattern that is backwards to that of the trees above. These two orchids, like ramps, then flower on leafless stalks in the weeks following leaf disappearance. Perhaps these species flower later in the season to take advantage of a more diverse and dependable pool of insect pollinators, compared to the insect fauna of spring. Not all deciduous forest wildflowers are ephemerals or backwards plants; other species emerge and flower in spring and then persist into the shady conditions of the deciduous forest summer.

▲ **Backwards**
The leaves of the Crane-fly Orchid emerge in the fall and senesce in the spring.

The study of nature's calendar

The seasonal alternations of summer and winter, and periods of wet and dry conditions, are prominent in the temperate zone. These seasonal patterns define the growing season and so are tied to ecosystem energy flow and carbon sequestration. Understanding seasonality is also important ecologically because particular biological interactions, whether they be antagonistic (such as caterpillars emerging after leaf-out) or cooperative (such as pollinators being available at flowering time), depend on the match between the responses of different species.

▼ **Early spring flowers**

In the early spring of deciduous forests, the ground warms before the overstory forest has leafed out, creating higher levels of light on the forest floor before shady summer conditions prevail. If moisture and nutrients are sufficient, the result is spectacular displays of spring wildflowers.

Nature's calendar

Seasonal responses are also dramatic examples of species adaptation. For instance, organisms ranging from trees to migrating birds have evolved to collect information, assess environmental cues, and predict, as a de facto risk assessment, when it is time to respond. Some cues, such as the length of daylight or, for many migrating animals, the magnetic field, are fixed by latitude and, in case of photoperiod, the calendar date and geographic patterns are precisely the same from year to year. Other cues, especially weather patterns, provide important information but are variable from year to year.

The study of the timing of biological events is formally called phenology, but it can also be thought of as the study of nature's calendar. In temperate forests, flowering, the return of migratory birds, the emergence of insects and hibernating animals, the bud-break that leads to a new flush of leaves, and the coloring and fall of leaves are all examples of biological events that are the subjects of phenological studies.

Climate change

Climate change has now introduced an immediacy to these studies. Are warming climates changing the relationship of temperature and precipitation timing to the fixed signals of day length? How will species respond? Do they have enough genetic or phenotypic variation to adjust in place? Will they have to migrate to keep up with the environments to which their phenologies are matched? Will interacting species find themselves mismatched in phenological timing, thereby resulting in flowers that aren't pollinated or reproductive failure in birds if their insect prey are not available when eggs hatch? What are the best climatic predictors of phenological responses?

Ecologists are looking for ways to answer these questions. Data fall into three categories: the records of observers and naturalists (these include written records, dated photographs, and museum specimens), the establishment of phenology networks tying current observations to weather data, and remote sensing of ecosystems from satellites and high-elevation aircraft.

Research is beginning to show how phenology is changing. One example from the temperate deciduous forest was made possible because the American naturalist Henry David Thoreau (1817-1862) carefully recorded seasonal observations in and around his home town of Concord in Massachusetts. In 2012, plant ecologist Richard Primack and his colleagues showed that spring blooming dates for 43 species observed in the 1850s by Thoreau were earlier in 2004-2010 and that, for 2010, the warmest year in their observations, it was three weeks earlier than in Thoreau's time. Thoreau also recorded the date of "ice-out" (the breaking up of pond ice) at his beloved Walden Pond over the years 1846-1860. Volunteers in Concord have recorded ice-out dates in recent decades and have found that, as of 2009, it was occurring two weeks earlier than recorded by Thoreau.

▼ **Spring awakening**
Seasonal events mark the calendar for animal species, including the emergence of insects and the end of the hibernating period for mammals.

Diversity in northern hemisphere temperate deciduous forests

The European voyages of exploration from the sixteenth to nineteenth centuries generated thousands of botanical and zoological specimens. In the 1700s, the Swedish botanist Carl Linnaeus (1707-1778), the father of modern taxonomy, noticed something odd—namely, the striking similarity of plants arriving from eastern North America to those from the Far East.

DISJUNCT GENERA

Five northern hemisphere centers harbor the genera derived from a much more widely distributed flora. From left to right these are the Pacific Northwest, eastern North America, Europe, the Middle East, and east Asia—some genera, such as *Acer*, are found in all centers.

	Temperate forest
	Tsuga (Hemlock)
	Acer (Maple)
	Hamamelis (Witch Hazel)
	Fagus (Beech)
	Liriodendron (Tuliptree)

Gray's puzzle

With time, this remarkable pattern was further documented, and today we recognize 85 genera of higher plants—among them *Magnolia, Liriodendron, Sassafras, Nyssa, Carya* (hickories), *Catalpa, Cladrastis* (yellowwood), *Wisteria, Pachysandra, and Halesia* (silverbell)—that are found as wild plants only in east Asia and eastern North America, half a world apart with no occurrences in between. When a taxon is found in widely separated areas, it is said to be disjunct. In the mid-1800s, the great Harvard botanist Asa Gray (1810-1888) was so intrigued with this America-Asia disjunction that it became known as Gray's puzzle.

However, that wasn't all. In almost all cases, the disjunct genera had more species in east Asia than in eastern North America. The east Asian forests were also richer in total species diversity than those of eastern North America, which in turn were

richer in species than European forests when places with similar temperature environments were compared. To take an example, *Acer* includes more than 50 species in Asia, ten species in eastern North America, and three species in northern Europe. Only a few genera reach a high point of diversity outside east Asia. For instance, the temperate zone in eastern North America has 13 species of hickory, while east Asia has only a few species and Europe none. Temperate deciduous forests also have many more oak species in North America (more then 40), with fewer in Europe and Asia.

The diversity anomaly

When places have similar environments but different diversities, they are said to have a diversity anomaly (to read about this in mangroves, see pages 172-173). But what accounts for the temperate forest diversity anomaly? The answers fall into two categories.

The energy-diversity theory states that the number of species in an area is correlated with energy flow, this flow usually being represented by net primary productivity or by a surrogate that is correlated with productivity, such as potential evapotranspiration. The good news for the energy-diversity theory is that east Asia, eastern North America, and Europe, considered alone, all have marked declines in diversity from warmer, more productive habitats to cooler, less productive ones in the transition to boreal forests. When we compare these gradients among the continents, however, we see striking differences. The three areas have similar diversities at high latitudes, but as we move south, the continents increasingly diverge so that, in the heart of the deciduous forest, east Asia is richer in species than eastern North America, which is, in turn, richer in species than northern Europe. To be fair to the energy-diversity theory, the problem includes a scale dependence: at small scales, the three areas are more similar in diversities (to exaggerate, at the scale of a single tree, all three areas can have one and only one tree species!), but as we move to larger and larger scales (for example, at a scale of 40 by 40 miles/100 by 100 km), the three deciduous forest centers are clearly ranked east Asia>eastern North America>northern Europe.

▲ **Hickory**
While most genera of the temperate forest reach a high point in diversity in east Asia, Hickory (Carya) *is one of the few that reaches its high point in eastern North America.*

Historical biogeography

In contrast to the energy-diversity theory, a second category of explanation for diversity anomalies is that of historical biogeography. This is the idea that diversity is specifically dependent on the history of evolution and the geographic template on which evolution has occurred, in addition to any effect of contemporary energy flow.

The story of the temperate deciduous forest diversity anomaly starts some 60 million years ago. Warm and wet climates at the time, especially in the far north, meant that temperate species were located farther north and there was genetic and species exchange across the supercontinent of Laurasia, in what is now the North Atlantic Ocean. The fossil record confirms this: genera that are now limited to eastern North American and east Asia (for example, *Magnolia, Nyssa, Halesia*) were found from Alaska to Europe until the Pleistocene Ice Ages. Intriguingly, some genera now confined to Asia were also found across the north temperate zone. *Ginkgo* and *Metasequoia* (dawn redwood), for instance, are classic examples—they are called "living fossils." Formerly widely distributed but now with a very limited range in China, Ginkgo (*Ginkgo biloba*) dates back to the Jurassic around 170 million years ago and, thus, dinosaur times. Metasequoia was known only from the fossil record before the species *M. glyptostroboides* was documented in the wild for the first time in a remote valley in China in 1943.

▼ Living fossils

Dawn Redwood (Metasequoia glyptostroboides) is called a living fossil because it was known from the fossil record before it was found, in 1943, as a living tree in a remote area of China.

As the continents drifted toward their current locations and the North Atlantic Ocean appeared and then widened, climates cooled and the interiors of continents became dry. Deciduous forest species moved southward to keep up with their optimal temperature regimes. They also required areas with summer rainfall, and thus moved to the eastern sides of North America and Asia and the western side of Europe. And so the picture comes into focus: there was once a more widespread temperate flora that became isolated in east Asia, eastern North America, and northern Europe because of continental drift and changing climates.

The Tertiary period ended with the beginning of the Pleistocene Ice Ages some 2 million years ago. Each advance of ice caused a fourfold expansion and contraction of temperate forest. Ice age extinctions were greatest

FOSSIL RECORDS OF MAGNOLIA

Many genera now restricted to North America and Asia, for example, Magnolia (fossil fruit pictured below right) were once known from Europe, as shown by the fossil record.

in Europe, presumably because east-west mountain ranges and the Mediterranean stand in the way of southward escape routes for the temperate flora. Ice age extinctions were intermediate in North America because mountains extended in a generally northeast-southwest direction rather than east-west. Extinction was lowest in east Asia because the ice sheets did not penetrate as far south here compared to the other temperate forest centers, and, additionally, because forest habitat extends continuously from temperate to subtropical and tropical latitudes. In summary, the higher the Pleistocene extinction rate for formerly widespread genera, the lower the current diversity of the three centers of the temperate deciduous forest.

As it turned out, extinction rates aren't the whole story. Molecular evidence, available only in the last decade, now shows that speciation rates have been higher in east Asia. One need only glance at a topographic map to see that tall mountains here extend over wide ranges of longitude and latitude, creating environmental heterogeneity and likely interrupting gene flow that would otherwise counteract speciation. Because mountains have multiple habitats over short distances, they may function to both lower extinction rates (adjusting to changing environments does not require as much spatial movement) and increase speciation rates.

Two hundred and fifty years after Linnaeus and 150 years after Gray, we can report that Gray's puzzle has been solved! Energy flow is important, but today's patterns were shaped by historical and geographical evolutionary patterns.

Temperate conifer forests in western North America

Western North America has an astounding 80 species of conifer in 16 genera, including 25 species of pine, some of the world's tallest trees (redwoods; Douglas firs, *Pseudotsuga*), and some of the most massive and oldest trees (redwoods; Giant Sequoia, *Sequoiadendron giganteum*). This diversity reflects the great areal extent and environmental variety of the western mountain ranges, including the Rocky Mountains, the Sierra Nevada, the Klamath Mountains, and the Cascades.

The Rockies themselves span 55 degrees of latitude, from Mexico to Canada, with 62 peaks that surpass 13,000 ft (4,000 m) in height. In the Pacific Northwest, oceanic air masses bring in more than 150 in (4 m) of annual rainfall, producing temperate rain forests (see pages 166-169). This is ten times the annual rainfall of semiarid piñon pine-juniper woodlands at low elevation in the central Rockies. Western coniferous landscapes also have broad-leaved deciduous trees—including maples, alders, birches, oaks, and mountain ashes—but only a few forest types are dominated by deciduous trees, such as cottonwoods and willows in lower-elevation riverside forests and aspen trees in the early successional stages after disturbance.

Elevation patterns

Sorting out the pattern of western coniferous forests begins with elevation. From low to high elevations, temperature and evaporation decrease and clouds, precipitation, snowfall, wind, and solar radiation increase. In Rocky Mountains National Park, temperatures decrease about 5.4 °F per 1,000 ft (9.8 °C per 1,000 m) of elevation rise and precipitation doubles from the lowest to highest elevations. Reflecting these environmental gradients, a typical slope in the central Rockies has five bands of forest: piñon pine-juniper woodlands at the lowest elevations; Ponderosa Pine (*Pinus ponderosa*) woodlands and Douglas Fir (*Pseudotsuga menziesii*) forests at middle elevations; and Lodgepole Pine forests (*Pinus contorta*) and subalpine spruce-fir forests (the latter related to the boreal forest in composition and structure) at the highest elevations. For the mountains that reach a sufficient height as a function of latitude, subalpine forests yield to alpine meadows. The critical elevation for treeline (see pages 156-161) declines from south to north, from about 11,500 ft (3,500 m) at 35°N to 6,500 ft (2,000 m) at 50°N.

▶ **Slope patterns**
*As one ascends the Rocky Mountains, temperature falls and precipitation increases, and the hiker encounters an ever-changing forest. Three elevational bands are shown here: the lowest elevations are dominated by a short-stature and open forest of piñon pine and juniper, the middle elevations are dominated by Ponderosa Pine (*Pinus ponderosa*) and Douglas Fir (*Pseudotsuga menziesii*), and the high elevations by subalpine spruce and fir forest.*

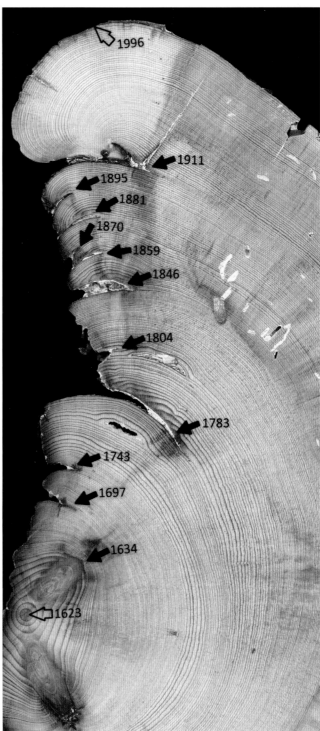

▛ **Adaptation**

Thick bark, shown here for Ponderosa Pine (Pinus ponderosa), reduces the temperatures experienced by the living inner tissues, thus protecting the tree.

▲ **Fire scars**

Fire scars on a Ponderosa Pine (Pinus ponderosa) show that 11 fires occurred from 1693 to 1996, an average of one fire every 27.5 years.

Fire in western coniferous forests

Elevation and topography provide the environmental setting for the diversity of western coniferous forests, but these forests are in the front-page newspaper headlines for another reason: fire. Fire has been an ecological and evolutionary force in these mountains for thousands of years, as is dramatically shown by species adaptations such as thick bark (which insulates the living inner bark from extreme fire temperatures), the serotinous cones of some species (which open only after exposure to the heat of a fire), and seeds that germinate and survive best on mineral soils exposed by burning. The Giant Sequoia is a case in point: its cones release the small seeds only after fire exposure opens them, thus showering the ground with multiple years of seed production right after a fire event. Although capable of producing massive 3,000-year-old trees, the seeds are small and perform best on fire-created seedbeds.

The importance of fire to these trees is ancient, but the frequency and intensity of fires has increased over the last decades, even as human development has placed an increased number of people and increased property values into this landscape. Fire has increased for five reasons: a century of fire suppression has allowed "fuels" (needles, twigs, branches, boles, and understory trees that create "ladder fuels") to build up; tree mortality from insect and pests has increased fuels; cheatgrass (*Bromus tectorum*), an invasive species, has increased the size and intensity of fire; changing grazing pressures from both livestock and wildlife species have influenced fine fuels (for example, grasses in forest understories); and ongoing climate change has brought warming and other extremes, including severe droughts. In the pre-European landscape, lightning and Native American practices served as ignition sources for fire; in more recent times, human ignitions, whether through accident, intent, or from powerlines, have become dominant.

To understand fire in western coniferous forests, we have to begin with its role before European settlement. Fires varied from frequent (5-20-year intervals) low-intensity fires in Ponderosa Pine, to infrequent (200-400-year intervals) but high-intensity fires in high-elevation Lodgepole Pine and subalpine spruce-fir forests. In Ponderosa Pine, fires tended to sweep quickly through the "fine fuels" of the forest understories, such as grasses. These fires resulted in little mortality to the thick-barked canopy trees and kept the forests as "open" woodlands—made familiar from western movies because it was easy to traverse them on horseback. At high elevations, rare but intense fires resulted in high mortality among canopy trees, and a wave of new seedlings and sprouts as the beginning of successional recovery.

The amount and structure of fuel are critical in Ponderosa Pine forests at lower to moderate elevations, where fuel loads and ladder fuels have increased. At high elevations, there is plenty of organic materials to act as fuels, but moist conditions limit fire ignition and spread. Fuels may be at higher levels than historical norms after decades of fire suppression, but drought conditions increase the likelihood of large and intense fires. In the lower-elevation forests, human influences have exacerbated both bottom-up factors (fuels) and top-down factors (extreme droughts).

Historical fragmentation of temperate deciduous forests

The temperate deciduous forest has long been home to human populations and today they are found in the world's most economically developed countries. The pressure of high human population here have resulted in forest fragmentation, with the original forest cover now largely reduced to isolated patches.

▶ **Forest fragmentation**
Agricultural development in the temperate zone has greatly fragmented the original forest cover. Habitat loss and fragmentation is a leading cause of species endangerment.

The moderate climate and dependable summer precipitation characteristic of the three centers of temperate deciduous forests allowed farmers to grow crops without irrigation. Temperate crops, as well as livestock production, were perfected over thousands of years. The deciduous forests also yielded fertile soils, although patterns of agriculture led to soil erosion and areas where the soils were "worn out" over time. Historically, farmers did keep some land in woodlots. The original forest provided construction materials, firewood, and an abundance of nut trees (chestnut, oak, beech) that were greatly valued by farmers because livestock was often turned loose in remnant forests when nuts were available. A few small areas of woods were also saved from agriculture for other values, including shipbuilding, hunting reserves, and sacred groves dedicated to religious practices and burials.

Patterns of fragmentation

In 1956, botanist John Curtis (1913-1961) of the University of Wisconsin published four maps of forest cover in Cadiz township in southern Wisconsin. From a starting point of a single large block of continuous forest in 1831, the 1882, 1902, and 1950 maps showed a steady loss of forest habitat, from about 90 percent of the landscape to just 4 percent. In 1831, there had been a single large tract of forest, whereas in 1950 there were approximately 54 small forest fragments. Curtis' simple figure inspired many similar maps that show increasing fragmentation over time for a wide variety of ecosystems in all parts of the globe. Today, habitat loss and fragmentation are counted as a leading threat to biodiversity.

The pattern of forest fragmentation has also changed over time as the human population has increased and land use patterns have changed. For instance, smaller family farms have often yielded to large agribusinesses and farms have generally shifted to irrigated but fertile grassland soils—although agriculture has, meanwhile, largely shifted to the application of fertilizers. It may come as a surprise that Thoreau (see page 287) lived at the time of maximum forest clearance in New England, when the landscape was only 30 percent forested. In the mid-1800s, agriculture began moving to more productive soils westward, leading to farm abandonment and reforestation in New England. The regrowing forest in New England that began in the decades after Thoreau's death in 1861 paralleled the fragmenting forest in John Curtis' Wisconsin.

FRAGMENTATION IN CADIZ TOWNSHIP

Cadiz Township, Wisconsin, was heavily forested in 1851 but
agricultural development steadily reduced the total amount
of forest and the size of individual patches (after Curtis, 1956).

1831

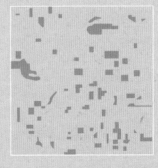

1882

1902

1950

Habitat loss

Habitat loss rarely happens without habitat fragmentation, but the two are separate aspects of the problem. Habitat loss is simply the area of habitat lost, while habitat fragmentation describes how that loss is configured; that is, the landscape structure of the remaining habitat—the number and size of the fragments, the shape of the fragments, and the distance apart and pattern of arrangement of the fragments. The most compact shape, in terms of the ratio of edge to area, is a circle. The narrower the shape, the greater the edge effect and the smaller the area of core habitat. Curtis' map showed not just habitat loss, but also fragmentation: the 4 percent of the original forest that remained in Cadiz township was not in a single tract, but rather in 54 separate tracts, each of which averaged just 0.07 percent of the original forest.

▲ **Deer populations**

Forest fragmentation can cause dramatic increase in some species. Deer populations rose in the temperate deciduous forests of eastern North America due to the loss of predators, the low hunting pressure, and the mix of open and forested habitats.

Species loss

A given fragmentation does not affect all species or habitats in the same way. When predators are affected differently from their prey, trophic cascades result. One example of this is the explosion of deer populations following the loss of Wolves (*Canis lupus*) and Mountain Lions (*Puma concolor*), along with the decline in hunting, throughout North American deciduous forests. Sometimes, these trophic cascades affect human populations directly. For instance, it has been hypothesized that exposure to tick-borne diseases has increased in eastern North America because fragmentation here has promoted the populations of small mammals and deer.

A 2019 study showed an alarming trend: North American bird populations in temperate woodlands had declined by 25 percent, a loss of about 482 million birds, over the last 50 years. Many interacting causes are suspected, but habitat loss and fragmentation, through human development and logging, is thought to be a major part of the story. The Wood Thrush (*Hylocichla mustelina*), a bird with a beautiful flute-like call and an emblematic species of eastern North America, is found in unbroken woods. Sustainable, reproducing populations of require woodland patches larger than about 0.1-0.4 square miles (0.25-1 sq km). This is small in comparison to the requirements of Mountain Lions, which need 3,800 square miles (10,000 sq km) for population sustainability, yet in much of eastern North America—especially at low elevations in urban and agricultural areas—forest patches are not sufficiently large to maintain Wood Thrush populations. An added problem is that the Wood Thrush migrates in the winter to the tropics and experiences threats in its winter range, as well as along its migration route.

▼ **Wood Thrush**
In eastern North America, the Wood Thrush requires deep woodlands. Populations therefore decrease with forest fragmentation.

The development of sustainable forestry

In 1850, at the dawn of the Industrial Revolution, the world was powered by the muscles of large beasts and the sweat of humans. For prior centuries, most of the energy that heated homes, fused sand to glass, smelted ore to metals, and powered other industrial activities was mostly derived from burning wood (see pages 320–321). Nations rose or fell on their wood resources, and for those that depended upon a navy of sailing ships wood for shipbuilding was a crucial military resource.

▼ **Man-of-War**

A British Man-of-War carried a mainmast 3 ft (1 m) in diameter at its base and 118 ft (36 m) tall, as well as shorter masts. At sea, masts are embrittled by drying and break under the load from winds.

The Venetian Arsenal

A stunning example of such a naval power, the Republic of Venice, combined building a navy and exercising its power over the seas with developing a sustainable forestry practice. At the republic's apex in the early sixteenth century, 16,000 workers at the Arsenale di Venezia (Venetian Arsenal), the city's armory and shipyard, built a ship a day on an assembly line of moving barges. The Arsenal consumed wood from forests managed using what today would be called sustainable forestry. This involved several different types of trees: oak and chestnut for the ribs of ships, beech for oars, and other timbers for masts and additional ship parts. Oaks were grown and harvested on sustainable rotations on Montello, a large hill in the province of Treviso in northern Italy. For every tree that was cut, a replacement was planted. In more mountainous areas, spruce trees were planted in canopy gaps to produce tall, relatively knot-free masts—again, with the proviso that harvested trees had to be replaced to maintain a sustained supply. The Arsenal was an exceptionally early case of several modern themes: industrialization, assembly-line production, and forest sustainability.

Forestry practices in Britain and France

In 1662, the commissioners of Britain's Royal Navy were in a global struggle with the Dutch and others for control of the seas. They were concerned about some of the very issues that the Venetians had worked to resolve: they needed tall oak trees and other timber to refurbish old ships and to build better new ones. Unfortunately for the British, the Cromwellian rule following the English Civil War (1642–1651) revoked feudal laws that protected forests. Further, for a century and a half, the need for firewood and house construction had depleted wood stocks, as had the industrial use of charcoal in glass factories and ironworks. The naval commissioners sought a report from the Royal Academy,

which was eventually headed by the gardener John Evelyn (1620-1706). His book *Sylva, or a Discourse of Forest-Trees and the Propagation of Timber in His Majesties Dominions* (1664) described different commercially valuable tree species, along with descriptions of how and when to plant, transplant, prune, and fell these trees to "increase the beauty of forests and their value of timber." *Sylva* was a bestseller, but it was effectively ignored. The British chose instead a mixture of two strategies: import natural resources from across the globe, and substitute materials that were becoming scarce. The replacement for the wood burned in the 1666 Great Fire of London came from Norwegian and American colonial forests; the lack of firewood was substituted by burning coal.

Sustainable source

Oaks grown on Montello Hill (above) provided the Venice Arsenal (below) with wood for warships and merchant vessels— what today would be called sustainable forestry.

France suffered from analogous wood supply problems. Facing the same concerns as the British, King Louis XIV stopped the sale of timber from the royal forests in 1661. Jean-Baptiste Colbert (1619-1683), adviser to the king, Finance Minister, and Secretary of the Navy, produced massive reforms that increased timber sales and royal revenue. Sadly, a combination of apathy, inertia, and difficult local personalities caused Colbert's reformation to fail. On the eve of the French Revolution in 1789, there was less woodland in France than there had been in 1669.

Nachhaltigkeit, or sustainability

The development of a sustainable practice of forest use has its origins in the historical use and abuse of the European temperate deciduous forests. We have looked at its origins in Venetian, English, and French attempts to develop a forestry practice, but the heir to this history is seen in the work of Hans Carl von Carlowitz (1645-1714), who was born in Chemnitz, Saxony. His family was long involved in the management of forested landscapes, and his father had been appointed by the Prince of Saxony to supply mines and smelters with timber from the forests of the Ore Mountains. In 1665, as a young German nobleman, Carlowitz spent five years on a Grand Tour of Europe. He was in France when Colbert's reformation of French forestry was underway, and in London at the time of the Great Plague (1665-1666) and Great Fire. From his later writing, he appears to have read *Sylva* and may have met its author, John Evelyn.

▼ **Mountain forests**

The Ertzgebirge Mountains on the German-Czech border. Timber from these locations were rafted down rivers to supply mining timbers and fuel for smelters.

On his return to Saxony, Carlowitz took up a position with the Saxon Mining Administration in Freiberg, which controlled hundreds of mines and smelters. Building sailing ships and maintaining mines and smelters have one thing in common: the consumption of prodigious amounts of wood. The mines of Saxony starved for wooden timbers and the smelters needed wood and charcoal fuel. In 1713, Carlowitz published a 400-page book, *Sylvicultura Oeconomica, Anweisung zur wilden Baum-Zucht*, on the cultivation of wild trees and forests. He recognized that the Europe-wide devastation of forests was well underway and felt it would produce a severe economic collapse due to timber shortage. Certainly, Saxony's silver mines and smelters would be closed by this shortage. Carlowitz saw the short-term focus on money as the driver for this coming catastrophe: land was being cleared of forest because agriculture seemed more profitable, and there was no reason to plant trees that would not be harvested in one's lifetime. Despite being written 300 years ago, Carlowitz's book offers advice relevant to modern issues: *Holtzsparkünste* (the art of saving timber)—insulate homes better and use energy-efficient stoves in houses and smelters; *Surrogata* (substitutes)—develop energy alternatives; and *Säen und Plantzen der wilden Bäume* (sowing and planting wild trees)—carry out reforestation and manage forests better.

Carlowitz referred to his overall system and its philosophical implications as *Nachhaltigkeit*, which means "going on forever." The word "sustainability" was subsequently coined as an English term with the same meaning.

▲ **Live Oak trees**
This Live Oak Reserve system is part of a naval forest reserve begun under U.S. President John Quincy Adams in 1828. Live Oak wood has enormous strength and is ideal for the interior hulls of wooden warships and their curved structural supports.

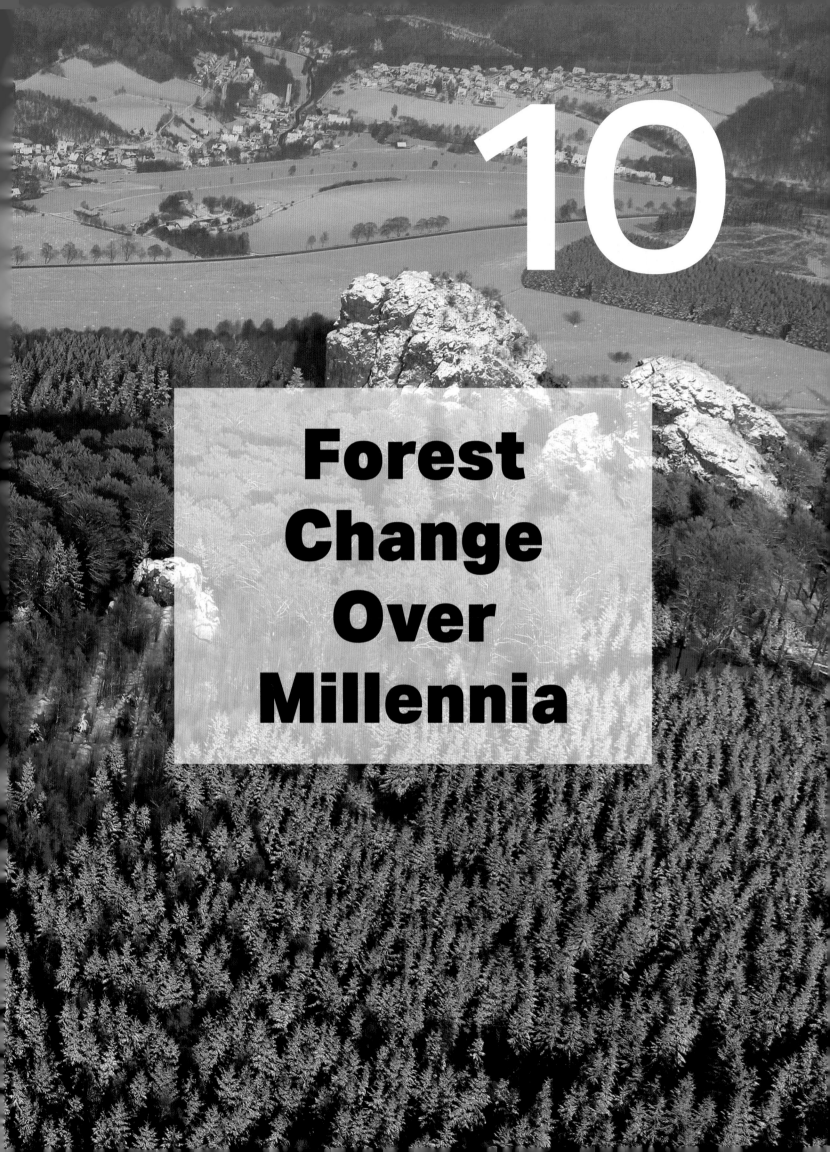

10

Forest Change Over Millennia

Discovering history through trees

Around 10,000 years ago, it is estimated that over half of the Earth's habitable land—equivalent to six times the area of the United States—was covered with forests. During the twentieth century, global forest cover dropped to 38 percent of habitable land. Humans have used forests since time immemorial, but we have also converted them, purposefully or not, into cultivated and grazed areas.

▶ **Dating**

Each tree ring in this ash tree slab corresponds to one growth year. Heartwood coloration is the result of a chemical process. The scar is a testimony of the tormented history of this tree.

Dendrochronology

Next to jumping from one log to another, counting the rings of a tree is among the best amusements for a forest visitor. Following the rings from bark to pith takes us on a journey from the present to many decades or even centuries into the past. One cannot help but wonder what the tree must have witnessed during its lifetime. Quite literally, scientists have used tree rings as time capsules to understand the climates of the past. A tree grows faster during wet, warm years than during cold, dry ones, thus, by measuring the width of its rings, one can tell a lot about the environmental conditions in which it has grown.

The science of tree-ring dating is called dendrochronology and, according to some scholars, it was polymath Leonardo da Vinci who first suggested that the rings could be used to infer past climates. However, it was only in the nineteenth century that dendrochronology became a rigorous discipline, with known years of exceptional weather being used to cross-reference the tree-ring time series of several trees. For instance, early tree-ring scientists used the Great Frost of 1709 as a reference point for Europe. This winter was so cold that the Venice Lagoon froze and water froze inside houses in southwest France. The event left a discernible growth mark on all trees growing across the continent at the time.

There are, however, several complications associated with dendrochronology. For a start, trees tend to grow proportionally faster when young than when they age, so careful data analysis is needed to account for tree age. Second, some tree species, such as poplars, produce erratic rings, so only selected species should be used for dating. These include the Great Bristlecone Pine (*Pinus longaeva*) in North America, oaks (genus *Quercus*) in Europe, and conifers such as Hinoki Cypress (*Chamaecyparis obtusa*) and *Picea brachytyla* in Japan and China, respectively. The tropics pose a specific challenge, because many trees here grow continuously, making dendrochronological work much more challenging. That said, important studies were conducted in 2014 using Spanish Cedar (*Cedrela odorata*) in Peru.

READING CLIMATE HISTORY THROUGH TREE RINGS

Tree rings reveal local climate conditions over decades or even centuries.

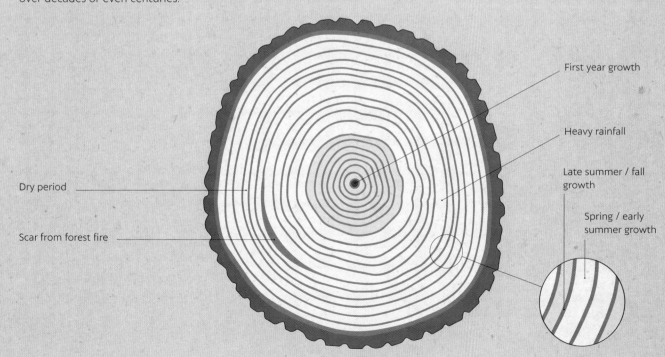

First year growth

Heavy rainfall

Late summer / fall growth

Spring / early summer growth

Dry period

Scar from forest fire

A venerable chronology

The most direct approach to dendrochronological dating is to find a very old single tree that can provide a single consistent tree-ring record over several centuries or even millennia. The search for such a tree is associated with American researcher Edmund Schulman, who in the 1950s initiated tree-ring studies on Great Bristlecone Pines in the upper treeline of California near the border with Nevada. After a long search, he discovered trees that were more than 4,000 years old, but unfortunately he passed away before he could publish his findings. It was Wesley Ferguson, Schulman's collaborator, who first published a 7,100-year-old chronology based on 18 Great Bristlecone Pines. The trees each spanned several hundred years in age, and one had lived for almost 3,000 years. Notoriously, this tree-ring reconstruction was used to calibrate one of the most celebrated dating methods in archaeology: radiocarbon dating (see box below).

Reconstructing past environments

All living organisms assimilate elements, notably carbon, oxygen, and nitrogen. These elements are present in slightly different forms: carbon is mainly of the ^{12}C type, but a rarer and slightly heavier form, ^{13}C, is a stable isotope. Plant tissues contain a lower concentration of ^{13}C relative to that in the atmosphere. This is expressed as a ratio of concentrations $[^{13}C]/[^{12}C]$ in wood relative to a standard, which is written $\delta^{13}C$. Typical values of

wood $\delta^{13}C$ are around −24‰ (parts per thousand), with departures caused by dry seasons. Oxygen, meanwhile, has two main stable isotopes: ^{16}O, which is the main form; and the heavier ^{18}O. Oxygen enters plants as water through their root system and the water inside the leaves is enriched with the heavier isotope through transpiration. The ratio of oxygen concentrations is written $\delta^{18}O$ and measured in parts per thousand, and like $\delta^{13}C$ is correlated to the intensity of the dry season. Crucially, both $\delta^{13}C$ and $\delta^{18}O$ can be measured using tiny samples of material, including single tree rings. Analytical methods have made impressive advances over the past decades, so that today $\delta^{13}C$ and $\delta^{18}O$ ratios can be measured using samples weighing less than 1 mg.

Radiocarbon dating is perhaps a better-known technique than isotope analysis. The ^{14}C isotope of carbon is fixed in living tissues and, after the death of the organism, its concentration decays with a half-life of about 5,730 years. The principle of radiocarbon dating is to measure the amount of ^{14}C relative to ^{12}C in biological remains: the older the remains, the lower the ratio. Analyses of Great Bristlecone Pine tree rings (pictured opposite) have been crucial to the calibration of the ^{14}C decay model.

Wood isotope analysis

The work on bristlecones also turned out to be a crucial opportunity to extract other information from tree cores, including stable isotopes. Carbon isotope ratios (written as $\delta^{13}C$; see box opposite) and oxygen isotope ratios (written as $\delta^{18}O$) in plant tissues affect the efficiency of photosynthesis and water uptake in a plant, and are therefore useful to quantify past environmental changes.

In 2021, scientists used $\delta^{13}C$ and $\delta^{18}O$ wood isotope analysis to reconstruct the central European summer hydroclimate for the past 2,100 years. This study identified periods with more frequent summer droughts at the beginning of the Common Era, around 900-1000 CE, the period of the great medieval deforestation, and also in the Renaissance during the fifteenth and sixteenth centuries. It has long been known that the cultural development of Europe was intricately linked to its climate, and trees offer a unique window on this. In turn, favorable periods for agriculture, and hence for population expansion, have inevitably been linked to a conversion of forests to cropland, especially during the Middle Ages (see pages 322-323). Research into why these shifts in climate have occurred over the past two millennia have revealed changes in sun-heating capacity, large volcanic eruptions, and human-induced climate change, although the latter is only clearly detectable through the past 50 years.

◀ **Historical data**

The massive trunk of a cut redwood tree, Redwoods National Park, California—tree rings provide a wealth of information on past climates.

TREE RINGS AND PAST DROUGHTS

A reconstruction of the June–July–August drought index based on oak tree-ring measurement of carbon and oxygen isotopes from central Europe. Scientists used this data to identify periods with more frequent summer droughts. (Source: Büntgen et al. *Nature Geosciences*, 2021.)

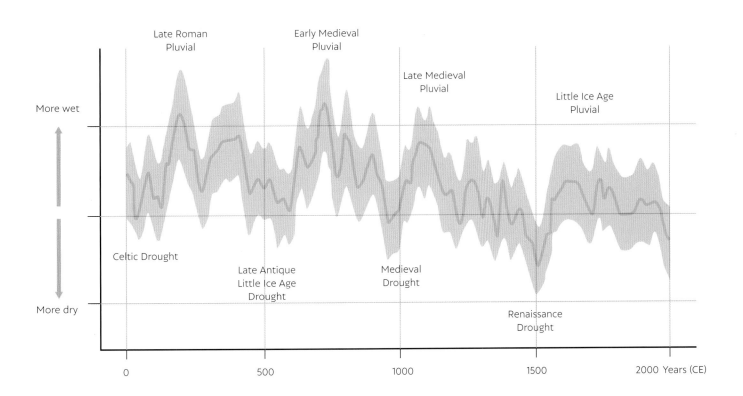

Millennial forest trends

Tree-ring studies have mainly been used to study regional climates, yet it is quite clear that forests themselves have been impacted by environmental changes. Looking back over millennia, or even millions of years, what types of forest covered the planet in the past? Understanding the historical perspective is crucial to our knowledge about how quickly forests have changed and are changing in structure and species composition. The lessons of the past help us put into perspective the major changes observed in recent decades.

▶ **Pollen**

Some plants release massive amounts of pollen, which are then dispersed by wind. Pollen spores are important markers of past vegetation, for instance in lake cores.

Pollen detectives

One method used to explore changes in the distribution of vegetation through time is based on the pollen record. Plants produce numerous pollen grains, many of which never find their target and are deposited in the environment. The outer pollen wall (called the exine) is morphologically diverse, and an excellent proxy to distinguish the presence of different plant types. The pollen structure is also extremely durable in sediments, persisting for millions of years. Oil prospectors have used pollen remains to detect the age of geological strata and to infer site quality, spurring an intense interest in palynology—the applied science of pollen-based environmental reconstruction.

Palynology is generally based on sediment cores taken from lake bottoms. Once collected, these cores require a great deal of preparation, being sliced period by period and then examined under a microscope to detect and identify any pollen grains. The reward for all this work is in the results, which can be spectacular. Our current knowledge of the changes in the vegetation at the end of the Last Glacial Maximum (LGM), for instance, is largely based on palynology. In North America, work by Margaret Davis and colleagues has revealed that the northward expansion of trees after the end of the last ice age has closely tracked that of the ice sheet. The impressive speed at which forests have reinvaded North America has been one of the greatest surprises of this research, demonstrating that forest trees are capable of long-distance dispersal and fast establishment. The study also shows that spruces and oaks have responded very differently to these changes, with spruces extending farther northward than oaks, which barely cross the boundary with Canada.

SPRUCE AND OAK MIGRATION

Pollen record of oak (top) and spruce (bottom)—shaded in
green—since the Last Glacial Maximum. The blue shading
shows the continental ice sheet. Spruce migrated northward
faster than oak (after Davis et al., 2001).

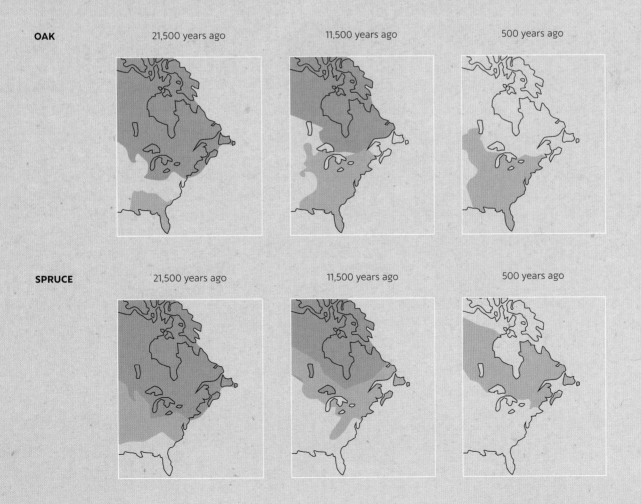

OAK   21,500 years ago   11,500 years ago   500 years ago

SPRUCE   21,500 years ago   11,500 years ago   500 years ago

During the last glacial period, oceans were more than 330 ft (100 m) below the current sea level. The islands of Java, Sumatra, and Borneo were connected to mainland Southeast Asia, which allowed for free migration of plants and animals across the region. Sulawesi and Papua New Guinea were always separated by the sea, generating a largely different fauna and flora. This biogeographic barrier is known as the Wallace line.

European migrations

Forests are a symbol of endurance and immortality. Yet, pollen research has demonstrated that they were absent in most of North America and Europe a few thousands of years ago, and they have been able to recolonize continents in just a few hundred years. In Europe, forest tree species, especially oaks and softwoods, also migrated northward after the retreat of the ice cap at the end of the LGM. Estimates of postglacial migration rates of temperate forests are as high as 550 yd (500 m) per year, although these figures have been disputed by some researchers, who argue that localized tree populations persisted in the north during the ice age but went undetected because of their sparseness. However, this hypothesis of favorable northern ice age favorable spots, or refugia, for forests has received little support, and the prevailing view remains based on the northward expansion model.

The history of this northward migration has been also recorded in tree genomes. European oaks (genus *Quercus*) persisted in three groups during the Ice Age, in Spain, southern Italy, and the Balkans, and thereafter they migrated northward as clearly distinct genetic pools, which can still be observed today. The oaks of western Europe migrated from Spain, through France toward England. These findings imply that most present-day European and North American forests are young, dating back to the end of the last ice age, and that they also have a low genetic diversity.

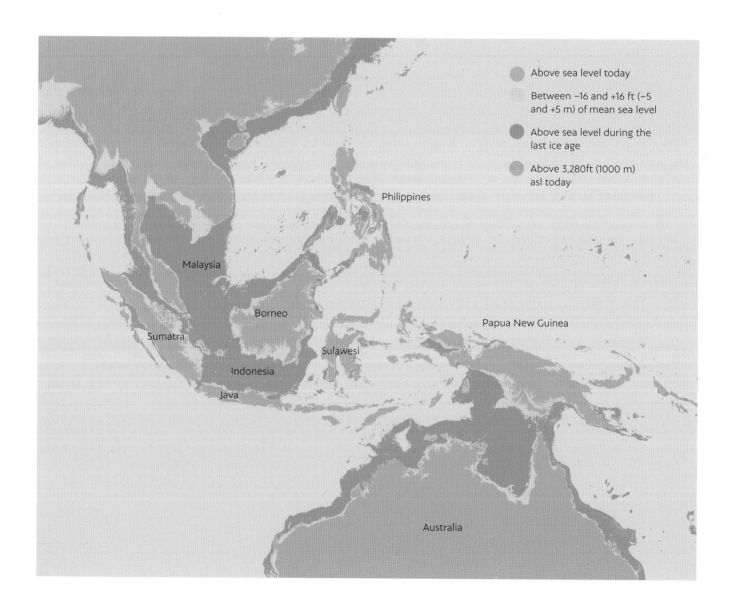

Above sea level today

Between −16 and +16 ft (−5 and +5 m) of mean sea level

Above sea level during the last ice age

Above 3,280ft (1000 m) asl today

Philippines

Malaysia

Borneo

Papua New Guinea

Sumatra

Sulawesi

Indonesia

Java

Australia

Southern hemisphere

The history of northern hemisphere temperate forests since the end of the last ice age is quite well known, but what happened elsewhere? There has been lots of speculation that the Amazon Forest retracted to a few refugia during the Pleistocene Ice Age. In fact, this process could have happened at each glacial stage over the past 2.6 million years, and it has even been speculated that a repeated contraction into refugia may have acted as a "speciation pump," explaining the outstanding biological diversity of Amazonia. This refuge theory has received limited support from palynology: cores taken at a site in the mouth of the Amazon River demonstrate that the Amazon Basin was not extensively replaced by grass-like savanna vegetation during the LGM, as has been suggested. Paraíso Cave, near the Tapajós River in Amazonia, has also provided important findings in relation to the refuge theory. Using $\delta^{18}O$ levels measured in the cave's stalagmites, researchers have reconstructed the Amazonian climate for the past 43,000 years. Both precipitation and temperatures appear to have been lower, such that evapotranspiration was consistent with a persistent rain forest vegetation during the last ice age.

Southeast Asia

The most dramatic changes during the LGM were experienced in Southeast Asia. At this time large volumes of seawater were taken up by the polar ice caps and the global sea level was about 400 ft (120 m) lower than it is today. As a result, the islands of the Indonesian and Philippine archipelagos were connected to the Indochinese Peninsula. It is difficult to imagine that Southeast Asian forests extended uninterrupted from Cambodia to Java in a large paleocontinent called the Sunda Shelf, but this is what the evidence reveals. Pollen and phytoliths (solid bodies of silica found on the surface of plant cells) from sediment cores taken on the southern South China Sea continental shelf and dating to the last ice age include high percentages from lowland rain forest and lower montane rain forest species, suggesting that the exposed shelf was covered with humid vegetation. Vegetation-inferred climate during the last ice age was cooler than it is today, but this was not sufficient to prevent rain forests from growing on the Sunda Shelf.

▲ **Oak tree migration**
Oak tree (Quercus robur) from Dartmoor National Park, UK. Oak trees migrated remarkably fast from southwestern Europe to England after the Last Glacial Maximum.

Uncovering the distant past

Pollens preserved in the fossil record shed light on long-term vegetation trends, stretching back before the last ice age. The story of modern broad-leaved forests probably began somewhere in the tropics around 66 million years ago.

▶ **The Andean cordillera**

Before 40 million years ago, the Andean range did not exist, and pollen fossils found there match a lowland forest vegetation.

▼ **Fossil trees**

This petrified tree from Lesbos Island, Greece was preserved after a volcanic eruption around 20 million years ago.

The Cenozoic era began dramatically, with the extinction of all non-avian dinosaurs and a perfect storm of catastrophes, including the impact of a large meteorite and massive volcanic activity on the—then insular—Indian tectonic plate. Post-cataclysm Earth experienced a massive diversification of mammals and of flowering plants. Fossils of large broad-leaved tree trunks suggest the existence of modern-day forests before 55 million years ago, early on in the Cenozoic.

Research conducted by Colombian palynologist Carlos Jaramillo and colleagues in the present-day Andes—which were the lowlands during the early Cenozoic—has revealed an amazing diversity of plant forms. The Earth went through a massive warming event 55-50 million years ago, called the Paleocene-Eocene Thermal Maximum. Throughout this period, plant diversity accumulated and tropical plant taxa—especially rain forest taxa—underwent a major diversification. It is no exaggeration to say that the present-day tropical flora was shaped during this period, when the Earth was so warm—some 22 °F (12 °C) warmer than today—that there were no polar ice caps.

After this long warm period, the Earth slowly cooled, and around 34 million years ago another major shift occurred. This was triggered by the formation of the Antarctic ice sheet due to changes in atmospheric circulation related to the rise of major new mountain ranges (the Andes, Himalayas, and Rockies). This led to a sudden drop in the diversity of pollen types globally, caused by a major retreat of forests, and spurred adaptations for plants to drier and colder environments. One of the most spectacular such adaptations was the appearance and rise to dominance of the grassy biomes. The period from 34 million to 23 million years ago was particularly favorable for open grasslands, and for the animals associated with this habitat (herbivores), but conditions were not so suitable for forests.

The ice ages

The ice ages comprise a smaller, more recent slice of time in the history of forests over the past 2.6 million years, yet were no less influential. During this period, major changes in forest cover occurred through a succession of about 50 glacial cycles. The Pleistocene Ice Age, lasting from 33,000 to 16,000 years ago, is the one that is best understood. The period since the last deglaciation has been accompanied by the last major forest expansion, but also the rise of modern humans.

DIVERSITY OF SPECIES

A graph showing the diversity of northern South American plants during the Cenozoic era—the most recent era of Earth's history—beginning 66 million years ago, until the Miocene epoch, beginning 23 million years ago. The curve shows the number of pollen-type forms, a proxy for plant diversity, highlighting the major diversification during the Paleocene–Eocene Thermal Maximum. Based on Jaramillo et al., *Science* (2006).

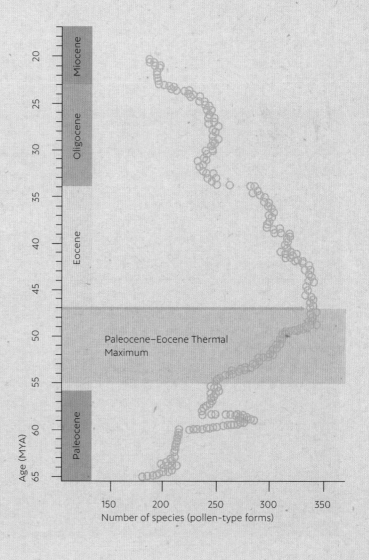

Paleocene–Eocene Thermal Maximum

Miocene

Oligocene

Eocene

Paleocene

Age (MYA)

Number of species (pollen-type forms)

Fire and Neolithic settlements

The history of archaic hominids remains so poorly known that a discussion on their interactions with forests is at best speculative. A long-held theory suggests that the bipedal habit of humans is associated with a change in habitat—the conquest of open savannas—but biomechanical evidence contradicts this theory. The hominid *Ardipithecus ramidus*, dated at 4.4 million years, was bipedal, but its hand was adapted for climbing, suggesting it lived primarily in forests.

Fire

The most significant event by far in the early development of humans was control of fire, which not only held enormous importance for the later success of the species, but also for forests. Even small human populations with a mastery of fire can have a disproportionate influence on vegetation. Unfortunately, it is difficult to distinguish the impact of human-caused fires from natural events far into the past. Even the timing of human control of fire is uncertain, ranging from first hints dating back 1.5 million years ago to clear evidence from 400,000 years ago. We tend to have a distorted perception of ancient time periods. A century is a long period compared with a human lifespan, and since forest recovery after a disturbance takes more than a century, we perceive forest dynamics as slow and gradual. However, a century-long forest disturbance would hardly be noticeable in the paleoenvironmental record of the past million years.

▼ **Aboriginal Australians**

Aboriginal Australians have long used fire to avoid lightning bush fires, but also to fertilize croplands, and as an aid for game hunting.

ARCHAEOLOGICAL EVIDENCE

The excavation of artifacts from Madjedbebe, a rock shelter North of Kakadu National Park in the Northern Territory provide the oldest evidence of human arrival in Australia, with the presence of hearths, hatchets, and grindstones.

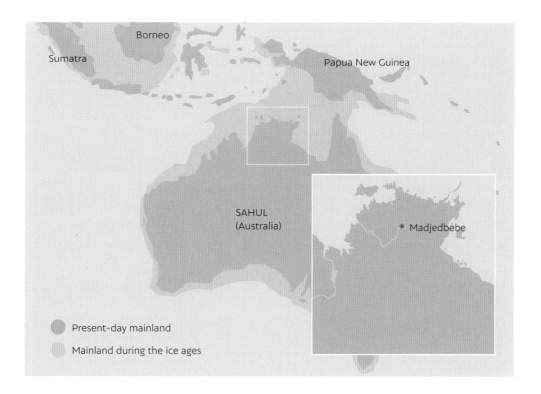

The case of Australia

Australia presents a test case for how humans have shaped forests by fire. The continent (technically called Sahul) was first colonized some 65,000 years ago, as testified by recent excavation at Madjedbebe in the Northern Territory. Paleogenomic studies have estimated that a major expansion of Aboriginal people across Australia took place some 10,000 years ago, although archaeological evidence supports the presence of humans across Sahul before 30,000 years ago. The view that Aboriginal people transformed the land by burning open woodland and grassland has frequently been cited in the literature, but fire adaptation of the Australian flora far predates the expansion of the human population. Both the pollen record and soil charcoal show that during the last ice age grasslands, shrublands, and open woodlands covered much larger areas of Australia than is the case today. After the end of the ice age, forests spread from remnants and present-day forest cover was established only around 5,000 years ago. Therefore, evidence suggests that burning by Aboriginal people did not stop the advance of the forests and in no way created vast areas of grassland.

The case study of Australia demonstrates the difficulty of distinguishing man-made deforestation from events caused by nature, especially through fire. It also demonstrates that powerful narratives around the alleged destructive activities of Indigenous cultures must be carefully examined against known evidence. In short, to paraphrase American journalist H. L. Mencken, "For every problem there is a solution that is simple, neat—and wrong."

The Neolithic Revolution

Europe and temperate Asia provide another glimpse into the interaction of humans with forests after the end of the last ice age. Both regions experienced the Neolithic Revolution around 10,000 years ago, which was marked by a transition to a sedentary lifestyle, agriculture, and animal husbandry. Agriculture must have led to a stepped increase in deforestation, but given the cost of clearing land with Stone Age technology, this deforestation was likely limited.

To gain an idea of how impactful the Neolithic period may have been on temperate forested areas, researchers have estimated metabolic calculations for humans living at the time. The rationale of this approach is that humans have minimal requirements to eat, keep warm, and build shelter. According to some estimates, the basic "basket of goods" for each Neolithic human included farming goods (wheat, cattle, sheep, or goats) and wood products (firewood and construction wood), and the estimated required agricultural land per capita is 2½–5 acres (1–2 ha). Thus, a 30-person village would need to convert less than 150 acres (60 ha) of land. In addition, they would also have gathered forest products over an area ten times this, or 2⅓ sq miles (6 sq km). This calculation suggests that both Europe and temperate Asia were far from fully deforested by the end of the Neolithic period: aside from a few areas where population density may have exceeded 13 people per square mile (five people per square kilometer), large regions were uninhabited. This evidence is supported by the scattered distribution of pottery artifacts in Europe, which suggests centers of occupation in north-central Europe and around the Mediterranean Basin during the middle of the Neolithic period. Although wood is less durable than pottery, it is highly likely that the material was a crucial component in the life of Neolithic humans—to the extent that innovations in wood technology, more than polished stone tools, may have been crucial in triggering the Neolithic Revolution.

▶ **European Beech**

European Beech (Fagus sylvatica) has numerous usages as firewood, timber, and for cabinetmaking. Beechnuts make a valuable oil, and beech wood tablets were in common use before paper. In English, German, Russian, and Swedish, ancient words for beech and book are the same.

How and when agriculture spread from the Fertile Crescent Asia to Western Europe from about 10,000 years ago, remains unclear, and could have involved the migration of both humans and technologies. The transition to agriculture marks the beginning of deforestation of European forests.

Neolithic pollen records

Temporal variation in the density of pollen for some plant groups reveals the impact of humans on their environment. This is most clearly observed in the density of grasses (Poaceae), as compiled in the European Pollen Database. In predominantly forested landscapes, we can expect that grasses will be present in only low densities. Grass pollen indeed declined at the end of the last ice age, coinciding with the northward migration of forests, and remained at a low density until 4,000 years ago. Another marker of the impact of humans is the slow increase in the abundance of Common Hornbeam (*Carpinus betulus*) and European Beech (*Fagus sylvatica*) from 6,000 years ago, in the later stages of the Neolithic. Both species make excellent firewood, are useful in carpentry and construction, and their fruits and leaves are edible for both animals and humans. Both trees are also associated with disturbed forests, and they regenerate quickly, being adapted to forest management. Overall, the pollen record suggests a gradual influence of humans on forests starting at the end of the Neolithic period.

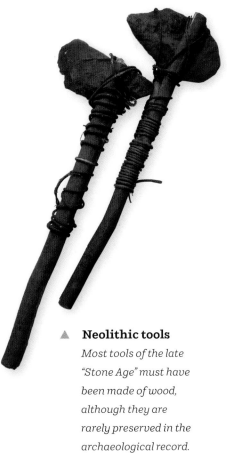

▲ **Neolithic tools**
Most tools of the late "Stone Age" must have been made of wood, although they are rarely preserved in the archaeological record.

Forest change since classical antiquity

Why did once powerful civilizations collapse? How was their overuse of resources involved in their decline? These questions have been a favorite topic among environmental historians, most of whom agree that several causal factors are generally involved, poor stewardship of the environment being one of them.

Cultures built on wood

Some historians have repeatedly suggested that the cultural collapses of the Harappan civilization in the Indus Valley, Mesopotamia, the Mycenaean civilization, and the Roman Empire can all be linked to deforestation. The proposed mechanism involves an overuse of resources, which may start with an increased demand for wood for shipbuilding in a time of war. This could then result in erosion and subsequent flash flooding, and in turn alter agricultural production systems. These narratives have been propounded because all of these cultures were built on wood, but they have seldom been demonstrated based on direct evidence. A universal feature of human cultures over the past 4,000 years has been their heavy reliance on forest products: forests provided firewood, construction lumber, and food. However, instead of leading to overuse of resources, this has led to major innovations in forest management and wood technology —likely the most important over this long period of human history—including techniques such as coppicing and pollarding.

▼ **Mesopotamia**

The collapse of ancient civilizations has been claimed to be related to overuse of wood resources. Other factors may be involved.

Theory suggests that in order for small communities to manage their environmental resources suitably, an institution is necessary, involving a long-term contract among the participants of the community and the means to enforce the contract. When this theory is applied to modern situations, it shows that sustainability can be achieved over long timescales, but only if several conditions are fulfilled, and it is therefore by no means guaranteed. Failures in the management of common resources can occur—and indeed have done in the past.

Cahokia

One often reported example of the unsustainable use of wood resources by a community is provided by Cahokia (pictured below), which was the largest city in North America until Philadelphia surpassed it in the mid-eighteenth century. It was located on the Mississippi River near present-day St. Louis, and was active from 800 CE to 1350 CE. With a population of up to 15,000, Cahokia relied largely on maize-based agriculture. According to archaeologist William I. Woods, the residents also made wide-scale use of forestry resources: a large palisade was erected around the city nucleus, and this had to be rebuilt three times. The famous Cahokia Woodhenge, comprising circles of cedar poles standing 20 ft (6 m) tall, suggests that forest resources were more than stock commodities and had acquired a symbolic value. However, there is no evidence for an unsustainable use of wood products in Cahokia. A far more likely contributing factor to the decline of the city was its heavy reliance on water for cultivation, and the fact that water management was not easy along the banks of the Mississippi River. Tree-ring climate reconstructions indicate that a drought hit the Cahokia region in 1276–1297, placing more pressure on water resources. Additional evidence suggests that the Anasazi people of the American Southwest and the Fremont people in what is now Utah were also significantly impacted by this millennial drought event.

▲ **Ancient forest practices**

In the Middle Ages, pigs were fed in the forest. Swineherds knocked down acorns for pigs, a practice called pannage.

Managing forest resources in Europe

While careful management of forest resources was likely at Cahokia, little remains of this history. In contrast, there is much direct evidence of wood management in Europe. The uses of forest products here were extremely diverse, and woodcrafting was advanced in many cultures. In rural areas forests were used as commons, where villagers grazed their livestock and collected firewood. One practice was to feed swine with oak acorns by clubbing the branches of the trees, and honey, beechnut oil, and beeswax were also key products in a world where sugar and artificial light were scarce. Technology historian Joachim Radkau has reported on a study in which 27 different wood species were found in the home of a poor nineteenth-century peasant living in a German forest, all chosen based on their suitability for a particular task. Spectacular examples of wood craftsmanship include the towering naves of major cathedrals and other buildings. A remarkable feature of these woodworks is that they were assembled from an exceptionally straight trunk, grown specifically for the occasion.

During the European Middle Ages, increased population sizes created a land-optimization challenge, where the space requirements for animal grazing, crop cultivation, and firewood collection all had to be balanced. This constraint for space became acute by 1000 CE, and was accompanied by rapid forest clearance. According to some estimates, forest cover in central and western Europe dropped from 40 percent in 1000 CE to less than 20 percent at the onset of the Black Death around 1350. In Germany, villages known as Waldhufendörfer were created by clearing long strips of forest, separated into farm holdings each measuring roughly 60 acres (24 ha) in area. In England, the situation was even more extreme.

Environmental historian Oliver Rackham has analyzed the Domesday Book of 1086 and shown that the country was already quite sparsely forested by that time, with about 15 percent wood cover. According to the Hundred Rolls, a survey of land ownership conducted in England in 1279, no more than a few percent of the land was left with wood cover.

Quite amazingly, none of this deforestation was conducted with the help of the saw. Use of the saw in woodcutting is a typical example of a protracted technological revolution. In Germany, Radkau tells us, woodcutters continued to favor axes even though sawing reduced waste by as much as 20 percent. It was only in the mid-eighteenth century that wood sawing took off. Rational explanations for this reluctance are the higher complexity of tool maintenance, the painful kneeling posture required while sawing, and increased cost of the technology. The next major technological innovation was not until the 1950s, with the widespread adoption of the chainsaw.

▲ **Pollarding**

Pollarded beeches in Epping forest, Essex, UK. Pollarding is a pruning technique that favors the production of firewood and fodder to feed livestock. It has been in common practice since the Middle Ages in Europe.

The interesting case of New Zealand

New Zealand separated from Australia with the opening of the Tasman Sea some 85 million years ago, and its flora and fauna are highly endemic. The country was originally covered with temperate forest vegetation, and the national forest inventory—based on more than 14,500 surveyed forest plots—includes 112 tree species. New Zealand forests are ecologically dominated by the genus *Nothofagus* (southern beeches) and by conifers in the family Podocarpaceae.

New Zealand is a hotspot of tectonic and volcanic activity, and Taupō Volcano in the North Island is responsible for some of the most violent eruptions ever recorded, including the Oruanui eruption 26,500 years ago and the Hatepe eruption around 232 CE. The frequency with which large eruptions have occurred in this region, although low, must have had a major impact on the landscapes and on forests. One open question is whether forest fires could have extended right across the islands as a result of the eruptions. Even if the impact of the eruptions themselves was major, especially due to volcanic ash downfall, the prevailing high average rainfall and moisture may have prevented widespread propagation of natural fires. A radiocarbon dating of soil charcoal collected from Kopuatai Bog, north of Taupō, shows a constant yet low frequency of fire events over the 10,000 years leading up to the Hatepe eruption.

▼ **Tāne Mahuta**

*New Zealand's largest Kauri (*Agathis australis*) tree, in Waipoua Forest in the North Island.*

Unlike the Australian flora, New Zealand tree species show none of the classic adaptations to fire. A study comparing the two countries found that New Zealand tree bark is thicker on average, especially in conifers, but that New Zealand tree species lack the ability to resprout from their root system. This indicates that New Zealand forests must have been quite susceptible to fire: in rare natural fire occurrences, trees are killed and the forests take many decades to recover.

Pollen stories

Fire is not the only proximal cause of vegetation change in New Zealand. The history of glaciation parallels that of Europe, with the South Island glaciers beginning their retreat around 14,000 years ago. Palynology reveals fluctuations in the vegetation over the past 10,000 years. Up until 7,000 years ago, the abundance of tree fern pollen in the record suggests a mild and wet climate. Later, the retreat of frost-intolerant species and the expansion of southern beech species suggest a colder climate in the south. In the north, meanwhile, drier summers and a more variable climate may have favored the expansion of the emblematic conifer Kauri (*Agathis australis*). The pollen record of Lake Maratoto in the Waikato lowlands of the central North Island, suggests a relatively stable vegetation and climate there from 12,000 to 2,000 years ago.

One surprising feature of paleoenvironmental research in New Zealand is the relative lack of dendrochronological studies. The oldest time series extend to 1200 CE, but they do not cover the prehistoric period. There is therefore a large potential for tree-ring studies to uncover the fine-scale variations in tree growth in response to climate and volcanic activity.

▲ **Southern beeches**
Southern beeches (Nothofagus) are dominant in New Zealand's forests.

◀ **Taupō Volcano**
One of the most active volcanoes of the world, with major eruptions every thousand years. In this part of the world, forests must be adapted to the high volcanic activity and to earthquakes.

▶ **Past vegetation of New Zealand**

The petrified forest at Curio Bay in the South Island is 180 million years old, and conifer fossils are related to modern Kauri. This is one of the best preserved remains of Jurassic forests.

Impact of Māori settlers

Archaeological evidence strongly indicates that the first wave of human settlement of New Zealand took place around 1280 CE, when Māori arrived by boat from west Polynesia. The earliest sites of detectable human occupation have all been radiocarbon dated to after this time. These sites include large deposits of moa bones, suggesting these large, flightless birds were a prized meal for early Māori populations.

The New Zealand fauna has largely evolved in the absence of predators, and flightless land birds have thrived, the most spectacular being the moa, a now-extinct group of ostrich-like birds, the largest of which weighed more than 400 lb (200 kg). Between 1280 and 1840, all moa species were hunted to extinction, and forest cover declined from 82 percent to 55 percent of the total land area. Why the presence of Māori resulted in such dramatic deforestation still remains a mystery. The hypothesis that they engaged in large-scale cultivation of the sweet potato is doubtful, as they were primarily hunter-foragers. The most significantly impacted region was the lowlands of the South Island, especially podocarp conifer forests here. One theory, put forward by paleoecologist Matt McGlone, is that these forests were fire-prone and that Māori accidentally set fire to them. The micro-charcoal record suggests that immediately following the settlement of New Zealand by Māori, there was a sharp increase in fire frequency. Throughout the eastern South Island, the driest area in New Zealand, charred *Podocarpus hallii* and *P. totara* logs on the ground have been dated to around 1100–1400 CE.

European colonizers began arriving in New Zealand in number from 1840. They set about deforesting the hilly regions, converting large areas to farmland, for sheep and dairy pasture. By some estimates, the sheep flocks totaled a million in the mid-1850s and 10 million in the early 1870s. The direct result of this land-use change is that forest cover shrunk from 55 percent to about 24 percent of the total land area.

Controversial dating

In the 1990s, controversy raged around a suggestion that Māori had sailed to New Zealand as early as 300 CE. This theory was based on the radiocarbon dating of the bones of Pacific rats (*Rattus exulans*), which were transported with human migrations throughout the Pacific. The early radiocarbon dating results of the bones provided the strikingly early dates, which were considered by many to be erroneous. In 2008, New Zealand paleoecologist Janet Wilmshurst and colleagues re-examined the archaeological sites where the original rat bones were collected, and found that no radiocarbon date was older than 1280 CE. They also reported on the dates of rat-gnawed seeds, which were found to date from after 1280 CE.

NEW ZEALAND LOSS OF FOREST COVER

Progressive loss of forest in New Zealand from 1000 CE to present. (Source: Ogden et al., 1998.)

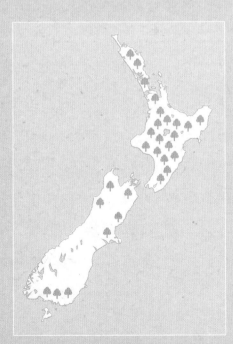

1280
Forest cover—82 percent of the island area

1840
Forest cover—55 percent of the island area

Present
Forest cover—only 24 percent of the island area

Lessons of the past

This chapter has explored the extent to which forests have informed past climate and land-use changes. Dendrochronology, stable isotope research, and palynology all offer unique insights into past environmental conditions and vegetation changes.

▶ **Eden-like forest**
Southern beech (Nothofagus) forest covered in lichen near Ushuaia, Argentina.

One key finding is that forests were able to respond quickly to the return of more favorable conditions following the end of the last Ice Age. Another is that tropical forests were much less affected by the ice ages and therefore retained a high level of species and genetic plant diversity. But how useful are these results in understanding how forests will respond to future climate change? One issue in looking to the past to inform the future is that the human-caused climate disruption we are currently experiencing is quite different from environmental conditions witnessed during the past few thousand years. And with the influence of humans on forests comes an inextricable tangle of narratives.

One of the major features of forest-human interactions over the past three centuries has been a radical shift in perception, from the forest as a key energy resource in the pre-fossil fuel era, to the myth of the forest Eden. There is ample evidence that pre-industrial civilizations were heavily reliant on forest resources, but the view that some collapsed by driving forest resources to extinction is now considered an anachronism. In 1532, the German theologian Martin Luther (1483-1546) wrote, "Who can enumerate all of the uses of wood? Wood is the greatest and most necessary thing in the world, of which man has need and cannot dispense with." Forests were carefully coppiced, or the trees pollarded to optimize their use. Fear of wood shortage was pervasive in Europe in the sixteenth century and beyond, and this fact alone shows that forest management was an essential economic and social activity.

▶ **Logging**
In the Cascade Mountains near Seattle, Washington, workers load 120 ft (36.5 m) long logs with sharpened ends, that will become fish-trap pilings.

Regional to global resource

The development of the wood trade was originally driven by regional demand. By the early seventeenth century, however, tropical wood was already highly valued in Europe. The Dutch imported large amounts of Mauritian Ebony (*Diospyros tessellaria*), using it for picture frames and other decorative objects, such that the prized ebony forests of Mauritius were largely gone by 1645. The creation of a global market for highly profitable commodities, including forest products also triggered the urge for better knowledge of nature as a resource, leading to the explorations of the seventeenth and eighteenth centuries.

A lesser-known aspect of this history has been told by environmental historian Richard Grove: along with colonial conquest, a sentiment of environmental stewardship developed early on. It was clear to the colonizers that their actions could alter their environment, especially forest resources, and many policy makers passed regulations to avoid forest overuse. However, protection policies established by one local governor could be revoked on his departure and, at best, policies merely slowed down the ineluctable destruction of forests. Crucially, this early colonial history generated a powerful narrative of the tropical forest of Eden, and the aesthetic and moral urge to protect "virgin" forests. The French botanist Bernardin de Saint-Pierre (1737-1814), the author of *Paul et Virginie* (1788), is probably responsible more than anyone else for the establishment of this narrative, which would seed nineteenth-century Romantic environmentalism.

It is difficult, and often politically challenging, to attribute past deforestation trends to particular factors. As this chapter shows, inferring forest cover change from paleoenvironmental proxies is error-prone and it is rarely possible to draw firm conclusions. A popular view is that the forest has always been a casualty of human greed, irrespective of culture. This universalist view has been useful in dispelling the concept of the "noble savage." It has also helped shift the focus from narratives of the colonizing countries toward those of the Indigenous populations. However, deforestation is an overwhelmingly modern phenomenon, a result of the global society we live in. Once forested lands have been encroached by crop cultivation and grazing land, and indiscriminately robbed of their resources to supply the global market. Global deforestation peaked from the 1920s to the 1980s, a period that generated environmental disruptions many orders above anything seen before.

◀ **Forest paths**
If looking at the history of forests over the past millennia teaches us a lesson, it is one of patience and of resilience.

GLOBAL LOSS OF FOREST COVER

Ten thousand years ago (8000 BCE), global forests covered 57 percent of habitable land. This proportion was down to 50 percent in 1800, a decline of 7 percent in 10,000 years. During the twentieth century, global forest cover dropped to 38 percent of habitable land.

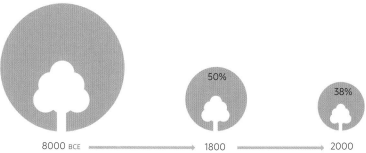

8000 BCE ⟶ 1800 ⟶ 2000

50%

38%

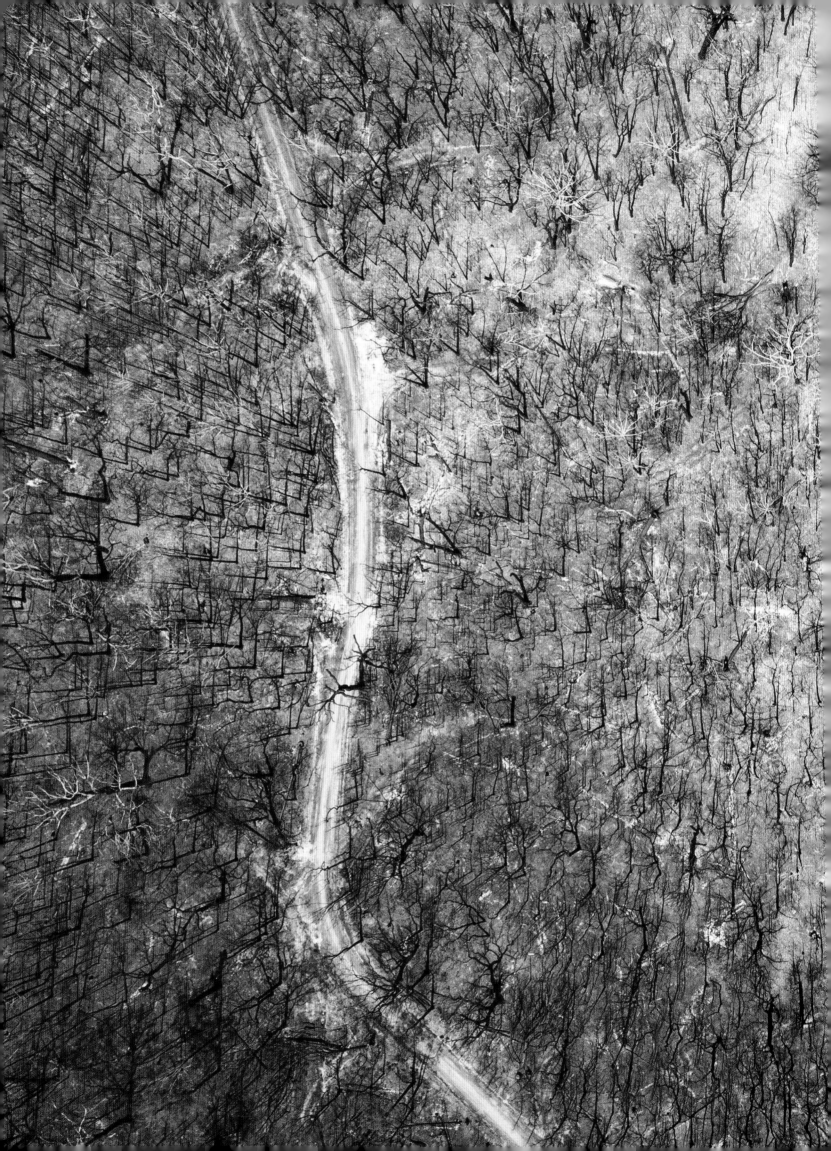

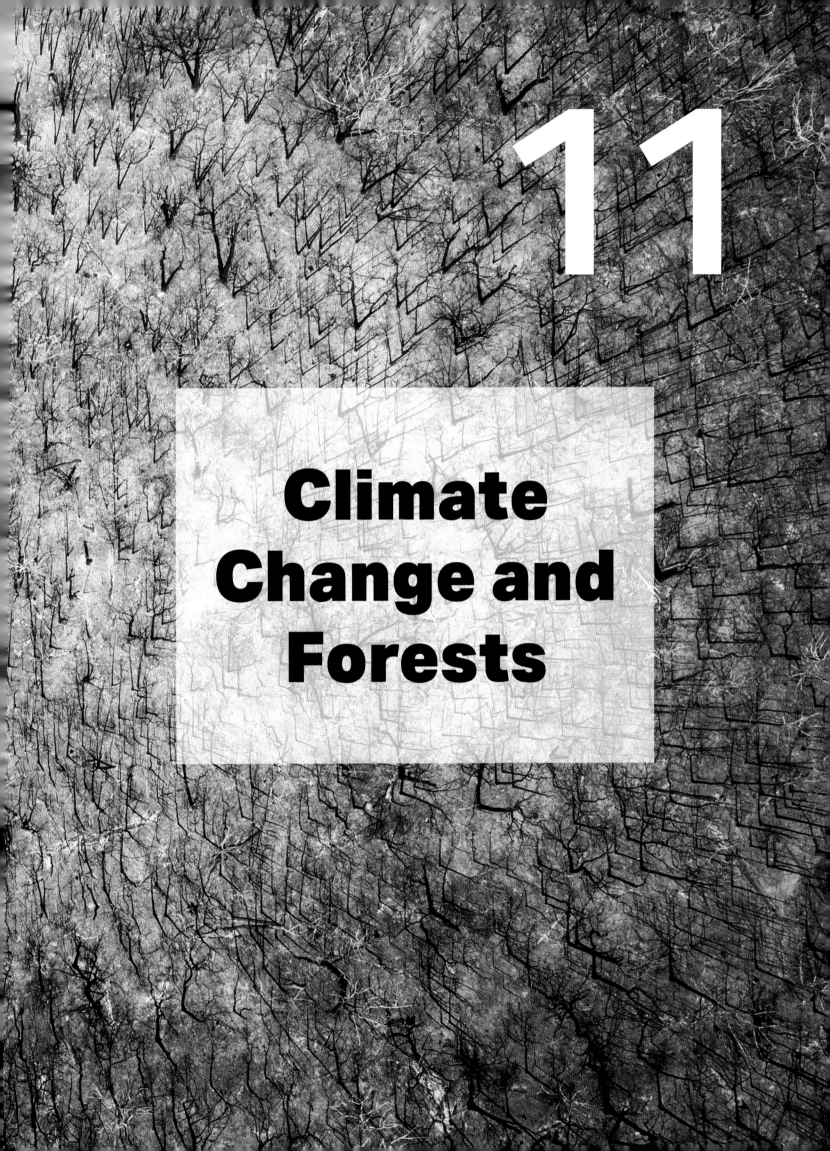

11

Climate Change and Forests

Climate change: ecology's big question

Ecological science abounds with explanations of how ecosystems look, function, and recover from disturbances. These explanations are based on observations of patterns of responses to events, or to natural gradients in water, nutrients, and other influencing factors. Ecology derives from biology, but unlike that discipline—with its "white rats" in laboratory conditions—it is logistically difficult to manipulate ecosystems to test ecological theories.

▼ **Slash and burn**

This practice rotates patches of land from forest to a sequence of crops and back to forest.

Forest ecology is rather like astronomy—the cosmos provides elaborate and sometimes plentiful observations. Progress develops from understanding observed patterns and the underlying processes that produce them. For forest ecologists, climate change is a two-edged sword. On the one edge, climate change experiments on forests—even when one can circumvent the logistic challenges—take place over

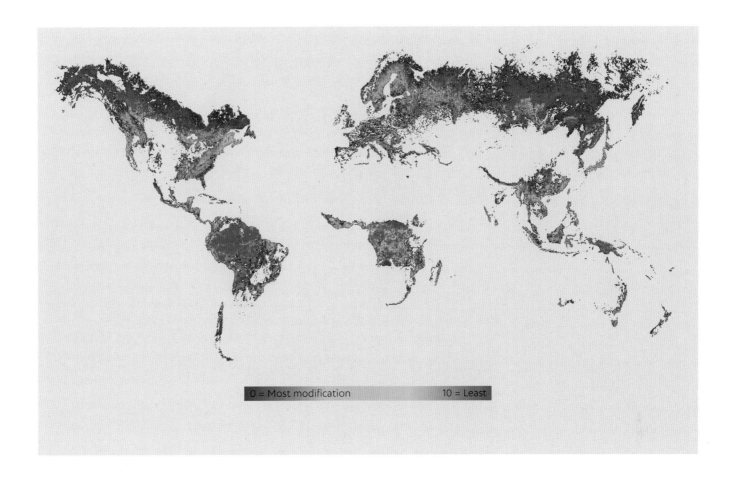

0 = Most modification   10 = Least

a relatively short term and so are blind to the actions of long-term processes, such as the centuries of generation cycles of trees, or the millennia it takes new species to migrate to the site of the climate experiment. On the other edge, the deep past may reveal the patterns of forests under altered climates, in the absence of putatively critical species, or under different concentrations of atmospheric carbon dioxide. These are effectively quasi-experiments from the past that could test our understanding of the way forests work. Given that we are in the process of inducing novel climates onto our planet, the big question in ecology today is: how do ecosystems change in response to climate change?

Climate change from human actions

The changes that have been wrought on our planet by human actions are easily seen. If one looks from the window of an airplane, the effects of the modern era of land conversion are discernible—often very clearly so. Perhaps more subtle but no less omnipresent are the changes to the atmosphere from releases of chemical compounds. Modern "civilization" is changing the planet, and there are persistent and difficult questions as to how this might affect "civilization" in return. One of these questions involves the increase in carbon dioxide in the atmosphere from burning fossil fuels, initially coal, followed by petroleum and natural gas.

Early climate change observations

In the dank, dark Stockholm winter of 1896, the Swedish physicist Svante Arrhenius (1859-1927) distracted himself from a painful divorce by solving between 10,000 and 100,000 physics-based equations relevant to our understanding of the transfer of heat to and from the Earth's surface using recently formulated theories. He focused on mathematical solutions to questions that resonate with findings

▲ **Human actions**
Degree of human modification of the world's forest. Black areas are non-forest. Industrialized regions are largely deforested; forest clearing in developing nations is correlated with population increases; the boreal forests and tropical moist forest have the greatest areas of least modified forest.

from Chapter 10—how could the Earth have warmed fast enough to melt the ice that covered North America and Eurasia 10,000 years ago? And how could it have been so cold as to create these ice sheets and glaciers in the first place? Sweden, as with other higher-latitude landscapes, was and still is a "glacial rebound," as the northern planetary crust continues to decompress from the weight of the now melted Pleistocene glaciers. As the crust lifts, giant boulders emerge from the Baltic Sea, forming the islands of the archipelago off Stockholm and bounding the Swedish coastline. Finding the answers to the questions above would certainly appeal to the curiosity of a geophysicist born and raised in this environment.

Arrhenius followed up on the observations made by French mathematician Jean-Baptiste Joseph Fourier (1768-1830) as early as 1821 that the atmosphere, like a greenhouse, lets through the sun's rays but retains the dark rays from the ground. The "dark rays" are what we now call infrared radiation. The Swede calculated the expected climatic effect of different concentrations of carbon dioxide in the atmosphere, creating tables with predicted temperature changes for every 10° of latitude, from 60°N to 60°S. For each 10° band, Arrhenius predicted the average temperature change for all four seasons across a year at atmospheric carbon dioxide values ranging from two-thirds to three times the average concentrations in 1896. The results of his calculations resemble those from modern general circulation models (GCMs) that are currently used in assessments of planetary climate changes from increased levels of so-called greenhouse gases in the atmosphere.

Arrhenius predicted that warming effects would be greatest at higher latitudes and in winter, and he estimated that the expected long-term increase in global temperature under a doubling of the amount of carbon dioxide in the atmosphere would be 9-11 °F (5-6 °C). This lies in the range of modern GCM predictions, albeit at the high end, although this agreement may, of course, be fortuitous. Arrhenius' calculations do not include significant changes in climate involving cloud formation and changes in vegetation, which are included in current models, and he made these calculations at a time when the principal source of carbon dioxide emissions to the atmosphere from human activities was forestry and land conversion.

CARBON DIOXIDE RELEASE

Release of CO_2 to the atmosphere from fossil sources (fuels, flaring of gases, and making cement) and from forestry and land use. At the time Svante Arrhenius first computed greenhouse warming changes in global temperature in 1886, most of the CO_2 to the atmosphere came from forests. A Gigaton (Gt) or the equivalent Petagram is 1 billion metric tonnes or 10^{15} grams. (Source: IPCC, 2014)

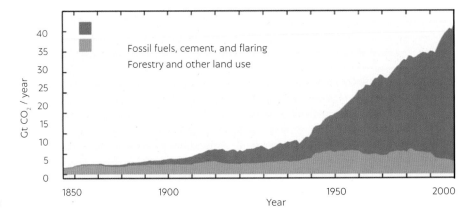

Forest change as an agent of climate change

The interactions between forest change and climate change work in multiple directions: climate can change forests, forests can change climate, and we can change both. Understanding cause and effect in dynamic systems with feedback loops presents a challenge, and even more so when parts of the interacting systems operate at different scales of time and space.

Early observations on forest clearance

When examining this topic, however, there is a straightforward, long-standing question: what are the consequences of clearing forests? In 1785, the American statesman Thomas Jefferson (1743-1826) wrote in his *Notes on the State of Virginia* that, "A change in our climate, however, is taking place very sensibly. Both heats and colds are become much more moderate within the memory even of the middle-aged." Fifteen years later, in 1799, the political writer and lexicographer Noah Webster (1758-1843), speaking to the Connecticut Academy of Sciences, related that, "It appears that all the alterations in a country, in consequence of clearing and cultivation, result only in making a different distribution of heat and cold, moisture and dry weather, among the several seasons." Webster's comments were based on his observations that the conversion of New England from forests to agriculture had changed the seasons, particularly to colder winters. At the time, he was a leading Federalist Party intellectual; Jefferson was the Democratic-Republican vice president of the United States and two years from his election as the third president. The tone of this scientific discussion and the politics of the two protagonists were acrimonious, and the event drips with historical irony. More than two centuries later, the United States has certainly returned to a time of politicization of climate issues. Hard questions are often good questions from the viewpoint of scientists.

In 1853, the French scientist Antoine César Becquerel (1788-1878) asked the good question, how do forests modify temperature? Given that people were deforesting landscapes at the time, it was also wise to wonder then, as it is now, what else happens through the agency of forest clearance. Understanding the effects of forest clearance on climate may be considered an old issue, but we are now beginning to comprehend better how it might work. Inspecting the Webster/Jefferson argument in 1999, Gordon Bonan from the National Center for Atmospheric Research used a climate simulation model and determined that the climate change expected from deforestation of the pre-colonial North American forest landscape should agree with Webster's conjecture, producing earlier and colder fall weather across the middle of a cleared continent.

1700

Pre-European-settlement forest of Massachusetts, and home of the Nipmuc people, indigenous corn-farmers, hunters, and fishermen. The landscape before European colonization would have shown natural ecological variation with both natural and human disturbances producing a landscape varying in the ages, densities, sizes, and species of trees.

1740

European settlers dramatically changed the land through forest clearing, hunting, and trapping. The abundance of many species changed rapidly, and mostly negatively. Old-growth forests were transformed into a rural landscape.

1830

Depending on location New England was largely deforested between 1830 and 1880. Sixty to 80 percent of the land was cleared for pasture, tillage, orchards, and buildings. Much of the remaining areas of woodland were subjected to frequent cuttings for lumber and fuel.

Climate change observations in the Caribbean

On the history of human modification of other aspects of climate, the explorer Christopher Columbus (1451-1506) wrote to his son Ferdinand in 1494 that the presence of forests on the islands of the West Indies caused more rainfall than he had seen on the deforested Azores. Some 500 years later, in 1984, the American meteorologist Richard Anthes analyzed modern weather records, which indicated that Columbus' observation was correct. Dominica, one of the most heavily forested islands in the Lesser Antilles at about 80 percent cover, has about three times the rainfall of the nearby deforested islands of Saint Kitts, Nevis, Antigua, and Barbados.

In the Caribbean colonial era, starting from about 1650, the introduction of sugarcane to the Antilles and the attendant rapid deforestation of the islands produced deleterious consequences over much of the archipelago. The vegetation-climate interactions postulated by Columbus inspired an appreciation of the role of forests in producing rain. The Tobago Main Ridge Forest Reserve on the island of Tobago is the oldest legally protected conservation forest reserve in the western hemisphere. According to the ordinance that established the reserve on April 13, 1776, it was "for the purpose of attracting frequent showers of rain upon which the fertility of lands in these climates doth entirely depend." This ordinance was the product of 11 years of work by the British member of Parliament Soame Jenyns (1704-1787), whose principal parliamentary interests were trade and plantations. In turn, Jenyns was influenced by the ideas of Stephen Hales (1677-1761), a clergyman and member of the Royal Society. Hales worked on many topics, but important here is his research on the movement of water from roots through plants into the air (evapotranspiration). He produced an argument that this flow of water could hydrate the air and produce clouds and rain.

Today, the American Society of Plant Biologists awards the Stephen Hales Prize annually to a scientist for exceptional work in plant biology. The Tobago reserve that was established on the basis of Hales' bright idea is now a major tourist destination and was voted the World's Leading Ecotourism Destination by the World Travel Awards over four consecutive years from 2003. It covers 9,780 acres (3,958 ha) and extends from sea level to 1,982 ft (604 m) in altitude. The Caribbean has suffered the extinction of many species and the islands are now a top priority for the development of protected area networks. The Tobago reserve is considered a leading example of what can be done and its historical importance was noted in *Scientific American* in 1992 for its importance as the first of its kind, a rain protection forest.

The western hemisphere's second such forest reserve was founded about 15 years later and only 111 miles (179 km) from Tobago, on the island of Saint Vincent. There, the Kingshill Enclosure Ordinance No. 5 of 1791 created a small forest holding "reserved and appropriated for the purpose of attracting clouds and rain." This and the Tobago reserve, both developed a decade or more before the Webster/Jefferson arguments, are prescient examples of our understanding about the effects of forest clearance on climate. The actions are an early case at a small scale of what might now be called bio- or eco-engineering, using scientific theory about climate and vegetation interactions to frame a governmental response with the direct intent to improve local climatic conditions.

▲ **Tobago Main Ridge Forest Reserve**

The oldest conservation/ forest reserve in the western hemisphere was created in 1776 to use forest to increase clouds and promote rainfall on the Caribbean island of Tobago.

◄ **Recovered species**

The White-tailed-Sabrewing Hummingbird (Campylopterus ensipennis) is an endangered species thought to be extinct in Tobago following Hurricane Flora in 1963. Rediscovered in 1974, it has now largely recovered in the Tobago Main Ridge Forest Reserve.

Scaling things up to a global level

But what are the larger-scale questions? What are the consequences of our total land clearance across the planet and all our other alterations to Earth as a functioning system? Understanding what we are doing to our shared home when the feedback consequences are tied up with our actions is difficult. To add to that challenge, forests are far from ideal experimental units: they differ from one another, they respond at different time scales, they are logistically hard to sample, they may have unknown histories that complicate understanding their responses to changes, and so on. Nonetheless, we cannot walk away from trying to improve our understanding of forests as an Earth system.

We have some fine new tools to aid us in our approach. These include advanced instruments on satellites and in the laboratory for analyzing ecosystems, ecological models that can be used to synthesize processes and investigate the possible consequences of change, and computational power as never before to inspect patterns in very large data sets. To quote William Shakespeare, "the game's afoot."

Using vegetation models

Ecological models are tools for understanding the potential effects of ongoing change in the environment on forests and other vegetation. However, the scales of time and space of the phenomena incorporated in the models constrain their applications. Furthermore, their ability to provide answers depends on the questions asked.

Modeling limitations

Consider two models of a horse race, one predicting the duration of the race based on prior and immediate weather conditions, and the other using the record of each of the competing horses in previous races and adjusting their speed for track conditions and any other factors that might be important in identifying the winning horse. The exactitude, data requirements, and nature of the predictions are as different as the utilities of the models. Predicting that the horse race should

last for 2 minutes and 15 seconds with great accuracy and precision might be of much less interest than simply the name of the likely winner. Ecological models of forests under climate change address analogous issues. They are developed in order to emphasize the scales of time and space in which forests work, and according to the questions that the model developers hope to answer. In model formulation, there is a challenge in knowing what should be included (or omitted) from a model and the conditions under which model predictions should be useful.

That the global patterns of climate and vegetation are strongly interrelated is an ancient ecological concept. The ancient Greek philosopher Theophrastus (c. 371-c. 287 BCE) observed the positive relationship between altitude and latitude with respect to their climates and vegetation. From this venerable knowledge, early global and regional climate maps were drawn from observations of vegetation (see Chapter 4, page 112). The converse—global vegetation mapped from climate observations only—were developed recently in the context of evaluating the global effects of climate change.

◀ **Lapse rates**

Temperature decreases with both latitude and altitude and is referred to as the lapse rate.

▲ **Theophrastus**

Greek philosopher called the "Father of Ecology." Among many accomplishments, he first observed the positive relationship between altitude and latitude with respect to their climates and vegetation.

CLIMATE-BASED GLOBAL MAPS OF EARTH'S POTENTIAL VEGETATION

The upper map shows the vegetation expected for the current climate; the lower two are equivalent maps but under two different greenhouse-warming climates. The current potential vegetation is changed in over 40 percent of the terrestrial surface under either of the two climate-change conditions. (Source: Smith, Shugart, 1993.)

Current

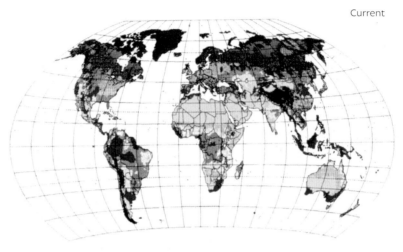

- ⬛ Rain forest
- ◼ Subtropical moist forest
- ◻ Dry forest
- ▨ Warm temperate forest
- ▦ Semiarid
- ◻ Hot desert
- ◼ Shrublands
- ◼ Steppe
- ◻ Cool desert
- ◼ Cool temperate forest
- ⬛ Boreal forest
- ◼ Tundra
- ◼ Cold parklands
- ⬛ Polar desert / ice

Oregon State University

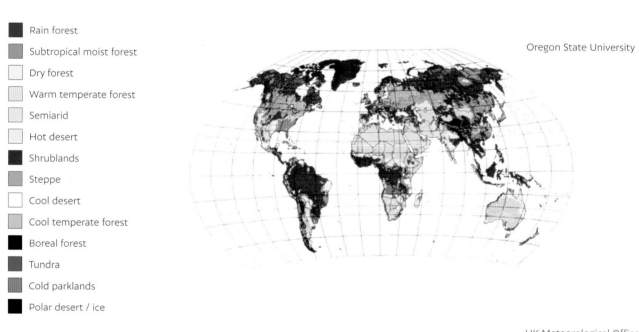

UK Meteorological Office

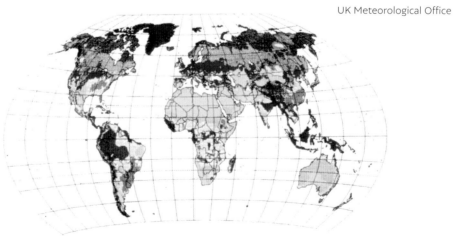

Painting a global picture

The global map from Emanuel et al. (page 134) is a map of the world's vegetation that was produced by collating monthly temperature and precipitation measurements from about 8,000 meteorological stations around the world. Computer-based interpolation can fill in the areas around these stations with equivalent estimated weather conditions based on the surrounding topography. One can resolve such a climate map into pixels—in this case of ½° of latitude by ½° of longitude on each side—and then "paint" the globe with the vegetation expected onto each pixel, given its estimated climate. The "paint" in this case was Leslie Holdridge's life zone classification system (see page 133), which relates vegetation life zones to three climatic indices for dryness, temperature, and annual precipitation. The resultant vegetation map was the first global map of vegetation based on climate and depicts the global terrestrial vegetation expected from the current climate conditions. The approach immediately found application in evaluating the potential effects of climate change.

For example, when the OSU (Oregon State University) model and UKMO (United Kingdom Meteorological Office) model were used in the 1980s to predict a climate with double the level of the then atmospheric carbon dioxide concentrations and applied across more than 8,000 weather stations worldwide, the resultant adjusted vegetation was quite different from that seen today. Under this scenario, more than 40 percent of the global terrestrial area changes to a different vegetation categorization. Both models predicted warmer global climates and higher precipitation than is currently the case. The UKMO model has more rainfall and more warming than the OSU model, but the OSU model is effectively "wetter" than the UKMO model because the increased evaporation caused by higher temperatures predicted in the UKMO model more than offsets the predicted increase in precipitation.

There are several common details across these predicted outcomes and those of similar studies. The possible vegetation changes in response to the climate changes predicted by global climate models are large. Even with relatively coarse vegetation categories, we potentially may be changing 40-50 percent of the world's vegetation to some other sort of vegetation. Applying these statistics to the world's network of biotic preserves implies a change to the broad biome-level vegetation of almost half our diversity protection network, such as converting forests to grassland, savannas to deserts, and so on. Should these predictions prove true, the consequence could be widescale ecological extinction.

PACKRATS AND ECOLOGICAL CHANGE

Packrats (*Neotoma* spp., above right) build nests (above left)
from material they collect within a range of about 100 ft (30
m) from their nests. In arid areas of the United States, these
nests have been preserved for up to 40,000 years and can
be aged using radiocarbon dating (see page 308). The nests
are primarily composed of stems, leaves, and other pieces
of plant species that were growing nearby at the time they
were being constructed. In 1982, the American paleoecologist
Kenneth Cole examined the changes in the distributions of
woody plants at different elevations near the Grand Canyon
of Arizona, and his discovery challenged the notion that the
plant communities in the western United States moved up and
down the mountain gradients as units. Cataloging the contents
of packrat middens of different ages and from different
locations, Cole found differences in patterns of different
vegetations and their elevation in response to environmental
change over the past 24,000 years. Communities that exist
today were not in evidence in the past, and vice versa. For
example (see graph opposite, adapted from Cole, 1985), piñon
pine-juniper woodland did not exist in this region 11,000 years
ago, when it developed in a narrow band on the mountains at
around 4,920 ft (1,500 m) elevation. More recently it expanded
upslope and now occupies a zone between 4,920 ft (1,500 m)
and 6,560 ft (2,000 m). The species making up the vegetation
of each mountain zone change in abundance with a degree of
independence from one another (see also page 292). There are
some clear challenges in assessing the effects of future climate
change on forests given some of the complexity of vegetation
differences evident under past climates.

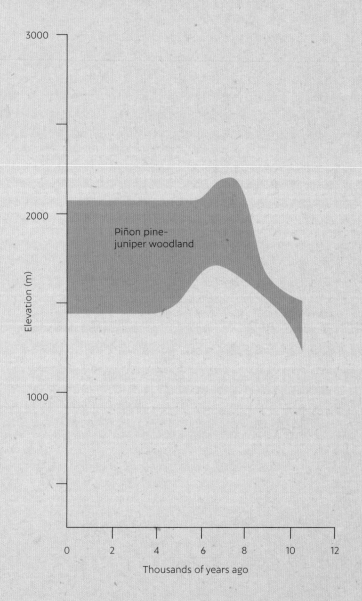

Piñon pine-juniper woodland

Elevation (m)

Thousands of years ago

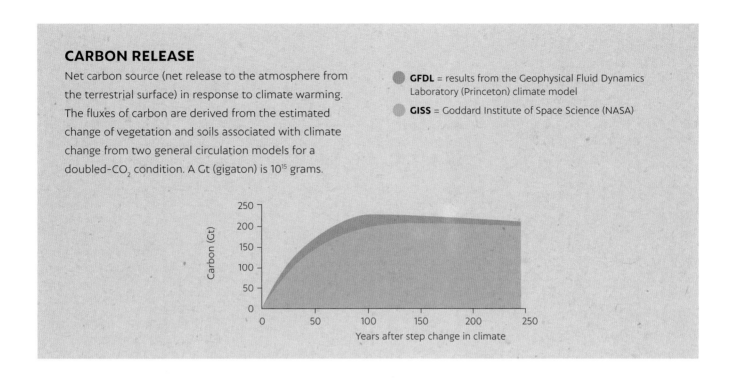

CARBON RELEASE

Net carbon source (net release to the atmosphere from the terrestrial surface) in response to climate warming. The fluxes of carbon are derived from the estimated change of vegetation and soils associated with climate change from two general circulation models for a doubled-CO_2 condition. A Gt (gigaton) is 10^{15} grams.

● **GFDL** = results from the Geophysical Fluid Dynamics Laboratory (Princeton) climate model

● **GISS** = Goddard Institute of Space Science (NASA)

Carbon (Gt)

Years after step change in climate

The good news

There is some potential good news, at least in certain kinds of locations. Pixels of ½° latitude by ½° longitude cover a large enough area that smaller (sub-pixel) areas could harbor patches of refuges for species from former vegetation. For example, if the pixel covers a mountainous area, then mountain refugia could still support forest at upper elevations with cooler conditions. However, paleoecological observations using fossil material and other indicators from the past (see pages 310-312) indicate this potential amelioration could be quite complex (see box opposite).

At a global scale, there are other issues around climate/vegetation change that involve fundamental processes (photosynthesis, water use in plants, and so on) and the role of forests and their soils on controlling greenhouse gases in the atmosphere. The changes that occur across different vegetation types could alter 40 percent or more of the vegetation on the terrestrial surface of the Earth. But what does such a change imply? One possible consequence could be a positive feedback, with climate warming producing the release of greenhouse gases to the atmosphere, which then cause additional warming. For example, a climate-warming transition from deciduous forest to grassland would likely occur under the predicted increase in wildfire frequency and intensity. The carbon stored in the trees could be released to the atmosphere quickly as carbon dioxide, and then be slowly replaced with the development of a prairie vegetation, which would take up carbon from the atmosphere but store less in the living grasses relative to the storage in the preceding living forest. Forest soils would change to prairie soils, providing a transfer of carbon dioxide to the atmosphere. As a mature prairie soil develops over a longer span of time, carbon would be taken from the atmosphere and stored in the soil.

Looking at the example above, and considering all the vegetation transitions under climate change, the landscape processes that release carbon tend to respond quickly and the ones that ultimately store carbon act slowly. Another example of this kind of positive feedback mechanism is seen in the regional case of boreal larch forests converting to "dark" conifer forests (see pages 236-237).

Dynamic global vegetation models

As we have seen, the use of biogeographical models focuses on the question of how climate change might alter the world's vegetation. Another equally important set of questions concerns how a change in climate might change the fluxes of water from the plant canopies, the uptake and release of carbon dioxide from the canopies, and the absorption of incoming sunlight and transmission of outgoing long-wave, infrared radiation.

▼ **Flux tower**

The GuyaFlux tower of Paracou has been measuring fluxes of heat, water vapor, CO_2, and other greenhouse gases in French Guiana since 2004. These meteorological tower observation systems provide data to calibrate and test biophysical models of forest and other plant canopies across the world.

"Big leaf" models

Models of forests and other ecosystems that pursue these questions initially visualized the forest canopy as a big leaf to try to capture the complexity of the manner in which a leaf balances the dynamics of heat, water, and photosynthesis. The relationships that control this balancing act are simple in the sense that they are physical formulas, even though the equations themselves may look complex. One can test the appropriateness for the parameter values used in these equations by measuring the responses of leaves under different conditions to see if these match the model's predicted values. Some of these observations can be made from meteorological towers in a forest and others from data gathered by airplanes or satellites.

Advances in global vegetation models

More advanced, kindred models known as dynamic global vegetation models (DGVMs) conceptualize the canopy as a swarm of leaves that can shade one another. There has been a creatively healthy evolution of these simple physics-based

models over several decades. One of their advantages is their potential capacity to be directly incorporated into atmospheric models to better represent the Earth's surface and its dynamics. A good example is the Integrated Biosphere Simulator model (IBIS model), developed in 1996 by American climate scientist Jonathan Foley and his colleagues, initially to simulate the changes in the physics of the land surface, balance of carbon, and vegetation dynamics in the watershed of the Amazon River. This IBIS model calculation represented the Amazon Basin as a gridwork of pixels measuring ½° latitude by ½° longitude.

The model was applied at the level of each of the pixels. The initial application model used two plant types: trees, which have first access to sunlight; and grasses, which have first access to soil water. Different parameter values for these plant types were used for six different vegetation covers for the Amazon Basin (rain forest, woodland, savanna, and so on). This meant that the implementation of the model required a digitized vegetation map for the Amazon Basin. In addition, each pixel included ten different soil types and multiple soil layers, implying a need for a soil map. If the soil contains as much water as it can hold, any excess drains into the groundwater or flows to adjacent pixels. To send the runoff to the correct places, the model application therefore also required a terrain map to determine runoff-water routing. From this, it becomes clear that even a simple biophysical model with only two kinds of plants becomes very demanding in terms of data in its application to a region.

▲ **Forest canopies**
So-called "Big Leaf" models computed the metabolism of the vegetation mathematically as the transfers of heat, water, and carbon dioxide from a single large leaf, which represented the canopy.

Testing global vegetation models against river flows

A clever aspect of the IBIS application was that Jonathan Foley and his colleagues creatively developed an independent model test. Predicting the runoff of water from all the parts of the surface of the Amazon Basin (from the IBIS model) and knowing which rivers should receive that water (from the routing of water across the terrain) in turn provides a prediction of the amount of water flowing in the Amazon River, its tributaries, and the tributaries of its tributaries. And the test? This was that the amount of water flowing in the rivers should match the model prediction. The annual river flows from 56 flow-measuring stations on small, medium, and large river tributaries, and including the main stem of the Amazon River, closely matched the predicted flows. It turns out that the model showed good fidelity to the results from rivers with large flows over the combined 12-month period, but had a more difficult time predicting the monthly flows of smaller rivers.

In most biophysical models of this sort, one also needs to know the weather data at a relatively fine time resolution (sub-daily or hourly). DGVMs couple with atmospheric models by extracting this meteorological information from the atmospheric model and then providing the atmospheric model with the information

it needs, such as carbon dioxide uptake or emission, evapotranspiration, and so on. Collecting such data locally is relatively straightforward, but doing so at a global level is a logistic and financial nightmare.

A combined approach

One way out of this conundrum might be to test coupled DGVMs and atmospheric models against one another to look for consistent outcomes. In 2006, climate modeler Pierre Friedlingstein at the University of Exeter and his colleagues compared 11 coupled climate-DGVMs to explore the central problem of positive feedback. The models all agreed that future climate change will reduce carbon dioxide uptake by the Earth's surface and increase atmospheric carbon dioxide levels. This is positive feedback—increased levels of atmospheric carbon dioxide promote additional increases in atmospheric carbon dioxide. However, there was no real consensus among the models as to the importance of ocean versus land in producing these results. We are already concerned about the possible effects of carbon dioxide to the atmosphere through human activities. These results imply that we know enough about how the Earth system functions to see the emergence of a difficult problem—that positive feedback may amplify our changes to the Earth's environment. However, we are less sure about the details of how this might work.

◀ **Predicting river flow**

The IBIS model was used to predict the river flow of the Amazon and its tributaries. The test compared the model predictions of water flow at 56 measuring stations for the monthly and annual flows of Amazonian rivers.

Gap models

So far we have discussed three different approaches to the knotty problem of predicting the interactions between global climate change and forests. However, there is a fourth approach. This emphasizes pattern-and-process concepts (see Chapter 2, pages 54-77) and the concept of the forest as a mosaic (see Chapter 3, pages 78-109) to create models that simulate the growth, birth, and deaths of individual trees in canopy gaps on small plots across the globe. Called gap models, these involve millions of such gaps and trillions of trees, all simulated by a high-speed computer.

Simulating forest gaps

Many of the processes in a gap model—such as the death of a tree, which seeds germinate successfully in a given year, and so on—have a degree of random chance of occurrence. Each gap model simulation is for an independent patch of land the size of the crown occupied by a large mature tree. The annual output of each simulated patch resembles a sample survey plot in a forest, with a tally of the diameter and species of each tree on the plot. Several hundred such simulated patches are averaged to produce an expected mean biomass and species composition of a forested landscape through time.

The biomass and species composition of the simulated forest are determined by competition between individual trees for light, water, and nutrients. Changes over time in seedling banks and individual tree processes (growth, regeneration, and biomass accumulation) are constrained by changes in the light profile, temperature, moisture, and nutrients—all computed each year in the model. Species-specific input parameters determine a maximum annual diameter increment of each simulated tree as a function of its size. This increment is then further reduced according to the environment (light, temperature, and resource availability). Different species respond in different ways to the values of these environmental factors.

Annual local environmental changes produced by a gap model for each simulation include the shading of light through the multilayer forest canopy resulting from tree growth and death, drying of the soils due to forest canopies transpiring away soil water, changes in the ratio of soil carbon and nitrogen (an important consideration for the rate of soil decomposition), and the overall availability of nutrients. Gap models have been developed over the past 50 years for hundreds of different forests in locations around the world. For global and diverse tropical applications, the use of model parameters based on functional types—groups of tree species that are similar with respect to their ecological attributes—has supplanted using actual species in these models. In 2017, American project scientist Jacquelyn Shuman and her colleagues implemented simulations for Russian boreal forests responding to climate change that involved modeling the growth, death, and regeneration of more than a trillion trees.

A SIMULATED FOREST PLOT

For every tree on a simulated forest plot, overall calculations are made for each simulation year and a number of factors— mortality, growth, and establishment—are taken into consideration. Every year, each tree has a probability of dying and trees growing poorly ("suppressed trees") are more likely to die. The establishment of seedlings depends on biological and environmental conditions. Tree growth is a function of the tree's size, species, and environmental factors. For each tree, the optimal growth is computed as the increase in a tree's diameter each year. This optimal diameter increment decreases as trees get larger. The increment also changes according to the environmental responses typical of the tree's species.

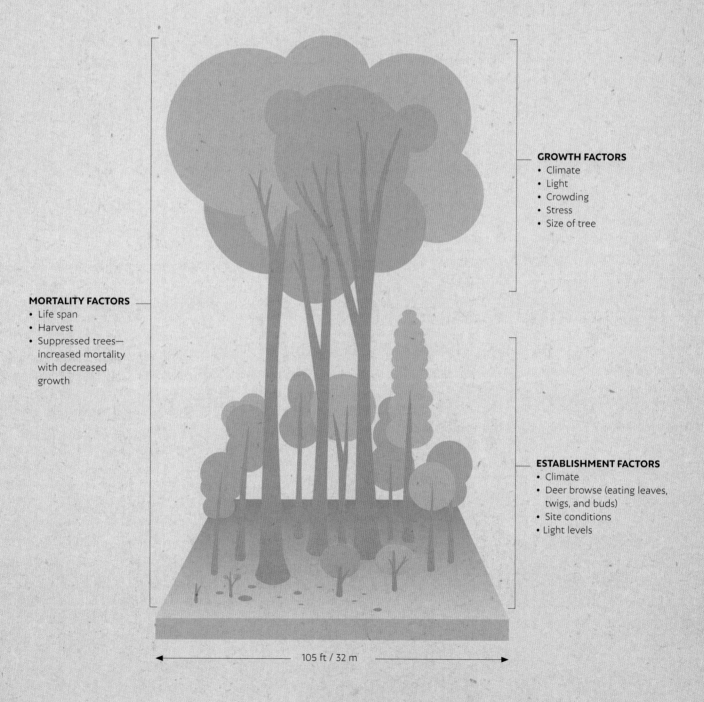

GROWTH FACTORS
- Climate
- Light
- Crowding
- Stress
- Size of tree

MORTALITY FACTORS
- Life span
- Harvest
- Suppressed trees— increased mortality with decreased growth

ESTABLISHMENT FACTORS
- Climate
- Deer browse (eating leaves, twigs, and buds)
- Site conditions
- Light levels

105 ft / 32 m

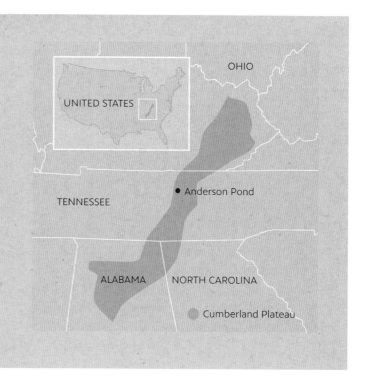

ANDERSON POND IN THE CUMBERLAND PLATEAU OF TENNESSEE

Beneath the surface of this small lake is a sediment record with fossilized pollen grains and charcoal deposited by wildfires dating back more than 23,000 years. The mechanisms for tree composition changes in this long record have been inspected using a gap model by A. M. Solomon and his colleagues. Some 23,000 years ago, this region was composed of trees now associated with the boreal forest. Over time, it transitioned to the diverse temperate forest we see today. The gap model evaluation indicates that the spruce and fir trees, which persisted at the site until 5,000 years ago, were relict populations surviving in shady, cool north-facing slopes.

OHIO

UNITED STATES

TENNESSEE

● Anderson Pond

ALABAMA NORTH CAROLINA

● Cumberland Plateau

Simulating past forests and predicting future change

The initial entry of gap models into climate change assessment was in reconstructing past forest changes, as seen in fossil pollen in sediment cores from lakes (see pages 310-311). In 1981, Allen Solomon and his colleagues at Oak Ridge National Laboratory applied a gap model to reconstruct a fossil pollen record of forests in the Cumberland Plateau in Tennessee, and later used it to predict changes in vegetation responding to climate change over eastern North America. While gap models can predict the changes in different tree species over time, pollen in sediment cores generally are resolved only to the genera of trees and other plants. Pollen data in sediments might "see" the presence of oaks (genus *Quercus*) at a time in the past, but these data are "blind" to exactly which oak species were there. Further, the data cannot "see" the presence of insect-pollinated trees, which do not deposit pollen in lakes.

These two problems can be filled in by the predictions of a gap model, which can produce predictions of the vegetation expected in the deep past. Predicting the genera at a given location in a past time in this way helps reconstruct whether a presumed past climate is consistent with the fossil pollen composition of the prehistoric forest. In some cases, "weird" prehistoric combinations of pollen genera are found in lakes but have no modern analogs. Gap models potentially can resolve which possible past climate or other conditions might produce such pollen results in lake sediments.

◀ **Cumberland Plateau**
View of the Obed River, which stretches across the Cumberland Plateau in Tennessee.

Modeling the forest's "ecosystem metabolism"

In a 2017 report, climate modeler Jianyong Ma and his colleagues produced the first global application of a gap model, called the FORCCHN model, to compute the "ecosystem metabolism" of the world's forests. This model predicted annual changes in the gross primary productivity (total carbon taken up by forests at a location), ecosystem respiration (amount of fixed carbon released by the forest), and net ecosystem productivity (gross primary production minus ecosystem respiration) for each year from 1982 to 2011. Gap model output can produce the vegetation variables used in DGVM models, including the leaf area of a forest at a location, the amount of plant tissue, and the vertical distribution of leaves, branches, and tree trunks. The FORCCHN model was tested on its ability to predict the uptake and emission of carbon dioxide, water, and heat for a forest at hourly intervals and summed to get monthly values. These essential forest ecosystem fluxes were calculated and compared to monthly measurements at 37 meteorological tower sites in different forests with statistically significant correlations between the patterns in the data and the model predictions.

Identifying boreal browning

A second type of model test, suggested by the FORCCHN model, could be conducted at completely different scales of time and space—globally and annually. The FORCCHN model can produce several important forest ecosystem measurements, one of which is net primary production, which is illustrated globally over the years 1982-2011 in the lower third of the graphic opposite. Satellite-based observations have identified several broad regions across global boreal forests that have been "browning"—showing loss of leaves. These regions, computed independently, coincide with the areas identified by the FORCCHN model, which may therefore have the capacity to identify such regions in advance. The causes of boreal browning are complex, including insect outbreaks and moisture stress, but all are conditions for which decreased net primary productivity is an antecedent. Predicted changes in productivity observations could be valuable adjunct warnings of possible forest change, since the onset of low net ecosystem productivity is often associated with tree death and insect outbreak, followed by wildfires as the dead trees become a source of fuel for wildfires.

FORCCHN MODEL

Applying the FORCCHN model for global-scale forest responses for the 1982–2011 period at a grid resolution of 0.5°×0.5°. Gross Primary Production (GPP) is the amount of carbon dioxide converted to sugar by photosynthesis; Ecosystem Respiration (ER) is the carbon dioxide emitted by the system; Net Primary production (NEP) is GPP minus ER.

If Net Primary Production is positive, then the forest is a sink and is removing carbon dioxide from the air—negative net ecosystem productivity shown in orange and yellow in the boreal-forest region independently matches the "browning" zones that have been seen in satellite imagery over parts of the boreal forests. (Source: Shugart, Foster, Wang et al., 2020.)

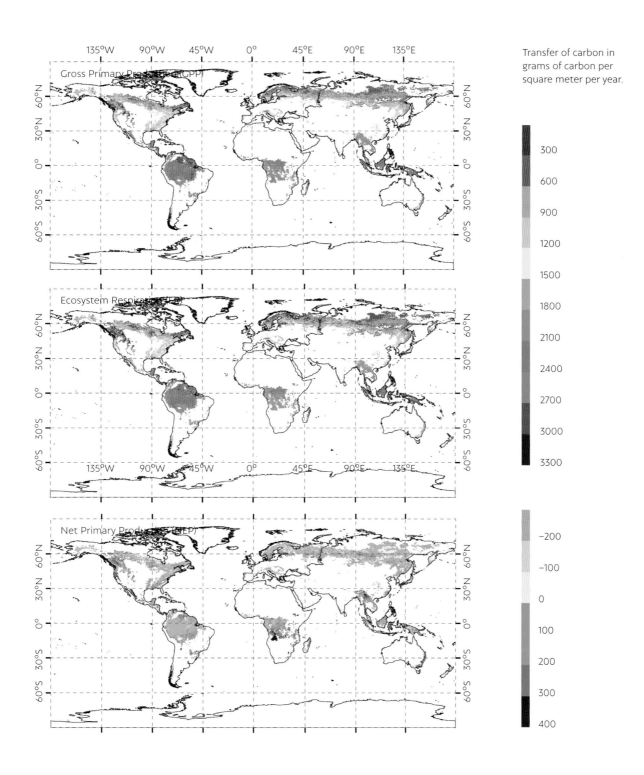

Transfer of carbon in grams of carbon per square meter per year.

Forests and geoengineering

The concept that human actions can control the weather is ancient and ingrained in early agricultural societies. In the Old World, the Book of Leviticus (26: 3-4) states, "If you follow my statutes and keep my commandments and observe them faithfully, I will give you your rains in their season, and the land shall yield its produce, and the trees of the field shall yield their fruit." In the New World, carvings of rain gods and rain dances abound across many cultures.

Modern rainmakers

There has been a checkered history of rainmakers in recent centuries, culminating in more scientific modern studies of seeding clouds to produce rain, initially at the Leningrad Institute of Rainmaking in the 1930s, and later, in the 1940s, at the General Electric Research Observatory Laboratories in Schenectady, New York. Eventually, rainmaking was deployed as a "weapon" by the United States in its protracted war in Vietnam. Cloud seeding (delivering chemicals into clouds from airplanes to promote rainfall) was implemented in Operation Popeye. This military operation ran 2,602 cloud-seeding missions over Vietnam from 1967 until 1972, with the intent of prolonging the monsoonal wet season and slowing the Viet Cong's ability to rebuild and resupply. The disclosure of this practice eventually led to international agreements against the use of weather as a military weapon.

▶ **Cloud seeding**

Cloud seeding by aircraft to induce rainfall in India.

▼ **Ancient geoengineering**

Vessel depicting Aztec rain god Tlaloc— humans have strived to control the weather for thousands of years.

Climate modification has become a topic of discussion within multiple learned scientific societies, including the Royal Society and the United States National Academy of Sciences, which have convened conferences and published special issues of scientific journals on the topic over the past decade. These discussions stem from the concern that human activities may potentially and irreversibly alter the planetary climate. There are historical precedents of nations contemplating changing the climate to alter the environment and better their situation. As early as 1948, Stalin developed plans to expand the Soviet economy by controlling climate at very large, even global, scales. One plan featured orbiting "rings" around the Earth, somewhat like the rings of Saturn, to reflect more sunlight upon the northern Soviet Union and other high-latitude areas. By their estimation, this would also have shaded tropical regions and made them more temperate. Other proposals have included damming and diverting the Congo River to water the Sahara, and blocking the Gulf Stream with a dam between the United States and Cuba. The Russian climatologist Mikhail Budyko calculated that covering the Arctic Sea with coal dust to darken the sea ice would cause it to melt, making for a warmer and wetter northern Russia. The most frightening aspect of this latter plan is that it would be relatively inexpensive to carry out. Of course, we are currently watching the Arctic Sea ice recede as an inadvertent consequence of human actions.

Bioengineering "solution" to climate change?

The planetary bioengineering questions of the past are now reemerging, but reframed for our current global climate situation: can we, and should we, modify the climate to "solve" the problem of global warming? Whatever is done in the future, the Earth's forests likely will play a significant role. More than twice the amount of carbon dioxide in the atmosphere is removed by the land surface (about 200 Pg) than by ocean uptake (about 90 Pg) per year, even though the land is only about 30 percent of the Earth's total surface area. Clearing forest in the northernmost latitudes (boreal forest clearing) can cool the Earth significantly. The result is that boreal forest clearing, perhaps by burning in the far northern parts of the forest, may be actively considered as a possible way to ameliorate climate warming.

It is important to realize in all of this that, while the question "Can we use planetary modifications of some sort to somehow rehabilitate a human-altered climate?" may be important, if we answer it then we face at least two existential questions. First, if in our planetary climate management all or some of our changes are undesirable, can we restore the former climate regime and get the climate genie back in its bottle? Second, if we can successfully "fix" the climate, then who gets to set the thermostat?

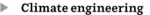 **Climate engineering**

Livingstone Falls at the lower Congo River—one climate engineering project proposed during the 1960s by the then-USSR was to route water from the Congo basin into the Sahara to irrigate the desert.

12

The Future: Seeing Forests with New Eyes

Seeing forests remotely

"If a tree falls in a forest and no one is around to hear it, does it make a sound?" This philosophical riddle touches on our perception of a physical phenomenon that can be observed and measured by instruments other than our own eyes and ears.

In the eighteenth century, Anglo-Irish philosopher George Berkeley (1685-1753) responded to the question by declaring, "*Esse est percipi*" ("To be is to be perceived"), meaning that an object or event is defined by its sensory qualities. If sound is defined as the vibration of airwaves, then a falling tree will make a sound that can be heard or detected by a recorder, regardless of any human presence in the forest.

To obtain information about a phenomenon, an object, or an area from a distance without direct contact is the science and art of remote sensing. Popular forms of remote sensing are images of the Earth's surface and its vegetation and landscape features captured by a sensor mounted on a platform stationed in the atmosphere or space. Most histories of remote sensing identify French photographer and balloonist Gaspard-Félix Tournachon (1820-1910), known by the pseudonym Nadar, as the first person to photograph the land surface from the air, in a hot-air balloon tethered 850 ft (260 m) above Paris in 1858. Nadar's original photos have since been lost, but later photos still exist (see opposite); the oldest-surviving aerial images belong to American photographer James Wallace Black (1825-1896), taken from a similar balloon about 2,000 ft (600 m) above Boston in 1860.

Developments in aerial photography

A bird's-eye view of the landscape permits new insights into the patterns and processes that govern vegetation formations. The first true unmanned aerial images were taken by amateur German photographer Julius Neubronner (1852-1932) in 1903, who used a camera mounted on the breast of carrier pigeons that automatically shot images at 30-second intervals along the birds' flight line.

▶ **Reconnaissance**

Reconnaissance aircraft during the First World War with the pilot trying to maintain a level plane so that the aviator can take vertical photographs of ground positions.

◀ **Early aerial shots**

An overhead view of Paris taken in 1868 by the French photographer Nadar, who pioneered the technique of aerial photography using a hot-air balloon.

American photographer George Lawrence (1868–1938) later perfected the method by recording panoramic images of the 1906 San Francisco earthquake and fire by strapping large-format cameras with curved film plates to 17 kites suspended about 2,000 ft (600 m) above the city.

During the First World War, observers in reconnaissance aircraft tried to obtain vertical photographs by holding a camera over the side of their plane and manually advancing the film. It was from the early 1930s and during the Second World War that aerial photography techniques were integrated in airplanes for automatic data collection during large-area surveys around the world. On October 24, 1946, a captured wartime German rocket launched from New Mexico provided a glimpse of the Earth in the first known photo from space, and the Cold War and Space Race of the 1950s and 1960s inspired further advances in aerial photography. Following the replacement of film-based technology by digital color photography and the use of cameras with images in both the visible (VIS) and near-infrared (NIR) light wavelengths, the opportunity for collecting photos over large areas and year-round, and the ease of interpretation of the imagery, made photography from air and space the primary tool for regional forestry and wildlife management.

REMOTE SENSING

Modern remote sensing platforms from ground, air, and space.

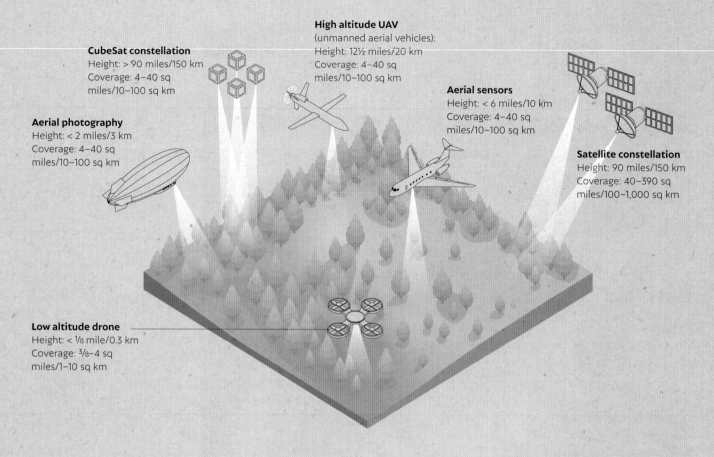

CubeSat constellation
Height: > 90 miles/150 km
Coverage: 4–40 sq
miles/10–100 sq km

High altitude UAV
(unmanned aerial vehicles):
Height: 12½ miles/20 km
Coverage: 4–40 sq
miles/10–100 sq km

Aerial sensors
Height: < 6 miles/10 km
Coverage: 4–40 sq
miles/10–100 sq km

Aerial photography
Height: < 2 miles/3 km
Coverage: 4–40 sq
miles/10–100 sq km

Satellite constellation
Height: 90 miles/150 km
Coverage: 40–390 sq
miles/100–1,000 sq km

Low altitude drone
Height: < ⅛ mile/0.3 km
Coverage: ⅜–4 sq
miles/1–10 sq km

WAVELENGTHS

The spectrum of light (top) and atmospheric transmission
(bottom) for remote sensing observations—the wavelength
regions along the spectrum transmit different types of
information about the trees and plants on the land below.

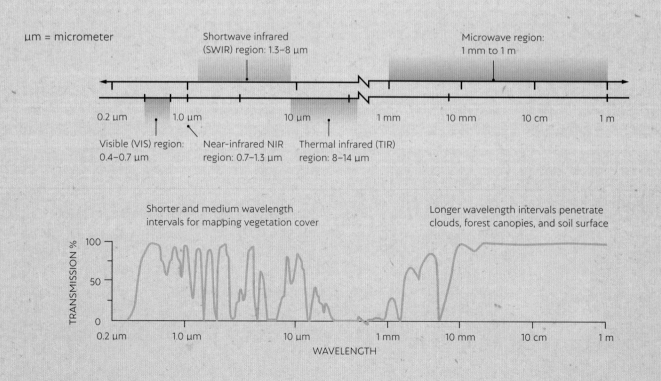

μm = micrometer

Shortwave infrared
(SWIR) region: 1.3–8 μm

Microwave region:
1 mm to 1 m

0.2 μm   1.0 μm   10 μm   1 mm   10 mm   10 cm   1 m

Visible (VIS) region:
0.4–0.7 μm

Near-infrared NIR
region: 0.7–1.3 μm

Thermal infrared (TIR)
region: 8–14 μm

Shorter and medium wavelength
intervals for mapping vegetation cover

Longer wavelength intervals penetrate
clouds, forest canopies, and soil surface

TRANSMISSION %

100

50

0

0.2 μm   1.0 μm   10 μm   1 mm   10 mm   10 cm   1 m

WAVELENGTH

Developments in remote sensing

The term "remote sensing" was first used in the United States in the 1950s by Evelyn Pruitt, a geographer at the US Office of Naval Research, to refer to the detection and measurement of electromagnetic radiation of different wavelengths reflected or emitted from distant objects. Remote-sensing measurements provide us with the ability to "sense" the condition (e.g., health), the form (e.g., structure), and the function (e.g., growth) of an object (e.g., plants) on the land surface. The information content of these measurements is used to characterize the physical, chemical, and biological state of ecosystems, along with natural processes (including vegetation, soils, and water) and human-induced processes (such as land-use activities).

Remote-sensing instruments are built at different wavelength regions on the electromagnetic spectrum (EMS). The VIS region of wavelengths (0.4-0.7 μm) coincides with the part of the EMS that our eyes are capable of sensing, and is used extensively in aerial photography and satellite spectral imagery for mapping vegetation cover. The NIR region spans 0.7-1.3 μm and lies beyond the human eye; it provides high sensitivity to leaf structure and morphology. The shortwave infrared (SWIR) region spans 1.3-8 μm; it gives information about the reflected solar radiation and moisture content of vegetation. The thermal infrared (TIR) region spans 8-14 μm; it captures the emitted energy of the land surface and detects vegetation stress and soil moisture. Longer-wavelength intervals, such as the microwave region, spread across wavelengths of 1 mm to 1 m. They include all the intervals that can penetrate cloud cover and also forest canopies and the soil surface to various depths, providing information on soil and plant water content, structure, and above-ground biomass.

The remote-sensing process generally includes a source of radiant energy, a sensor on a platform that detects and records radiation, and a set of activities that contain processing, interpretation, and visualization of the data. There are two types of remote-sensing instruments: passive and active. Passive instruments detect natural energy (e.g., from the sun) that is reflected or emitted from the observed scene. Active instruments provide their own energy (electromagnetic radiation) to illuminate the object or scene and then receive the radiation that is reflected or backscattered from that object. The most common instruments for studying vegetation characteristics and patterns are imaging spectrometers, which are passive sensors similar to cameras that detect and record surface radiation in VIS and infrared (IR) wavelengths. Among active sensors, radar (radio detection and ranging) and lidar (light detection and ranging) function in microwave and visible NIR ranges of the light spectrum, respectively, and provide information about vegetation structure.

Cover: changes in forest from disturbance and recovery

Perhaps the single most important factor that has impacted the Earth's surface is the clearing of woodlands by humans. As suggested by Welsh geographer Michael Williams in his seminal work *Deforesting the Earth* (2002), "the thinning, changing, and elimination of forests—deforestation, no less—is not a recent phenomenon; it is as old as the human occupation of the earth."

No wood, no kingdom

As discussed in Chapter 10, the need for wood-based fuel to generate heat, to smelt metals, to cook, and to build structures and ships, among other uses, has been the driving force behind changes in forest cover and part of the biography of modern forest life since the end of the ice age just over 10,000 years ago. For most Western countries, the forces that unleashed the large-scale use of timber magnified after 1750 following the onset of the Industrial Revolution. Within the span of a hundred years, the face of the globe changed. Humans gained control of nature and its resources with the invention of more effective tools and machines, faster transportation and communication systems, and movements of large amounts of goods and materials from various parts of the world.

▼ **Lumber production**
By the end of the nineteenth century, a vast amount of US forest land had been exploited for lumber production.

By the mid-nineteenth century, the United States was the world's predominant producer and consumer of timber by far. Over a period of 30 years (1869-1899), more than 100 million acres (40 million hectares) of US forests were cleared for agricultural expansion. By 1906, lumber production in the United States had reached about 3.8 billion ft^3 (108 million m^3), or almost two-thirds of the global output. William Greeley (1879-1955), chief of the US Forest Service in 1920-1928, estimated that more than 80 percent of US forest land was cleared between 1620 to 1920, when new laws on forest management and conservation were established and the exploitation of forests shifted to the tropics. In the early 1920s, about 27 million acres (11 million ha) of forests worldwide were cleared each year, with at least 70 percent of these in tropical areas. Between 1950 and 1980, more than 790 million acres (320 million ha) of tropical forests disappeared to provide land for grazing (cattle farming) and agriculture.

US DEFORESTATION 1620–1920

Almost all of US virgin forest land had been cut down by the
early twentieth century as depicted in these maps based on
the original work of William. B. Greeley, chief of the US Forest
Service from 1920 to 1928.

1620

1850

1920

LANDSAT DATA

Map of the intensity of forest cover change from 2000 to 2020 (green areas show no change) using Landsat data from the Global Land Analysis and Discovery (GLAD) laboratory at the University of Maryland.

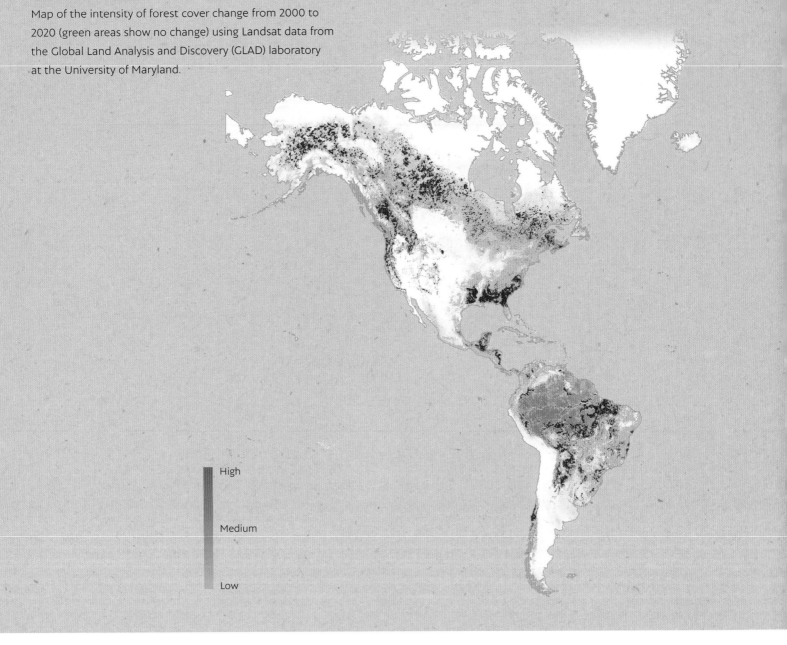

High

Medium

Low

Measuring deforestation

Estimates of forest clearing up to the early 1970s and before satellite observations were mainly based on timber statistics and wood volume produced and exchanged in the lumber market. Starting from 1972 and the launch of the Earth Resources Technology Satellite by NASA, Landsat data provided a new approach for mapping forest cover changes across the globe. The Landsat satellites (the latest, Landsat 9, was launched in September 2021) have acquired millions of images, which are digitally archived in the United States and in several receiving stations globally and are freely available for public use. The images are collected at different spectral bands, displaying vegetation cover, types, phenology, and canopy structure at spatial resolutions of 15–60 m every 16 days. A notable advantage of such a vast archive of digital imagery of the Earth by Landsat and other remote-sensing instruments is the establishment of large-area vegetation mapping programs conducted by government agencies for resource management and scientific applications. With

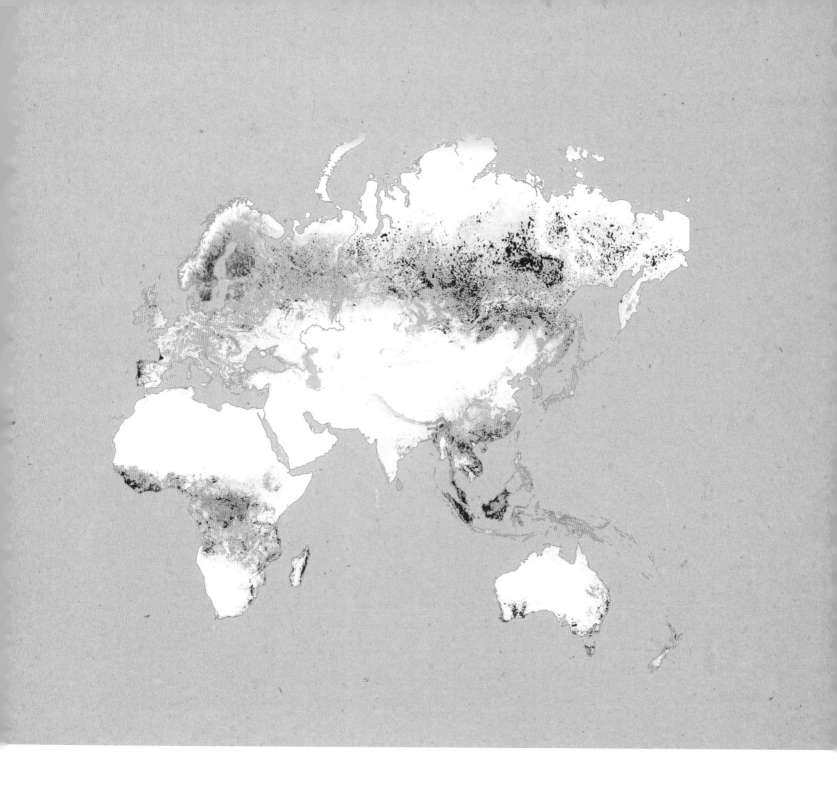

recent advances in cloud computing, such as the Google Earth Engine, the systematic mapping of forest cover changes has become readily accessible. Timely and precise evidence of human activities on land provided by these maps is then used for planning forest conservation, devising policies to reduce carbon emissions from land use, and generating natural climate solutions.

▶ **Three dimensions**

This 3D image of part of Pasadena, California was created using a shaded relief map from the Shuttle Radar Topography Mission (SRTM) elevation data (February 2000) and visible imagery from the Landsat 7 satellite.

Interpreting the data

The research on mapping land-use change has brought together social scientists, economists, and anthropologists to understand patterns and processes of human interactions with nature. Linking people to pixels using remote-sensing observations and geographic information systems (GISs) has ushered in a new area of multidisciplinary research. For a social scientist, remote-sensing data help provide the spatial and temporal contexts that shape social phenomena, which in turn provide information on individual and household behavior in and with the surrounding environment, including landscapes, patches of forest, and administrative or political units.

Moderate- and fine-scale optical images in the VIS and NIR spectral bands have produced reliable estimates of forest types and disturbance events, such as deforestation, fire scars, landscape fragmentation, and forest regeneration. For example, the contextual data in Landsat images and patterns of forest cover change have contributed to our understanding of the national and global economic drivers of forest fragmentation in the Amazon Basin (see graphic opposite).

▶ **Deforestation over time**

This series of photos shows a satellite view of large-scale deforestation over time in a remote part of the Amazon—Para, on the western outskirts of the town of Sao Felix de Xingu, Brazil. After forest areas are cleared, the brush is left to dry out. Satellites capture huge deforestation fires in 2017. The cleared land becomes cattle pasture in 2018.

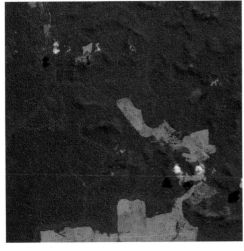
2013

2015

2017

2018

AMAZON FOREST FRAGMENTATION PATTERNS

During NASA's Large-scale Biosphere-Atmosphere Experiment in Amazonia (2000–2010), the interpretation of Landsat imagery by American geographer Eugenio Arima and his colleagues provided a typology of dominant patterns of land clearance that link forest fragmentation with social processes. Geographer Eugenio Arima and his team classified these fragmentation patterns as follows:

Fishbone fragmentation
Dominant in the state of Rondônia as a result of national-level forest colonization programs that resulted in smallholder settlements.

Rectangular fragmentation
Mostly seen in the state of Mato Grosso and related to large landholders and land companies.

Dendritic fragmentation
Seen in a region between the Xingu and Tapajos Rivers in the state of Para, reflecting the irregular behavior of loggers in generating road networks and avoiding topography.

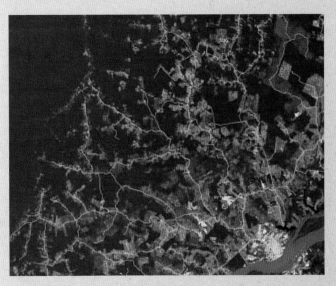

Radial fragmentation
This forms like a wheel of forest clearance radiating from a town or village and usually reflects spontaneous demographic growth of smallholders in the absence of government regulation.

Form: forest structure and dynamics

Trees and vascular plants play a major role in balancing energy and matter in the Earth's terrestrial ecosystems. The evolutionary processes of growth, survival, and reproduction—Darwinian selection—in diverse environments has led to a wide variety of forms and functions across and within ecosystems.

▶ **Structure**

The forest canopy is hailed as the greatest source of biological diversity on Earth. The horizontal and vertical distribution of layers of leaves, branches, and stems create a unique structure at fine scales that affects the entire forest ecosystem function and its interaction with the environment. Canopy structure distributes light into the forests, moderates temperature, acts as a windbreak and intercepts rainfalls, and produces myriad climate conditions, and specialized niches for plants, animals, birds, and insects.

The existence of a causal relationship between the forms/structures of ecosystems and their functions has historically informed the science of biology. Knowledge of variations in form and structure is essential to understanding the physiological processes that regulate plant growth. For example, crown characteristics influence the rate of plant growth, expressed as the increase in stem diameter, height, and seed and fruit production. Leaf structure is essential to understanding how the functions of photosynthesis and transpiration are affected by environmental stressors or human disturbance. Learning about stem structure helps in understanding the ascent of sap and translocation of carbohydrates, and knowledge of root structure allows an appreciation of plant hydraulics and the flow of water and nutrients.

Measuring form to understand function

The growth of a tree is inextricably intertwined with its corresponding form and structure. In general, trees are constrained in their geometry and display striking structural regularities. These may be explained by the constraints of constructing tall structures in wood and of transporting water up a tall structure made of hollow tubes. Trees "solve" both of these constraints, and the result in either case can be predicted by allometric models. These models are developed statistically from tree size measurements and are used to predict the tree's biomass and the area of its foliage from its diameter. However, most trees do not grow symmetrically over their life span, and small trees have a disproportionally larger number of leaves and less woody tissue than larger trees. Furthermore, the structure of trees and forest stands depends strongly on a combination of processes involving growth, mortality, competition, and a self-thinning strategy, which in turn rely on landscape features such as soil conditions and climate. Hence, recognizing variations in the form and size of individual trees and the structure of forest stands across environmental gradients has been one of the main goals of field ecologists for understanding the function of forests.

Remote-sensing techniques, particularly from active lidar and radar sensors on the ground and in air and space platforms, have provided measurements of forest structure with unprecedented precision in recent years. Three-dimensional vegetation structure is the spatial arrangement of leaves, branches, and stems. Precise measurements of this structure, from the level of a single tree (such as the stem height and diameter, crown size, and volume) to the level of a forest stand (such as above-ground volume and biomass, and horizontal and vertical variations of tree density and gaps), are routinely produced by active remote-sensing observations.

EXTRACTING INDIVIDUAL TREES

Individual trees can be extracted from terrestrial lidar point clouds using tree segmentation. Here a tree-level point cloud (brown) from a larger-area point cloud (green) is taken from terrestrial laser scanning in tropical forest in Nouragues Nature Reserve, French Guiana.

Lidar

A lidar emits nanosecond pulses of coherent light at the characteristic wavelength of its laser in the nadir or near-nadir direction, which are then scattered back by the land surface and its vegetated structures and recorded by the lidar sensor. The elapsed time between the firing of each pulse and its reception by the instrument determines the distance from the scattering events and the underlying terrain surface. The recorded signal, or lidar waveform, is a history of the laser's return energy as a function of time. The shape of the waveform is a function of canopy height and vertical distribution of foliage, trunks, twigs, and branches at varying levels within the lidar footprint.

A lidar sensor also provides the geolocation of all measured returns, allowing the calculation of the detailed vertical structure of forests and the underlying topographic elevation. In addition to forest structure, forest biomass can be inferred from the height information contained in the vertical lidar waveforms. Lidar observations from ground measurements taken by terrestrial and airborne lidar scanners have revolutionized the study of forest ecology over the past two decades. These instruments have provided precise measurements of tree structure, volume, and biomass, forest stand structure, and tree density and gaps, with unprecedented spatial and vertical resolutions of 10-50 cm. In space, lidar observations performed in a sampling mode along the orbital tracks of satellites are providing billions of measurements across global forests. These include the ICESat and ICESat-2 sensors in 2003-2008 and from 2018 to present, respectively, and the recently launched Global Ecosystem Dynamics Investigation sensor onboard the International Space Station.

Radar

Radar remote sensing, with its advantages of oblique observational geometry and all-hours, all-weather data collection, provides frequent imagery of the land from air and space. The imaging radar sweeps the landscape, and its radio waves penetrate the forest canopy and scatter from the large woody components (stems and branches) that constitute the bulk of the biomass and carbon pool in forested ecosystems. Recent innovations in radar technology have resulted in three-dimensional radar tomography, which allows the sensor to measure the vertical profile of forest biomass across a variety of old-growth and regenerating forest structures globally. With the launch of the NASA-ISRO Synthetic Aperture Radar and European Space Agency (ESA) BIOMASS missions in 2023, three-dimensional mapping of global forest dynamics at fine spatial resolution will become widely available for scientists and forestry managers.

By combining lidar and radar remote-sensing data with ground measurements, ecologists can now scale their understanding of form and function, from the level of individual trees, to ecosystems, to the global scale.

AMAZON TREE CANOPY STRUCTURE

As lidar satellites fly over the land they capture the structure of forests along their tracks, showing the vertical profile of the forest canopy at fine scales. The GEDI track across the Amazon broad-leaf forests shows on average 100–130 ft (30–40 m) tall trees shadowing dense canopies underneath at 30–65 ft (10–20 m) height.

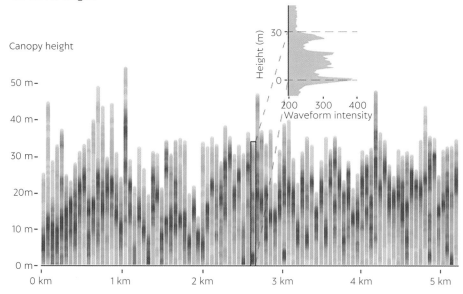

Canopy height

——— GEDI beam location

PACIFIC NORTHWEST TREE CANOPY STRUCTURE

The GEDI track across conifer forests of the Pacific Northwest shows trees reaching above 160 ft (60 m) tall but with open understory.

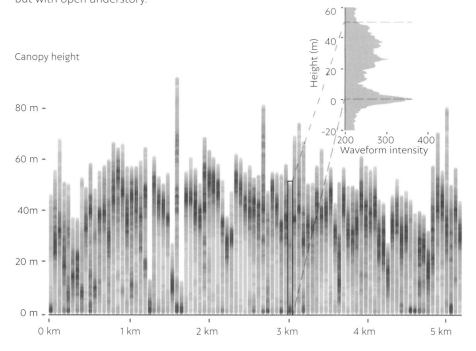

Canopy height

——— GEDI beam location

Vegetation function and dynamics

According to American forest scientist Stephen Pallardy, "To plant physiologists, trees are complex biochemical factories that grow from seeds and literally build themselves." Plant processes that collectively produce growth depend on the structure of trees, from leaves to branches, to stems, and to root systems.

The importance of physiological processes in regulating growth is reflected in the production of several tons of biomass in a patch forest every year from the simple raw materials of water, carbon dioxide, and some nitrogen. Trees follow the same processes as other seed plants, but their large size, slow growth, and longer life make them different from the shorter-lived herbaceous plants. The most obvious physiological differences between the two is that in trees the structure influencing the hydraulic flow of water from roots to leaves extends over a longer distance, there is a larger percentage of nonphotosynthetic tissue, and their long life exposes them to larger variations of extreme climate, soil conditions, and disturbance. Understanding these processes requires measurements that can span different tree species, ecosystems, and environmental conditions. Remote-sensing instruments therefore have to be able to measure vegetation attributes that can help quantify or model important and complex physiological processes, such as photosynthesis, transpiration, productivity, growth, and other metabolic activities. This section focuses on observations related to vegetation phenology and photosynthesis as the dominant processes controlling the exchange of carbon and water between forests and the atmosphere.

Measuring vegetation phenology

When sunlight strikes objects, certain wavelengths of its spectrum are absorbed and others are reflected. In plant leaves, chlorophyll strongly absorbs visible red light (VIS) for use in photosynthesis. The cell structure of the leaves, on the other hand, strongly reflects near-infrared (NIR) light. Leaf optical properties change significantly through the seasons. Plant phenology is the study of the timing of these seasonal events as they relate to the life cycle of plants. During leaf senescence, when leaf chlorophyll content degrades and other brown pigments persist, the RED reflectance in the visible spectrum increases, giving the leaves a yellow color. The NIR reflectance, on the other hand, decreases at the end of a seasonal cycle in the advanced stages of senescence. These properties of leaf optics that relate to its chemical changes and structure are reflected in various spectral functions and empirical vegetation indices. One of the most popular vegetation indices for capturing the green foliage status of the tree canopy is the Normalized Difference Vegetation Index (NDVI)—see graphic opposite—which was introduced for a wide range of vegetation remote sensing by NASA scientist Compton Tucker in 1979.

NORMALIZED DIFFERENCE VEGETATION INDEX (NDVI)

NDVI measures the green foliage status and is calculated from the visible red (VIS) and near-infrared (NIR) light reflected by the observed vegetation and is associated with intensity of photosynthetic activity.

The formula is: $\dfrac{(NIR - VIS)}{(NIR + VIS)} = NDVI$

The result is a number that ranges from minus one (−1) to plus one (+1), with a value near zero or negative indicating

no vegetation surfaces (rock, soil, snow, ice, water) and values close to +1 (0.8–0.9) indicating the highest possible density of green leaves. Vegetation phenology can be detected from NDVI changes from greenup to browndown or senescence (below) and the seasonal changes of vegetation observed by leaf chlorophyll and structural changes; chlorophyll strongly absorbs the VIS light and structure strongly reflects the NIR light (bottom graph).

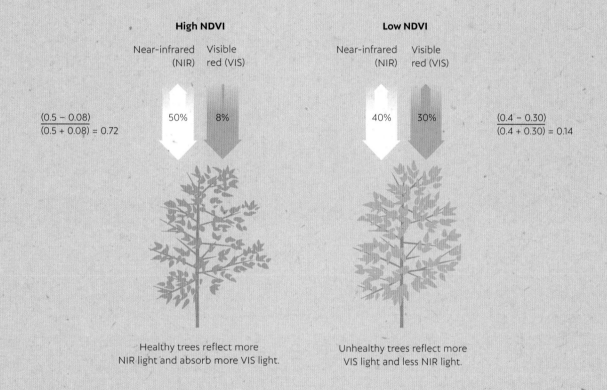

High NDVI

Near-infrared (NIR) Visible red (VIS)

$\dfrac{(0.5 - 0.08)}{(0.5 + 0.08)} = 0.72$ 50% 8%

Healthy trees reflect more NIR light and absorb more VIS light.

Low NDVI

Near-infrared (NIR) Visible red (VIS)

40% 30% $\dfrac{(0.4 - 0.30)}{(0.4 + 0.30)} = 0.14$

Unhealthy trees reflect more VIS light and less NIR light.

Seasonal foliage changes

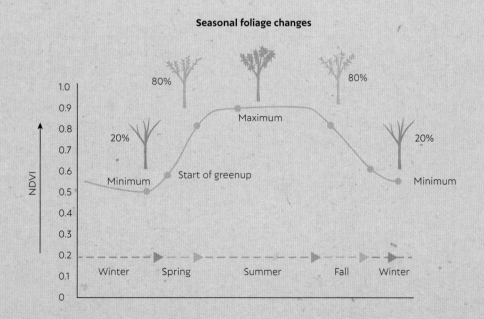

80% 80%

20% 20%

NDVI

1.0
0.9
0.8
0.7
0.6
0.5
0.4
0.3
0.2
0.1
0

Maximum

Start of greenup

Minimum   Minimum

Winter   Spring   Summer   Fall   Winter

US VEGETATION GREENUP CYCLES

The start of the annual growing season is among the most important climate-sensitive measures for vegetation. This map shows the average greenup dates for natural vegetation across the United States, calculated using MODIS satellite data from 2000 to 2013. The timing of spring greenup can affect growing season duration and productivity and is an important indicator of climate warming.

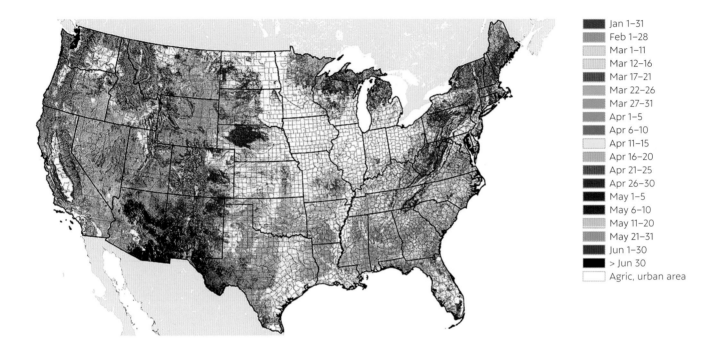

Monitoring phenological events with NDVI and detecting any shifts in the timing of the cycles has provided us with new insights into plant-environment interactions and has served as a powerful biological indicator of global climate change. For the first time, an analysis of satellite data gathered over the Amazon Basin has revealed the strong seasonal life cycle of this vast "evergreen" forest. Researchers have discovered that the large swing in leaf area—from new leaves to flowers and fruits—observed by NASA's Moderate Resolution Imaging Spectroradiometer (MODIS) was tightly synchronized to the increasing levels of sunlight during the dry season and its transition to the rainy season, with spatial patterns varying across different climate zones.

Measuring photosynthesis

Photosynthesis harvests light from an often quite variable stream of photons and converts this energy to carbohydrates, which ultimately fuel all plant processes. The efficiency with which absorbed photons are used for photosynthetic activity and for carbon fixation is highly regulated by climate. Plants have to solve an incredibly challenging problem in naturally fluctuating environments and deal with very large differences in temperature, light, and humidity depending on the time of day, the season, and the places where they grow. Focusing on phenology and life-cycle events using remote-sensing observations has helped scientists understand the seasonal demarcations in photosynthesis.

MONITORING PHENOLOGICAL EVENTS

The spectral vegetation index (NDVI) from Africa for four seasonal periods of spring, summer, fall, and winter, showing seasonality of vegetation across the continent. Areas of low seasonality in the middle of the Congo Basin rain forests, and high seasonality in savanna woodlands across the Sahel zone in the north and Miombo region in the south.

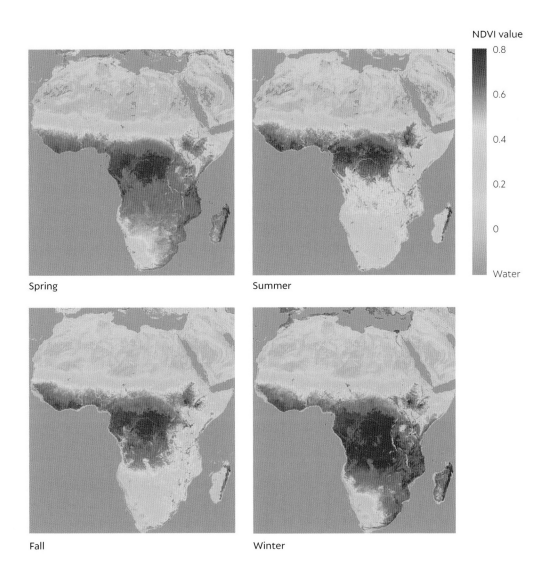

NDVI value

0.8

0.6

0.4

0.2

0

Water

Spring

Summer

Fall

Winter

Photosynthesis is perhaps one of the most important processes on Earth. It supports the production of food, fiber, wood, grain, and fuel, and sets the limit for the planetary boundary of production. Land plants are estimated to produce about 125 billion metric tonnes of dry matter per year (assuming 45 percent carbon content), of which three-quarters has been attributed to woody plants in forests and savannas. An indicator of the planetary boundary of production is the net primary productivity (NPP), defined as the gross primary production (absorption of carbon) of plants minus their respiration (release of carbon). This requires precise measurements of global photosynthesis. Vegetation indices such as NDVI or a more complex use of optical remote-sensing spectrum and scaling models have produced estimates of global vegetation photosynthesis and NPP.

Composition: plant functional types and diversity

Ecologists and plant geographers have long been interested in relationships between plants and their environments, organizing groups of plant species into functional categories. As discussed in Chapter 4 and earlier in this chapter, functional groups capture structural, physiological, and phenological properties of vegetation and are used to predict how certain species assemblages respond to anthropogenic impacts. Changes of these properties due to natural or anthropogenic disturbance affect several functions of the ecosystem at both local to regional scales, including productivity and biogeochemical cycling.

These functional groups are referred to as plant functional types (PFTs) in the ecological literature and are synonymous with other characteristics, including life form, plant community, and strategy. There is no universal agreement on the key traits of PFTs, whose classification depends on how they are being applied and the scale of the ecological study. Nonetheless, some visible indicators are used to define PFTs, including phenology (evergreen versus deciduous), life history (annual versus perennial), and morphological traits (leaf area versus volume), or more hidden physiological traits such as nitrogen fixation or photosynthetic pathways (C_3 versus C_4 plants; see pages 242-243). Remote-sensing measurements that include detailed information on vegetation characteristics across different spatial scales provide a new approach for defining and classifying PFTs.

Conventional remote-sensing measurements, such as Landsat imagery in the VIS spectrum and radar sensors in the microwave spectrum, can map broad categories of vegetation types at spatial resolutions of meters to kilometers. Pattern-recognition techniques and spectral classification approaches have been successful in routinely mapping general vegetation types and changes caused by human disturbance. In image classification, spectral information is represented by pixels that are grouped together using either a supervised (statistical classification) or unsupervised (clustering) approach. In-depth knowledge of the spectral information itself is not required to produce vegetation maps, which instead rely on the similarity of spectral and radiometric measurements spatially and over time. By adding more information to the classification approach, it is therefore possible to distinguish more distinct types of vegetation. In both supervised and unsupervised classifications, additional environmental layers such as topography, soil, geology, and even climate have been used as ancillary or collateral data to improve the accuracy or number of categories in regional vegetation maps. This is because although Landsat data identify general horizontal patterns of vegetation, they cannot reliably discriminate PFTs and species compositions.

MAPPING VEGETATION CHARACTERISTICS

Spatial composition of the physiological traits leaf chlorophyll, carotenoids (plant pigments), and water content of the Lägern mountain (pictured above), a temperate mixed forest ecosystem located near Zurich, Switzerland. The color composite shows the relative abundance of the three traits at each pixel of 6 x 6 m.

Carotenoids

Leaf water   Chlorophyll

The future of vegetation mapping

Constant advances in remote sensing are allowing researchers to increase the detail and accuracy of vegetation mapping. PFTs can now be mapped and monitored at different scales using data on the light spectrum reflected from vegetation, which provides additional information to help detect different levels of functionally important plant compounds. Sensors that measure the spectra of plants at leaf, branch, and canopy scales in field experiments have shown distinct levels of light absorption for different species, which can help contribute to separating them spectrally. Likewise, different levels of chemicals in plants observed in the optical spectrum, such as nitrogen and chlorophyll, tend to be associated with different patterns of canopy structure, further helping to separate functionally distinct species or communities of plants in a landscape. These plant properties are used as distinct spectral information to identify vegetation categories and other land-cover types, including water, soils, and dry plant material. Imaging spectroscopy from airborne and satellite platforms has allowed scientists to map PFTs and plant composition with increasing accuracy and to classify vegetation functions across landscapes and globally in novel ways.

▶ **Caldor fire scar**

WorldView-3 satellite images (1.24 m resolution) showing before and after the Caldor fire in California. The second image shows the scar that burned more than 220,000 acres (89,000 ha) of forests in El Dorado and Amador counties of the Sierra Nevada Mountains.

▶ **Caldor fire**

The fire started on August 14, 2021 and was contained after almost two months.

In recent years, researchers have applied more complex statistical models, machine-learning algorithms, and cloud computing techniques to integrate a variety of spectral information from different remote-sensing observations and platforms, allowing vegetation forms, functions, and composition to be mapped in yet more detail. Earth observation systems launched by national agencies such as NASA and ESA, along with a suite of commercial satellites built and maintained by private companies, have transformed the way scientists and decision-makers use tree-level information in myriad applications, from forestry to solutions to climate change.

▲ **Advances**

Recent advances in very high resolution remote sensing data at centimeter scales allow species-level study of tree structure.